# Leadership in Disruptive Times, Second Edition

# Leadership in Disruptive Times, Second Edition

## Negotiating the New Balance

Sattar Bawany

**BEP**
BUSINESS EXPERT PRESS
Leader in applied, concise business books

*Leadership in Disruptive Times: Negotiating the New Balance,*
*Second Edition*

Copyright © Business Expert Press, LLC, 2023.

Cover design by Charlene Kronstedt

Interior design by Exeter Premedia Services Private Ltd., Chennai, India

First published in 2020 by
Business Expert Press, LLC
222 East 46th Street, New York, NY 10017
www.businessexpertpress.com

ISBN-13: 978-1-63742-452-0 (hardback)
ISBN-13: 978-1-63742-234-2 (paperback)
ISBN-13: 978-1-63742-235-9 (e-book)

Business Expert Press Human Resource Management and Organizational Behavior Collection

Second edition: 2023

10 9 8 7 6 5 4 3 2 1

*To my extended family (siblings, nieces, nephews, grandnieces, and grandnephew, particularly Ameer) who make my life worth living during my times of crisis and make me realize that there is nothing better than being a family.*

# Description

As the world becomes more complex and connected, the threat of a corporate crisis grows. There are instances everywhere: We have experienced firsthand how a pandemic, when spread worldwide, caused massive global business disruption and a public health disaster; a corruption scandal causes a corporate leader to step down; the sudden death of a CEO without succession planning in place causes instability; a data breach shakes customer confidence; and quality issues trigger a widespread product recall. These are just a few examples among many of the recent corporate crises (Bawany 2020).

Today's businesses face unprecedented challenges operating in a global environment that is highly disruptive and increasingly volatile, uncertain, complex, and ambiguous (VUCA). Disruption has significantly impacted the way the world works, as many of us have experienced today and in recent years. Apart from businesses, government and individuals are also responding to shifts that would have seemed unimaginable even a few years ago. The current wave of disruption, including the recent coronavirus (COVID-19) pandemic, the known forces of Industry 4.0 (such as artificial intelligence (AI) and robotics), globalization, geopolitical tensions, and demographic change, is reinventing the workforce. Internet technologies have enabled drones and driverless cars, which are transforming supply chains, logistics, health care, and even defense and security, such as the war against terrorism (Bawany 2020).

Organizations face challenges that present varying levels of severity. But handled poorly, even a seemingly minor shock has the potential to escalate into a crisis that threatens the viability of a business. A crisis and disruptive event can disrupt operations, damage reputations, destroy shareholder value, and trigger other threats.

As the business community has learned through the COVID-19 pandemic, it's more important than ever for leaders to anticipate and plan for the possibility of an unplanned disruptive event. The more prepared you are to manage shocks, the less likely you'll fall victim to the serious harm a crisis has the potential to inflict.

Whereas risk management is traditionally a proactive discipline, crisis management is reactive. Crisis management can be viewed as a specialized discipline within risk management, where specific practices are instituted in response to unexpected events that threaten a company's stability. Having an effective plan and resources in place mitigates the destructive nature of that reactivity.

Crisis management is one of several interrelated core disciplines comprising enterprise risk management, along with emergency preparedness, disaster response, business continuity planning, supply chain risk mitigation, and cyber liability prevention. Crisis management practices can help lessen the magnitude of emergencies and disasters while decreasing the uncertainty and anxiety associated with these events.

We face a new era of radical uncertainty and disruption brought about by other challenges such as climate change, financial crises, terrorism, demographic changes in the labor market, health/disease risk from the pandemic, and rapid developments in innovative digital technologies and its impact on transformation at the workplace.

Over the past 20 years, successive economic and geopolitical crises have quickly sent shockwaves throughout the world, affecting every country, economy, trading relationship, and business operation. Amid continuing uncertainty around how the war in Ukraine may end or escalate, business leaders are faced with the challenges of navigating in the dark, accelerating already urgent transformation plans, and building organizational resilience for impacts that may yet strike.

The disruptive events of the past often have had short-term business impacts as leaders seek to return to a state of normalcy. However, we are now in an era of cumulative and extreme disruption that should more sustainably change future decision making. For example, some immediate consequences of the war in Ukraine could be medium- to long-term sanctions and countersanctions, commodity shortages, and supply chain disruption—so companies need to factor them in as part of their agenda.

The management of shocks and crises is becoming an everyday occurrence. Organizations also need to be agile, leverage opportunities, and drive innovation to remain competitive in the face of challenging conditions.

Right leadership is critical for organizations to thrive in a disruptive business environment. The book aims to answer the following questions:

1. *What are the megatrends of future disruptive forces that organizations need to take into consideration in their crisis management and business sustainability plan?*
2. *How do organizations negotiate the new balance of enterprise risk management (ERM) with corporate sustainability?*
3. *How do leaders transform their organizations to be agile, adaptive, and innovation-driven in the era of constant disruption and crisis?*
4. *What are the key considerations for an organization to consider as they adopt digital transformation to reinvent people, processes, and technology in the disruptive World-of-Work (WOW)?*

Long-term trends already in play before both current crises (the COVID-19 pandemic and the war in Ukraine) are accelerating digitalization, changing consumer and employee expectations, and causing a pendulum swing-back toward regionalization from globalization as we've known it. Leaders need to plan accordingly without getting stuck in the minutiae of the current moment.

## Keywords

crisis; crises; crisis management; crisis leadership; disruption; creative innovation; creative disruption; disruptive leadership; disruptive leader; digital leader; disruptive digital leader; disruptive innovation; disruptive forces; megatrends; VUCA; fourth industrial revolution; Industry 4.0; new normal; next normal; postpandemic; digitalization; digital transformation; digital transformation culture; cognitive readiness; critical thinking; organizational resilience; resilience; agility; future leaders; high potentials; future of work; ESG; climate change; metaverse

# Contents

# List of Figures

# List of Tables

# Testimonials

*"Leaders in organizations are continually confronted with increased competition, globalization, demand for social responsibilities, and a stream of technological advances that disrupt the marketplace. For those looking to navigate the turbulent and complex landscape of digital evolution,* Leadership in Disruptive Times *is the perfect blueprint for future-proofing their organization. Prof. Bawany provides insights into the role of 'disruptive digital leaders' that transform the organization into a more agile, innovative, and adaptive workplace in times of disruption and successfully lead digital transformation efforts. Must-read."*—**Dr. Marshall Goldsmith is the New York Times best-selling author of Triggers, MOJO, and *What Got You Here Won't Get You There. Thinkers 50*—#1 Executive Coach and the only two-time #1 Leadership Thinker in the World**

*"*Leadership in Disruptive Times *is an invaluable tool for executives, managers, and leaders in business, academia, non-profit organizations, government agencies, and more. This is a well-written and well-researched practical guide for leaders who want to overcome the disruptive challenges resulting from the COVID-19 pandemic and how organizations can adopt the best practices in the development of a digital-driven culture at the workplace. The book provides effective techniques, real-world examples, and expert guidance for organizations seeking to implement a digital transformation strategy in today's era of Industry 4.0."*—**Professor Howard Yu, Author of *LEAP: How to Thrive in a World Where Everything Can Be Copied* (2018), and LEGO Professor of Management and Innovation, IMD Business School, Lausanne, Switzerland**

*"The book* Leadership in Disruptive Times: Negotiating the New Balance *by Prof. Sattar Bawany is essential reading for all business leaders in today's world of constant disruption and crises. In his latest work, Prof. Bawany uses real-life case studies to illustrate the challenges companies face in the modern world and explains why some have managed to adapt effectively and even thrive during times of crisis, while others have quickly fallen by the wayside.*

*Each company will face unique challenges; however, Prof. Bawany explains that the underlying themes are remarkably similar, and lessons can be drawn from across different geographies and even unrelated industries. The pace of change is unlikely to slow and increasing complexity has become the norm for most organizations. This is the backdrop we must contend with, and this novel is a valuable resource for business leaders as they lead their organizations through disruptions and uncertainty."*—**Simon Sinclair, Chief Operating Officer, Commodities, Standard Chartered Bank**

*"A digital transformation strategy gives a company a competitive edge in Industry 4.0. Digitally mature companies are fundamentally more efficient and responsive to customer demands. Successful employee attraction and retention are rewards for companies with a realized digital transformation strategy.*

*Creating and implementing a digital transformation strategy is no small undertaking, especially in a VUCA environment, but it is essential to remaining competitive in the marketplace. It helps save money with more efficient business processes, and at the same time provides a superior customer experience. Transforming the way, a company does business opens new opportunities, provides an exciting new direction and attracts new customers. Prof. Sattar Bawany lays the ground sharing what it takes to future-proof for the next potential pandemic in this latest edition of his book* Leadership in Disruptive Times: Negotiating the New Balance.*"*—**Dr. Timothy Low, CEO and Board Member of Farrer Park Hospital, Singapore; Healthcare Investment Consultant, Pavilion Capital (Temasek)**

*"Business leaders have been breaking down traditional barriers, working across functional silos to drive innovation, and using data and AI to sense and respond to changes in the external environment. Essentially, we saw traditional players acting much more like digital natives. How can we learn from these experiences to create a digital and innovation-driven culture, especially when our world has become even more digital in the era of the post-pandemic 'new normal'? The answer is found in the latest edition of the book by Prof. Sattar Bawany, which provides CEOs and business leaders with proven tools, frameworks, practices, and strategies on how best-in-class organizations have been successful in improving their sustainability without negatively impacting*

*their profitability. I would recommend this book to all leaders from both private and public sector organizations.*"—**Dato' Mohammad Azlan Abdullah, Chairman, Sapura Energy Bhd; Group Chief Executive Officer, PROLINTAS Group of Companies, Malaysia**

*"Disruptive times—this is an often-used term of late, but Prof. Sattar Bawany has been able to crystalize what this means and more importantly how it impacts businesses and lives in general. His thoughts on leadership through these trying times are certainly fresh and innovative and a model for leaders and upcoming leaders to ponder over and adopt as a best practice.*"—**BS Teh, Executive Vice President, Global Sales and Sales Operations, Seagate Technology, CA**

*"Prof. Bawany's* **'L.E.A.D.E.R.' Framework** *enables organizations to develop their leadership team's relevant skills to manage future disruptions while staying focused on the mission of the transformation agenda. A highly recommended book to those who like to develop their resilience and disruptive mental agility which is crucial in today's digital and innovation-driven workplace.*"—**Mr. Pote Narittakurn (Lee Pit Teong), Founder & CEO, iGroup; Founder, MangoSTEEMS**

*"In preparing for a crisis, Prof. Sattar Bawany advocates the need for the development of* **'C.R.I.S.I.S.'** *leaders who have responsibility for conceptualizing a blueprint plan, advocating for appropriate resources, communicating crisis initiatives, and constantly updating response steps and initiatives so they remain relevant. A must read for Board members and leaders at all levels.*"—**Bonnie Hagemann, CEO of EDA, Inc. and Co-Founder of WomenExecs on Boards**

*"Prof. Sattar Bawany examines how strategic leaders deal with the challenges they face, the political risks and the opportunities they encounter, the pitfalls they must avoid, and the paths toward reform they may pursue. They will need to master the disruptive and* **'C.R.I.S.I.S.'** *leadership competencies in this new era. These new sets of skills complement the other contemporary leadership skills that leaders leverage in creating high-performing organizations and communities are the same as leading in a time of transformation mired in complexity.*"—**Michael Wooi, Dean, PPA Business School, Paris and CEO, International Professional Managers Association (IPMA), UK**

*"What makes leaders operate better is their ability to maneuver around complex situations and unpredicted scenarios. This ability has always focused on the role of leaders' assuming their influence on followers is the game changer. This book went further to discuss the role of teams as the collective body of leadership that co-creates the response to disruption and gave more understanding of how collective leadership can make a difference through the SCORE™ Framework of development of High-Performance Teams."*—**Dr Ibrahim Jamal Alharthi, CEO, Madinah Institute of Leadership & Entrepreneurship (MILE)**

*"The importance of leadership cannot be over-emphasized, particularly in disruptive times. But what does the right leadership look like? In this revised edition of his earlier book* Leadership in Disruptive Times, *Prof. Sattar provides guidance to leaders, to not just survive but thrive. The C.R.I.S.I.S. Leadership Model captures the specific competencies that leaders have used to successfully manage disruption during a crisis. This book provides the resources to help leaders prepare themselves as well as their organizations for disruptions, and to thrive in a VUCA environment."*—**Sim Gim Guan, Executive Director, Singapore National Employers Federation (SNEF)**

*"Prof. Sattar Bawany's* Leadership in Disruptive Times: Negotiating the New Balance *is a powerful and educating book. The book starts by sharing how the different megatrends and technologies are playing out and enlightens the reader with numerous case studies of best practices of how companies around the world are stepping into this new world. The book is full of notions, tools and techniques which will help you to lead in complex times and transform your organization into a high-performing, digitally-led, customer-centric and empathetic organization. Highly recommended read!"*—**Simon McKenzie, CEO, Bridge Institute**

*"Another comprehensive, thought-provoking, and eye-opening opus of the 2nd edition of* Leadership in Disruptive Times *from Prof. Sattar Bawany. Inspiring & Timely! The 'new normal' requires renewed leadership mindset to match the overall speed of digitization and innovation, and the literature delivered here truly helps us leaders of today and tomorrow rethink the way we see the world, the way we lead and the way we progress and move forward as an individual as well as a community."*—**Philip Panaino, Global Head of Cash Management, Standard Chartered Bank**

*"Having been a leadership consultant and coach in crisis communications for 25 years, I am familiar with the literature in this space. Quality hasn't quite kept up with the quantity. Theories and regurgitations are aplenty. Sattar's* Leadership in Disruptive Times: Negotiating the New Balance *stands out. The ideas are fresh, the counsel is practical, insights are researched, and the articulation is refreshingly bold. My biggest takeaway is the timely emphasis on 'values' and 'soft skills' in building crisis resiliency. Call it the 'digital paradox' where people have once again become the center of gravity spurred by unrelenting digitalization. The book provokes thought, invokes introspection, and gives hope. I recommend it."*—**Viswa Sadasivan, CEO, Strategic Moves Pte Ltd; Former Nominated Member of Parliament, Singapore; Retired Colonel (NS) in the Singapore Armed Forces**

*"Indeed, we are currently living in a volatile and disruptive world. Prof. Sattar Bawany provides insights into an understanding of disruptive leadership in times of crisis. A highly recommended book from Prof. Sattar Bawany as it provides essential guidance for leaders to navigate through inevitable periods of disruption and crisis with the* **'L.E.A.D.E.R.' Framework**. *The book also examines the fundamental qualities of disruptive leadership that would successfully distinguish leaders as they guide their organizations through the impact of the post-COVID-19 pandemic and the digital transformation at the workplace and provides very practical solutions for leaders who want to future-proof their businesses in this current disruptive world we are living in. A must-read!"*—**Datuk Wan Razly Abdullah, President and Group Chief Executive Officer, AFFIN Group**

*"The latest book on* Leadership in Disruptive Times: Negotiating a New Balance *by Prof. Sattar Bawany is a must-read for leaders looking into insights about leading in a 'new normal' way. For HR leaders, our top priority is to create an engaged workforce and ensure employee wellness initiatives are integrated into the hybrid way of working. This book gives further insights, case studies, and examples of innovative ways of doing things. It is very inspiring and a pleasure to read."*—**Janet Quek (Ms), Global Human Resource Business Partner (HRBP), FrieslandCampina AMEA**

*"*Leadership in Disruptive Times—Negotiating the New Balance *is an apt continuation of the first edition that has provided practical insights*

*for leaders of all levels and corporations to navigate the pandemic-ridden world of business. This edition comes at a time when the world is still grappling with the best approach to transition from the pandemic to yet another new normal.*

*Prof Sattar Bawany has written a must-read material for any leaders aspiring to succeed in the ever-changing world of technological advancement and unpredictable ecological evolution. The book gives a useful guide full of important information and contemporary analysis for leaders who want to future-proof their businesses and be not only responsive but also agile, adaptive, and innovative."*—**En. Mohamad Helmy Othman Basha, Group Managing Director, Sime Darby Plantation Berhad**

*"Prof. Sattar Bawany has done it again with his 2nd Edition book entitled* Leadership in Disruptive Times: Negotiating the New Balance. *The nuances that he has touched on in his 1st Edition have been planned and fully built upon in this book. As leaders of businesses and managers of people, we are constantly striving for professional and operational excellence. Prof. Sattar Bawany has provided frameworks and thought-starters that will push any business leader into reframing her/his thought process and that of the supporting team. The **C.R.I.S.I.S. Leadership Model** as well as the Disruptive Leadership Competencies are not only practical to apply but equally easy to communicate to all. Clearly a must-have on the list of books to read for the year."*—**Taranjeet Singh, CEO, Quantum Steppe Advisory; Professor of Practice Saito Business School; Chair Regional Board of Chartered Management Institute Malaysia**

*"The COVID-19 pandemic has turned the world topsy-turvy. It has mercilessly shaken global economies, wiped out corporations, destroyed small businesses, and brought immeasurable suffering to people around the world. Professor Sattar Bawany's latest book on* Leadership in Disruptive Times: Negotiating the New Balance *could not have come at a better time. As the world is still reeling from the shock and crippling effects of the pandemic, his book offers practical advice, invaluable insights, and contemporary case studies to help businesses and individuals navigate the highly unpredictable business environment.."*—**Dave Phua, Managing Director, Training Edge International, Singapore**

*"The changing world of work throws up many challenges as well as opportunities. Organizations need to address the megatrends and disruptions that are transforming the world we live in including debates on climate change, demographic changes, technological advancements, geopolitical trends, etc.* Leadership in Disruptive Times: Negotiating the New Balance *by Prof. Sattar Bawany is a playbook that advocates quite rightly for a human-centered approach to digital transformations in the workplace. It covers very practical solutions for negotiating our disrupted world. I strongly recommend this as a must-read!"*—**Professor Dato' Dr. Ansary Ahmed, Founding President and Group Managing Director, Asia e University, Malaysia**

*"Even if the technologies themselves are evolving and relatively easily acquired and deployed, having the right team of 'disruptive digital leaders' who can successfully lead the digital transformation implementation will be scarce. Digitally talented leaders are already so highly in demand that many large, traditional companies must reinvent themselves to attract them. Organizations should respond to this challenge by building new pools of skilled digital talent. The* Leadership in Disruptive Times: Negotiating the New Balance *provides the playbook on how to go about achieving that. A must-read!"*—**Dato' Azmi Mohd Ali, Senior Partner and Executive Chairman, Azmi & Associates; Independent Non-Executive Director, UMW Holdings Berhad**

*"Leaders today need to be equipped to face ever-evolving challenges. Without the right tools and skill sets, disruptions and 'black swan events' can overwhelm and derail even the most effective and trained leader. Professor Sattar's latest book* Leadership in Disruptive Times: Negotiating the New Balance, *is an excellent read and provides a deep-dive analysis, of global best practices in the digital age.*—**Dato' Mona Suraya Dato' Kamaruddin, Chief Executive Officer, Affin Hwang Investment Bank Berhad**

*"Prof. Sattar Bawany's Second Edition of* Leadership in Disruptive Times *is a seminal masterpiece in understanding the interrelated and interconnected issues related to the disruptions that are currently confronting humanity. He built upon his earlier insights into an understanding of disruptive leadership and provides the case for organizations to revisit and, at times, reinvent their people strategy, internal systems, and processes, and deploy the technologies that would suit disruptive times. A must-read for strategic thinking CEOs and policymakers*

*and indeed those aspiring to leadership roles in both private and public sectors."*
—**Ambassador Dato' Thanarajasingam Subramaniam, Member of Ambassadorial Advisory Panel, InvestKL, Malaysia; Deputy Secretary-General, Ministry of Foreign Affairs, Malaysia (2004–2006); Chief of Staff, President of the United Nations General Assembly (1997)**

*"In his latest book, Prof Sattar Bawany has built the case that when faced with these disruptive events, business leaders are finding it challenging to navigate the insurmountable challenges, reinvent their businesses and ensure their survival. His* **'C.R.I.S.I.S.' Leadership Model** *provides tools in a best practice framework for a comprehensive approach to building organizational resilience when facing emergencies including those related to pandemics, financial crises, cybersecurity, supply chain disruptions, and climate change."*—**David Chan, Regional Director, Material Sales, Boeing Global Services**

*"Businesses and leaders don't have the luxury of time to experiment if they want to stay relevant and will need to transform with agility and embrace bold actions with courage. Prof. Sattar Bawany has very candidly highlighted these in his latest book, and he offers global best practices, practical and proven frameworks, and approaches to realign the organization's digital agenda for acceleration ahead. The book also highlights the trusted role of a mentor and mentee as they together navigate unchartered territories leaning on the experience and helping in building the next generation of leaders."*—**Sanjay Prabhakaran, Co-Founder Asia Mentors Circle; Former President—Asia Pacific, Hologic, Inc., and Baxter International Inc.**

*"Few leaders can't do without reading Professor Sattar Bawany's latest book simply because it is not an option as conventional leadership practices simply can't do a good job any longer. The hard reality of leading in disruptive times requires a completely new way of thinking and the development of a new breed of* **'disruptive digital leaders'** *pipeline for the sustainability of organizations in this era. All in all, Prof. Sattar's superior knowledge of leaders in disruptive times. Surpasses many that I know for his work is his life mission compared to many others. It is undisputed that he is a guru in this field, not just an expert."*—**Dr. Michael Heah, MCC, CEO and Founder, Corporate Coach Academy Sdn Bhd; Chairman, Malaysian Association of Certified Coaches; Adjunct Professor, University Utara, Malaysia**

# Acknowledgments

Once again, this book would not have been possible without the unwavering support and encouragement of Mr. Lee Pit Teong (Pote), the founder and CEO of iGroup and Business Expert Press (BEP). Mr. Lee is a true visionary and inspires me with his passion and entrepreneurial drive, especially during the pandemic when he acted with deliberate calm and bounded optimism. By demonstrating these qualities, he helps the employees to feel a sense of purpose, giving them hope that they can face the challenges ahead.

I would like to express my gratitude to the iGroup and BEP colleagues, Susan Peh, Sky Chen, and Charlene Kronstedt, for their assistance in getting the images and graphics for this book.

Finally, I would like to thank all clients, business partners, and readers of the first edition of the book for their continuous feedback and suggestions of topics to be included in this second edition, which has been addressed in this book.

# CHAPTER 1

# Leading in an Era of Constant Crisis and Disruption

## Introduction: The Current Realities

The world is facing significant disruption and increasingly urgent global challenges affecting individuals, families, organizations, governments, and society. This volatility, uncertainty, complexity, and ambiguity (VUCA)-driven age of disruption brings new complexities, opportunities, as well as risks for businesses (Bawany 2020). The potential for crises has intensified, driven by rapid technological change and amplified by societal expectations linked to environmental, social, and governance (ESG) phenomena.

Throughout the COVID-19 crisis, we've seen an acceleration of these trends. We have seen how some businesses have been successful in looking beyond the pandemic and into recovery, while others have failed and many perished, especially the small and medium enterprises (SMEs).

The global outbreak of coronavirus (COVID-19) has created significant challenges for leaders at all levels in industries across the world. A postpandemic era will require us to embrace new definitions of leadership. The disruptive and seismic effect of the pandemic was felt by organizations across diverse industries. Leaders and employees are all asking far-ranging questions about the future: What will be the legacy of the pandemic? What kinds of leadership skills will they need to successfully navigate the various challenges in a disruptive and digital-driven workplace? How do organizations balance business sustainability and risk management while supporting the needs of the various stakeholders including their employees?

Those who have been leading organizations for some time will attest to the fact that disruption, in its various forms, can happen at any time, in any market segment, or in any industry. The reality is that its impact on traditional organizations can be disastrous if not managed effectively. It has and will continue to fundamentally change the way we live and work in decades to come. A leader must see beyond the horizon to anticipate these possible disruptions and develop relevant strategies to mitigate the associated risks (Bawany 2019).

Today's global disruptions (e.g., geopolitical tensions, supply chain bottlenecks, technological innovations, and climate change) and economic headwinds (e.g., soaring inflation, rising interest rates, decelerating growth, and currency fluctuations) have created a complex, once-in-a-generation, competitive environment with significant variations across geographic areas and sectors.

Navigating this unprecedented complexity requires business leaders to develop a dynamic perspective not only on the most likely scenarios for how their operating and economic environments will evolve but also on the distinct opportunities and risks these scenarios present for their organizations (Bawany 2018a).

To achieve organizational high performance in an era of constant disruption and crisis, both agility and resilience are important.

*Agility* refers to the ability to make a rapid change and achieve flexibility in various aspects of the operations, in response to changes or disruptive events in the external environment. It can also be viewed as the capacity for responding with speed and flexibly and decisively toward anticipating, initiating, and taking advantage of opportunities and avoiding any negative consequences of change.

*Resilience* refers to the ability to anticipate, prepare for, and recover from disasters, emergencies, and other disruptions, and protect and enhance workforce and customer engagement, supply network and financial performance, organizational productivity, and community well-being when disruption occurs.

It can also be viewed as the capacity for resisting, absorbing, and responding, even reinventing, if necessary, in response to fast and/or disruptive change that cannot be avoided such as "black swan" events (Taleb 2007).

The war in Ukraine marks a devastating shift across the worlds of society, geopolitics, and business—they will not be the same for a long time. Yet, the war is only the latest in an increasing number of unexpected disruptions impacting the global economy, and it won't be the last.

Over the past 20 years, successive economic and geopolitical cri-ses have quickly sent shockwaves throughout the world, affecting every country, economy, trading relationship, and business operation. Amid continuing uncertainty around how the war in Ukraine may end or escalate, business leaders are faced with the challenges of navigating in the dark, accelerating already urgent transformation plans, and building organizational resilience for impacts that may yet strike.

The disruptive events of the past often have had short-term business impacts as leaders seek to return to a state of normalcy. However, we are now in an era of cumulative and extreme disruption that should more sustainably change future decision making. For example, some immedi-ate consequences of the war in Ukraine could be medium- to long-term sanctions and countersanctions, commodity shortages, and supply chain disruption—so companies need to factor them in as part of their agenda.

Long-term trends already in play before both crises (the COVID-19 pandemic and the war in Ukraine) are accelerating digitalization, changing consumer and employee expectations, and causing a pendulum swing-back toward regionalization from globalization as we've known it. Leaders need to plan accordingly without getting stuck in the minutiae of the current moment.

The likely general redesign of business priorities from extreme effi-ciency and short-term profit to sustainable performance, resilience, and values affects strategic priorities. It may become more important to build a sustainable, flexible but strong business model that is fit to contrib-ute to the solution of big societal and environmental challenges as well as to sustain shocks and disruptions than to maximize short-term gains. Business leaders should focus on strengthening organizational resilience and addressing operational concerns such as supply chain bottlenecks and enhancing leadership readiness to navigate these challenges effectively to ensure sustainable business continuity.

Many of the challenges businesses are facing now echo what has trans-pired throughout the COVID-19 pandemic, from the initial uncertainty and initiatives to keep employees safe, to new ways of working and navi-gating broken supply chains.

We live in a constant era of disruption in which powerful global forces are changing how we live and work. The new world order is leading to growing challenges to globalization, geopolitical tensions, the rapid spread of new disruptive innovation, shifts in demographic forces, and the challenge of reaching net-zero greenhouse gas emission. These trends offer considerable new opportunities to companies, sectors, countries, and individuals that embrace them successfully. They are bringing forth dynamic and innovative new players on the world stage and could give a much needed boost to productivity and prosperity in many countries.

The past two and a half years have been extraordinary. What we are seeing is surely more than the progression of just another business cycle. The unnerving combination of a global pandemic compounded by energy scarcity, rapid inflation, and geopolitical tensions boiling over has people wondering what certainties are left (Bradley et al. 2022).

The Ukraine conflict has also caused food, fuel, and fertilizer prices to skyrocket. It has further disrupted supply chains and global trade and caused distress in financial markets. By current estimates, the war could cut global economic growth by 0.9 percentage points in 2022, as well as undermine development aid to the world's poor (United Nations 2022a).

The six megatrends of future disruptive forces that would lead to potential crises in the coming decades (the details will be elaborated on in Chapter 2) are given in Figure 1.1.

## Climate Change

According to the United Nations, the global temperature has already risen 1.1°C above the preindustrial level, with glaciers melting and the sea level rising. The impacts of climate change also include flooding and drought, displacing millions of people, sinking them into poverty and hunger, denying them access to basic services such as health and education, expanding inequalities, stifling economic growth, and even causing conflict. By 2030, an estimated 700 million people will be at risk of displacement by drought alone (United Nations 2022a).

A critical mass of the world's largest companies and countries have now made net-zero pledges, creating a snowball effect that will encourage others to join. As net-zero rapidly becomes the standard for government and corporate commitments, it's appropriate to stop and ask: Is net-zero a sufficient tool to address climate change? How can businesses leverage net-zero emissions strategy to offer the abatement of climate risk for

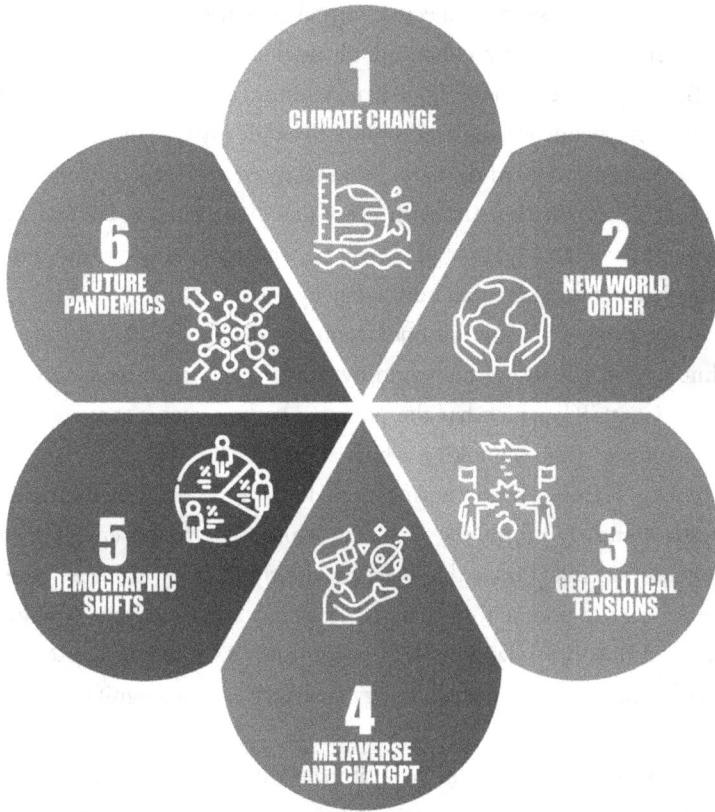

*Figure 1.1  The megatrends of future disruptions*

shareholders without abrupt disruption to near-term returns, and achieve reputational benefits for companies that serve customers or businesses that are climate-conscious? What are the significant limitations to the approach, which, if unaddressed, could easily misrepresent and undermine progress toward the ultimate goal of environmental sustainability?

## Metaverse and ChatGPT

Across technology platforms, the key drivers of the most recent era's digitization and connectivity seem to be approaching saturation. Yet, a set of already potent transversal technologies, particularly artificial intelligence (AI) and bioengineering, may combine to create another big surge of progress in the next era. According to technology research specialist

Gartner, a metaverse is a collective virtual shared space, created by the convergence of virtually enhanced physical and digital reality (Wiles 2022). It is persistent, providing enhanced immersive experiences, as well as device independence and accessibility through any type of device, from tablets to head-mounted displays. The metaverse will impact every business that consumers interact with every day. According to Gartner, the metaverse is where a quarter of us will be working, studying, shopping, and socializing for at least an hour a day by 2026.

At the time of writing this book (January 2023), the other disruptive technology that is taking the world by storm is the rise of generative AI such as ChatGPT, which has the potential to be a major game-changer for businesses. This technology, which allows for the creation of original content by learning from existing data, has the power to revolutionize industries and transform the way companies operate. By enabling the automation of many tasks that were previously done by humans, generative AI has the potential to increase efficiency and productivity, reduce costs, and open up new growth opportunities. As such, businesses that can effectively leverage the technology are likely to gain a significant competitive advantage.

The big questions remain. What impact will this next wave of disruptive innovation technologies have on businesses, work and social order? How are organizations ensuring their workforce readiness to leverage these latest technologies?

## The New World Order

In the world order, there is a tendency toward multipolarity, which in turn may imply realignment into regionally and ideologically aligned groups. This immediately raises questions of what might that multipolarity look like in practice. According to the Boston Consulting Group research, the global economy will lose up to $10 trillion in GDP in 2025 unless governments repeal or reduce tariffs and nontariff barriers that currently obstruct global merchandise trade, according to a new report released today for G20 governments (Anaya et al. 2020). Will the economy remain global in nature, and will we find new workable mechanisms to cooperate beyond the economy? Moreover, years of relative moderation in international politics seem to be giving way to more political polarization between blocs. How effectively will global and local institutions and leaders adapt to, and shape, this different world order?

## Geopolitical Tensions

The first geostrategic theme will be continued shifts in geopolitical power and the international system. The two-tiered world will contribute to these shifts. So too will relations among the great powers—the United States, Russia, and China—which will be somewhat inwardly focused while also competing with each other for global influence. While these great-power dynamics are creating a multipolar system, how will the variety of middle powers play a larger role in their regions and on the global stage? To what extent will the conflict between Russia and Ukraine create further severe geopolitical and economic shockwaves with lasting effects? What are the implications if the South China Sea geopolitical flashpoint evolves into a truly global conflict?

## Metaverse

Across technology platforms, the key drivers of the most recent era's digitization and connectivity seem to be approaching saturation. Yet, a set of already potent transversal technologies, particularly artificial intelligence (AI) and bioengineering, may combine to create another big surge of progress in the next era. According to technology research specialist Gartner, a metaverse is a collective virtual shared space, created by the convergence of virtually enhanced physical and digital reality (Wiles 2022). It is persistent, providing enhanced immersive experiences, as well as device independence and accessibility through any type of device, from tablets to head-mounted displays. The metaverse will impact every business that consumers interact with every day. According to Gartner, the metaverse is where a quarter of us will be working, studying, shopping, and socializing for at least an hour a day by 2026. The big questions remain. What impact will this next wave of technologies have on work and social order? How are organizations ensuring their workforce readiness to leverage these latest disruptive innovation technologies?

# Demographic Shifts

In demographic forces, a young world will evolve into an aging, urban world, and inequality within countries may increasingly challenge the social fabric. The majority of the world's workforce is aging rapidly while, at the same time, we see the rise of Generation Z, also known as "digital natives." This major demographic shift is bringing an end to the abundance of labor that has fueled economic growth since the 1970s. Thanks to longer and healthier lives, many people are working well into their 60s and beyond, but the trend toward later retirement is not likely to offset the negative effects of aging populations. As the total size of the labor force stagnates or declines in many markets, the momentum for economic growth should slow. How will governments and businesses address the major challenges, including surging healthcare costs, old-age pensions, and high debt levels? How will countries, institutions, and individuals adapt to demographic changes—will we age "gracefully"?

# The Next Global Pandemic

In the wake of COVID-19, there have been calls for the world to be better prepared for the next pandemic. These calls are driven by a sense that the outbreak could have been foreseen and prevented or that the spread could have been more effectively contained, causing less social and economic disruption and averting deaths. Yet, the world tends to move on quickly, with new crises taking center stage, resulting in the now familiar cycle of "panic and neglect." This is a concern: Although the timing and nature of the next pandemic spark are unknown, it is certain to happen. How can governments and businesses address the limitations of past efforts and the need for a more ambitious and sustained approach to preparedness? What roles do global institutions play in ensuring more financing, reform of global governance for health-related crises, and fresh thinking around global public goods?

# Conclusion: Is Crisis a Threat or Opportunity?

Each of the megatrends highlighted earlier would be challenging on its own; taken together, they can seem daunting. Yet, the opportunities for the economy, business, and society that these global forces generate are equally compelling and there is indeed new prosperity for those quick to embrace them. We cannot ignore the potential challenges, chief among them the growing social inequalities that could arise as a result. As societies, we will face challenges related to the future of work as well as inclusive growth; the two are closely linked. Embracing the trends while mitigating their negative impact on those who cannot keep up and our environment is the new imperative of our era.

Taking advantage of the opportunities that these trends offer—and avoiding or taming the challenges—will require big adjustments. In the next two chapters, we sketch out the impact of these six mega disruptive forces and what businesses can consider in achieving a balancing act toward how a more sustainable society might look like. These ideas do not amount to a comprehensive action plan and are not meant to be exhaustive.

# CHAPTER 2

# Megatrends of Future Disruptive Forces

## Introduction

Overlapping factors, including geopolitical tensions, regulatory pressures, skills shortages, and climate change, now present major threats to supply chain operations.

Global supply chains have experienced ongoing and unprecedented disruption since 2020 (Bawany 2020). The challenges presented by a confluence of multiple factors have forced businesses across the world to reassess how products are moved around on regional, national, and international levels. As lockdowns were imposed across the world in 2020 to mitigate the spread of COVID-19, shockwaves were sent across the global supply chains. In particular, the pandemic-related disruption exposed the heavy reliance on China's manufacturing and logistics sectors for many businesses. Even though economies around the world are reopening, reliance on China continues to present supply chain issues, as the country continues with a zero-COVID strategy.

The pandemic disrupted the global supply chain—Asia and parts of Europe were initially hit hard with workers who fell sick with COVID, as well as factories shut down or factories at partial production and lockdowns. Once the factories were not fulfilling supply, the transportation piece of the supply chain also began to falter. Many companies did not have a plan in place when their primary sources of supply were cut off or delayed.

There are many factors at play, including the political impact of the U.S.–China trade war, the global economic impact of COVID-induced reductions in manufacturing volume, and the practical implications of vehicles and vessels being in the wrong place at the wrong time.

Supply chain transparency was affected during the pandemic when businesses scrambled to find alternative partners amid lockdowns and labor shortages. It remains a serious challenge for businesses worldwide, indicating widespread awareness of the importance of visibility along entire supply chains, particularly when multiple partners and countries are involved.

We will now examine the nature of these identified six megatrends of disruptive forces and their potential impact on businesses, individuals, and society at large.

# Climate Change

The UN's 27th annual Conference of the Parties (COP27) took place in Sharm El-Sheikh, Egypt, from November 6 to 18, 2022. The summit theme was "implementation." It aims to shift the focus from negotiations and planning to action on the ground, where it is most needed. It wants to ramp up adaptation to climate change impacts, in parallel with emission reductions. The push is for major polluters to accelerate their phasedown of coal, oil, and gas. Russia's war on Ukraine makes clear the danger of relying on fossil fuels. Russia's exports are financing its war machine, while the tightening of global supplies has caused energy shortages and cost-of-living spikes around the developed and developing worlds (UN Climate Change 2022a).

## The Paris Agreement

The United Kingdom hosted the COP26 in Glasgow from October 31 to November 13, 2021. The COP26 summit brought parties together to accelerate action toward the goals of the Paris Agreement and the UN Framework Convention on Climate Change (UNFCC).

The Paris Agreement is a legally binding international treaty on climate change. It was adopted by 196 parties at COP21 in Paris on December 12, 2015, and entered into force on November 4, 2016. Its goal is to limit global warming to well below 2°C, preferably to 1.5°C, compared to preindustrial levels. To achieve this long-term temperature goal, countries aim to reach global peaking of greenhouse gas (GHG) emissions as soon as possible to achieve a climate-neutral world by mid-century (2050).

The Paris Agreement is a landmark in the multilateral climate change process because, for the first time, a binding agreement brought all nations into a common cause to undertake ambitious efforts to combat climate change and adapt to its effects. Implementation of the Paris Agreement requires economic and social transformation, based on the best available science. The Paris Agreement works on a five-year cycle of increasingly ambitious climate action carried out by countries.

Nationally determined contributions (NDCs) are at the heart of the Paris Agreement and the achievement of its long-term goals. NDCs embody efforts by each country to reduce national emissions and adapt to the impacts of climate change. The Paris Agreement (Article 4, paragraph 2) requires each Party to prepare, communicate and maintain successive NDCs that it intends to achieve. Parties shall pursue domestic mitigation measures, to achieve the objectives of such contributions.

The Paris Agreement requests each country to outline and communicate their post-2020 climate actions, known as their NDCs. Together, these climate actions determine whether the world achieves the long-term goals of the Paris Agreement and reaches global peaking of GHG emissions as soon as possible and undertake rapid reductions thereafter following the best available science, to achieve a balance between anthropogenic emissions by sources and removals by sinks of GHGs in the second half of this century. It is understood that the peaking of emissions will take longer for developing country Parties and that emission reductions are undertaken based on equity, and in the context of sustainable development and efforts to eradicate poverty, which are critical development priorities for many developing countries.

The Paris Agreement recognizes that the long-term goals specified in Articles 2 and 4.1 will be achieved through time and, therefore, builds on a ratcheting up of aggregate and individual ambition over time. NDCs are submitted every five years to the UNFCCC secretariat. To enhance the ambition over time, the Paris Agreement provides that successive NDCs will represent a progression compared to the previous NDC and reflect its highest possible ambition.

Parties are requested to submit the next round of NDCs (new NDCs or updated NDCs) by 2020 and every five years thereafter (e.g., by

2020, 2025, 2030), regardless of their respective implementation time frames. Moreover, Parties may at any time adjust their existing nationally determined contribution to enhance their level of ambition (Article 4, paragraph 11).

In their NDCs, countries communicate actions they will take to reduce their GHG emissions to reach the goals of the Paris Agreement. Countries also communicate in the NDCs actions they will take to build resilience to adapt to the impacts of rising temperatures.

Although climate change action needs to be massively increased to achieve the goals of the Paris Agreement, the years since its entry into force have already sparked low-carbon solutions and new markets. More and more countries, regions, cities, and companies are establishing carbon neutrality targets. Zero-carbon solutions are becoming competitive across economic sectors representing 25 percent of emissions. This trend is most noticeable in the power and transport sectors and has created many new business opportunities for early movers.

By 2030, zero-carbon solutions could be competitive in sectors representing over 70 percent of global emissions.

A report published by UN Climate Change ahead of COP27 shows that while countries are bending the curve of global GHG emissions downward, efforts remain insufficient to limit global temperature rise to 1.5°C by the end of the century. Since COP26 in Glasgow, only 29 out of 194 countries came forward with tightened national plans (UN Climate Change 2022).

### The United Nations Sustainable Development Goals

The UN Sustainable Development Goals (SDGs) are a universal call to action to end poverty, protect the planet, and improve the lives and prospects of everyone, everywhere. The 17 goals were adopted by all UN Member States in 2015, as part of the 2030 Agenda for Sustainable Development which set out a 15-year plan to achieve the goals.

On January 1, 2016, the 17 SDGs of the 2030 Agenda for Sustainable Development, adopted by world leaders in September 2015 at a historic UN Summit, officially came into force. Over the next 15 years, with these new goals that universally apply to all, countries will mobilize efforts to end all forms of poverty, fight inequalities, and tackle climate change, while ensuring that no one is left behind.

It is clear that the SDGs not only identify where we have to be in 2030 to create a sustainable world, but also outline new markets and opportunities for companies all over the world. To succeed, we must turn global goals into local business.

Taking urgent action to combat climate change and its devastating impacts is therefore imperative to save lives and livelihoods and is key to making the 2030 Agenda for Sustainable Development and its 17 goals—the blueprint for a better future—a reality.

In 2020, concentrations of global GHGs reached new highs, and real-time data point to continued increases. As these concentrations rise, so does the Earth's temperature. In 2021, the global mean temperature was about 1.1°C above the preindustrial level (from 1850 to 1900), with glaciers melting and the sea level rising. The years from 2015 to 2021 were the seven warmest on record (UN Climate Change 2022b). The impacts of climate change also include flooding and drought, displacing millions of people, sinking them into poverty and hunger, denying them access to basic services, such as health and education, expanding inequalities, stifling economic growth, and even causing conflict. By 2030, an estimated 700 million people will be at risk of displacement by drought alone (United Nations 2022a).

To limit warming to 1.5°C above preindustrial levels, as set out in the Paris Agreement, global GHG emissions will need to peak before 2025. Then they must decline by 43 percent by 2030 and to net-zero by 2050. Countries are articulating climate action plans to cut emissions and adapt to climate impacts through NDCs. However, current national commitments are not sufficient to meet the 1.5°C targets.

### "Climate Justice"—Case of Pakistan

With catastrophic floods that submerged a third of the country under water, Pakistan became a prime example of 2022 of the devastation that can be wrought by climate change. The flooding—caused by melting glaciers and torrential monsoon rains, both linked to climate change—made lakes out of villages, killed more than 1,700 people, displaced tens of millions, and caused upward of $30 billion in damage, with vast swaths of cropland destroyed and rampant disease.

When rains in June–September 2022 began to inundate villages, logistically the country was hardly prepared. It took at least two months for Pakistan to accept the scale of destruction and loss. Even after the disaster, there was hardly any emphasis on the country's total lack of preparation (Brohi 2022).

As Pakistan asked the world for support for flood relief and recovery, it framed it as a call for climate justice, not humanitarian assistance. It is responsible for less than 1 percent of global carbon emissions but is the eighth most climate-vulnerable country in the world. But those calls for climate justice—a fraught issue for developed nations—didn't find widespread traction, other than a forceful advocate in UN Secretary-General António Guterres. So Pakistan set its sights on COP27 to advocate its case and sent a solid delegation to Sharm el-Sheikh, headed by its prime minister, foreign minister, and minister for climate change. It made its case (as did Guterres), but the matter is beyond its control alone.

The most likely framework for climate justice for Pakistan and other vulnerable countries is the concept of loss and damage, which is helpfully on the agenda of COP27 for the first time and which has started to collect some funding from European capitals, but which still finds resistance from the United States and other developed nations. The expectations of anything major coming out of the meetings in Egypt in terms of a well-financed loss and damage facility are slim. Realistically, Pakistan's calls for climate justice aren't likely to receive a full, positive resolution anytime soon—but at least the issue, finally, is on the agenda.

According to the United Nations Children's Fund (UNICEF), schools for more than two million children in Pakistan remain completely inaccessible after the most severe flooding in the country's history destroyed or damaged nearly 27,000 schools in the country. Almost overnight, millions of Pakistan's children lost family members, homes, safety, and their education, under the most traumatic circumstances. Now, faced with the uncertainty of when they'll be able to return to school, and having already endured some of the world's longest school closures due to the pandemic, they are experiencing yet another threat to their future (UNICEF 2022).

UNICEF warns that the longer schools remain closed, the greater the risk of children dropping out altogether, increasing their likelihood of being forced into child labor and exposure to other forms of abuse in the impoverished South Asian nation of about 220 million people.

Pakistan already has the world's second highest number of out-of-school children, with an estimated 22.8 million children aged 5 to 16 not attending school, representing 44 percent of the total population in that age group, according to UNICEF. Many of the districts hit the worst by the flooding were already listed among Pakistan's most vulnerable areas, where a third of boys and girls were already out of school, and 50 percent of children suffered from stunting.

During the height of the coronavirus pandemic, schools across Pakistan were fully or partially closed for 64 weeks until they were reopened in March 2022, one of the world's longest school closures. Less than six months on, the destruction caused by the extreme floods means schoolchildren are once again locked out of learning. Excessive damage to infrastructure, including electricity and Internet connectivity, has left remote learning largely inaccessible.

### The Business Challenge

As customers demand greener products and services, investors seek out the next big climate solution, and governments legislate to cut emissions, companies know they need to decarbonize and fast. Advice and tools on how to cut emissions abound, so many companies remain confused about how to prioritize their efforts and understand what "good" climate action looks like.

Many companies are falling short of their carbon pledges. A new guide defines the four As of what companies must do to deliver on net-zero commitments and avoid accusations of greenwashing. *Ambition*: Has the company set the right decarbonization targets? *Action*: Is your company prioritizing the most impactful climate actions? *Advocacy*: Is your company's lobbying in line with your climate goals? And *accountability*: Is your company's sustainability reporting clear and transparent (Mendiluce 2022)?

The Russia–Ukraine conflict has also caused food, fuel, and fertilizer prices to skyrocket. It has further disrupted supply chains and global trade and caused distress in financial markets. By current estimates, the war could cut global economic growth by 0.9 percentage points in 2022, as well as undermine development aid to the world's poor (United Nations 2022).

These situations will only deteriorate with climate change, which acts as a "crisis multiplier" and whose impacts are already being felt across the globe. Increased heatwaves, droughts, and floods are affecting billions of people worldwide, contributing further to poverty, hunger, and instability. The COVID-19 pandemic and the war in Ukraine have further delayed the urgently needed transition to greener economies. Based on current national commitments, global GHG emissions are set to increase by almost 14 percent over the current decade.

## The New World Order

According to the Boston Consulting Group research, the global economy will lose up to $10 trillion in GDP in 2025 unless governments repeal or reduce tariffs and nontariff barriers that currently obstruct global merchandise trade, according to a new report released today for G20 governments (Anaya et al. 2020).

For the past few years, in many parts of the world, a protectionist mindset has been challenging the continuing trend of globalization. This mindset, if it spreads further, could endanger the many benefits of more open international trade, which include allowing multinational supply chains to become more flexible and versatile, giving consumers throughout the world better selection and lower prices, and helping pull hundreds of millions of people out of poverty. Open trade has also facilitated innovation and economic cooperation. A notable example is the expansion of international e-commerce, which has given smaller businesses and those in developing economies access to global markets.

The COVID-19 pandemic has delivered perhaps the greatest shock to international trade since the Great Depression. Regardless of when the top-line numbers fully recover, the global trade landscape will still look dramatically different as companies shift their focus from fighting the pandemic to winning the post-COVID-19 future. As it destabilizes economies, intensifies geopolitical frictions, and exposes the risks of current global manufacturing and supply networks, the pandemic is also likely to redraw the map of world trade.

## Protectionism

The current wave of protectionism, which has seen the imposition of new tariffs and other trade restrictions, is slowing down these positive developments. The COVID-19 pandemic represents a further deep shock to global trade. It is prompting a reconfiguration of value chains around the world, as countries look to reduce their reliance on certain foreign suppliers and increase their self-sufficiency in strategic industries, and as firms seek to reduce their dependence on single sources of supply. There is a real risk that these trends may further fuel a damaging spiral of trade restrictions and retaliation.

The risk of a trade war came sharply into focus in 2018, as protectionist threats by the U.S. Administration of President Donald Trump and its trading partners were followed by concrete actions. Tensions rose over the summer and, while these have been defused on some fronts, the risk of further escalation remains material. The impact of the measures implemented so far on the global and euro area economic outlooks is expected to remain contained. However, large negative effects could materialize if trade tensions were to escalate further. Uncertainty related to protectionism is weighing on economic sentiment and it may raise further, potentially eroding confidence and affecting the euro area and the global economy more significantly. The complexity of intertwined international production chains could also magnify the impact.

There is widespread consensus among economists on both the overall net benefits of trade openness and the need to cushion the negative impact it has had on certain groups in society. However, raising trade barriers is not the solution to the latter. Reversing trade integration may put at risk the net economic gains that it generated. By unraveling the long-term benefits of closer trade and investment links, retreating into protectionism also has the potential to unsettle global financial markets.

## The Business Challenge

Trade barriers make it more costly, or more difficult, for domestic businesses and consumers to buy goods from abroad, reducing trade flows. These barriers often take the form of tariffs, which for a given exchange rate increase the price of imported goods relative to those that are domestically produced. Nontariff measures, including import quotas or changes to regulatory standards, can also create trade barriers. A rise in the cost of imported goods due to tariffs will lower real incomes and, in turn, weigh on domestic demand growth. Some domestic production that uses imports as inputs might also be constrained if trade barriers cause supply chain disruption.

Lower trade can reduce productivity growth as businesses are less exposed to global competition and new ideas, less able to exploit comparative advantages by specializing, and less able to benefit from economies of scale. Historically, there has been a strong relationship between trade openness and output via productivity. A study by Feyrer (2019), for example, suggests that a 20 percent reduction in trade flows tends to drag on output by around 5 percent in the long run. The integration of global supply chains in recent decades may have intensified that link.

The impact may spill over to other countries. Countries that are not directly exposed to an increase in trade barriers might nonetheless feel some effect from their imposition elsewhere. Some might benefit from positive "trade diversion" effects if they produce close substitutes for products supplied by those countries that become subject to tariffs. However, most countries are likely to be negatively affected by the reduction in global demand, particularly if they supply inputs for affected countries' exports.

Spillovers could also occur via reduced business confidence and increased uncertainty. The introduction of trade barriers may make businesses more uncertain about the potential market for their products and services, and whether further protectionist policies will follow. That uncertainty is likely to reduce business investment, lowering the rate of global capital accumulation and so supply growth.

Global financial conditions could also be affected. The price of companies' equity or corporate bonds might fall, for example, if investors expect trade barriers to reduce profitability or increase the risks around it.

An increase in uncertainty, coupled with financial stress, could also amplify the impact of rising protectionism on economic activity. There are several ways in which elevated uncertainty about future trade policies can dampen demand. For example, households may delay spending when economic prospects become more uncertain. Furthermore, firms may reassess their economic prospects amid rising uncertainty, taking a "wait and see" approach and postponing investment.

In response to uncertainty shocks, firms can also adjust their inventory policies by disproportionately cutting their foreign orders of intermediate goods, with a disproportionate impact on international trade flows. An uncertain trade policy outlook may also give firms a reason to delay entering a foreign market or upgrading their technology. Finally, elevated uncertainty may push up borrowing costs for households and firms as investors demand greater compensation to protect themselves against future risks. The materialization of a global uncertainty shock, such as a trade war, may also drive investors to shift their portfolios to safe-haven currencies, with implications for the allocation of capital flows across countries.

Higher trade costs can also weigh on productivity. The tighter financing conditions associated with rising uncertainty can raise the cost of capital, with a negative impact on investment that could hinder productivity growth in the countries affected by the tariffs. Trade barriers can also lead to the misallocation of production factors across firms and countries. Less-open markets diminish global competition, thereby reducing incentives for innovation and technological advances and keeping less-productive firms in the market. As a result, aggregate productivity may decline.

## Geopolitical Tensions

In 1905, Britain was the ruler of the waves and watched with concern as the United States rose to become a potential challenger. While a shared heritage between the two nations helped avoid military conflict as the United States inevitably overtook British international power, the rise of Germany and Japan in the 20th-century global power struggle did precipitate war.

After the Soviet Union's collapse in December 1991, the United States became the de facto enforcer of the geopolitical order. This role of the United States was supported by a common view among Americans on this foreign policy. However, in recent years, ideological lines between the U.S. parties grew starker and foreign policy views began to mirror broader trends in the U.S. electorate. As a result, the United States has retreated from its role as the global superpower.

This fact is having far-reaching consequences, and other countries are trying to fill the resulting power vacuum. Some are increasing their efforts to have a central role in a more communal, but not necessarily more stable world geopolitical order. This is the case particularly for China and Russia at the global level.

## U.S.–China Rivalry

In a special report on China and America, *The Economist* explains that, with the rise of a richer and defiantly authoritarian China, the then U.S. President Barack Obama is likely to face a far more "nettlesome" challenger to the world order than his own country had been a century ago. Since the United States is still struggling to emerge from the crisis, and China's economy is still growing at pace (albeit somewhat slower than before the crisis), many experts see the balance of power shifting rapidly in favor of China. Recent references to a U.S.–China "G2" indicate a shift in relative nation strengths and that these two countries are now seen as "near-equals," whose cooperation is vital to solving the world's problems (Economist 2019a).

China is willing to become a global power. President Xi of China has pledged "to complete the modernization of China's armed forces by 2035 and build a world-class military capable of winning wars across all theatres by 2050." At the center of the efforts to modernize China's People's Liberation Army, there is a strong focus on technologies, particularly big data and AI (Economist 2019b).

China's geopolitical power is not solely based on its military force but derived from its capacity to take advantage of geo-economic factors such as the direct control of resources (e.g., rare earth), data logistics, trade imbalances, extraterritorial control, and sanctions. In December 2020, China enacted an export control law that tightened restrictions on the shipments of "strategic goods." This form of extraterritorial control, involving also the use of "blacklists," is a tool that has typically been used by the United States and is now also used by China to expand its economic influence and its rule of law in foreign affairs (Tan 2020).

In Asia, the U.S. House Speaker Nancy Pelosi's trip to Taiwan in August 2022 touched off a serious crisis between the United States and China. Indeed, given the way the two countries' interests are now colliding in hot spots throughout the Western Pacific, the question is not whether they will find themselves in some sort of perilous showdown but when, where, and under what circumstances (Huang 2022).

These aren't the only global flash points: Washington is currently laboring under the threat of renewed nuclear crises with Iran and North Korea. But showdowns with even the most roguish of rogue states aren't as consequential as great-power military crises—incidents that have a meaningful prospect of war. So buckle up for a period when the world's mightiest actors engage in high-stakes tests of strength.

Crises are terrifying, but they can also be clarifying. Diplomatic or military confrontations illuminate the intentions of an adversary. They vividly illustrate the stakes of geopolitical competition. Crises are also opportunities for constructive action: They can catalyze initiatives and investments that will help the United States triumph in the protracted rivalries ahead.

### Russia–Ukraine War

In Europe, Russia's invasion of Ukraine has destabilized the continent's eastern half, triggered a proxy war with NATO, and created an ever-present risk of escalation. The invasion began on the morning of February 24, 2022, when Russian President Vladimir Putin announced a "special military operation" for the "demilitarisation and denazification" of Ukraine. However, the conflict has been ongoing between Russia and Ukraine since February 2014 following Russia's annexation of Crimea in eastern Ukraine (BBC 2022).

With the current Russo-Ukrainian war, much of the focus by organizations naturally has been on managing the immediate impact: making sure that people and operations are as safe as possible; resetting, exiting, or idling operations in Russia and Ukraine; navigating sanctions; securing immediate resources; circumventing breaks in the supply chains; and supporting refugees and others immediately impacted by the war. While solidarity and crisis management will continue to be urgent necessities for however long the war lasts, leaders must start to develop strategies for the mid-term—and they must act fast.

The war in Ukraine has further compounded impacts still playing out from the pandemic, and the transformation timescale continues to compress. What would have happened in a 10-year horizon under a "business as usual" trajectory is now happening over 10 months. The pressure on leaders to act has never been so great or urgent, just as the data informing those decisions are increasingly volatile.

The conflict between Russia and Ukraine has created severe geopolitical and economic shockwaves with lasting effects. Sanctions on Russia have escalated, Russia's relations with the west have deteriorated, and disruptions to energy and food markets have become even more severe. As of this writing in November 2022, contingencies previously considered by some to be far-fetched, such as Russia shutting off natural gas flows to Europe or a rise in political instability in emerging markets, are becoming a reality. Reduced and disrupted flows of Russian oil and gas to Europe and the recent upheaval in Sri Lanka are notable examples (Shih 2022).

### The South China Sea Disputes

The main conflict in the South China Sea (SCS) dates back to 1279 when China drew a territorial map of its influence that included the entire SCS. Since then, control over the region has changed hands between regional powers and, later, colonial states. However, most people agree that the bulk of the current problems stems from the 1951 San Francisco Treaty, which followed Japan's defeat in World War II. Within the terms of its surrender, Japan gave up its rights to its islands in the SCS, leaving a power vacuum in the region. No country was explicitly granted sovereignty over these waters, and China (the Kuomintang Government) asserted its advantage by submitting the now infamous "nine-dotted line" claim covering almost the entire SCS in 1947. This line became its official claim and is known today as the "Nine-Dash Line" (Khoury 2017).

In 1982, the United Nations law established exclusive economic zones (EEZs). Right after, China reiterated its nine-dash line, refusing to clarify the limits of this line and rejecting the claims of other claimant countries. Ever since, tensions have built up over who owns the SCS.

In the meantime, the conflict has focused on the Paracels and Spratly Islands, an archipelago located in the heart of the SCS. Currently, China, Malaysia, the Philippines, and Vietnam claim part of the Paracels and Spratly Islands chain. They have asserted their claims by setting up small ships, ports, and even people on what is essentially a rock in the middle of the ocean.

The SCS is of vital importance for the Asia-Pacific, a fact further emphasized by the U.S. foreign policy rebalance toward Asia. The United Nations Conference on Trade and Development (UNCTAD) estimates that roughly 80 percent of global trade by volume and 70 percent by value is transported by sea. Of that volume, 60 percent of maritime trade passes through Asia, with the SCS carrying an estimated one-third of global shipping. Its waters are particularly critical for China, Taiwan, Japan, and South Korea, all of which rely on the Strait of Malacca, which connects the SCS and, by extension, the Pacific Ocean with the Indian Ocean. As the second largest economy in the world with over 60 percent of its trade-in value traveling by sea, China's economic security is closely tied to the SCS (China Power 2017).

As a vital artery of trade for many of the world's largest economies, the SCS has garnered significant attention. The high concentration of commercial goods flowing through the relatively narrow Strait of Malacca has raised concerns about its vulnerability as a strategic chokepoint. Reports on the SCS frequently claim that $5.3 trillion worth of goods transits through the SCS annually, with $1.2 trillion of that total accounting for trade with the United States. This $5.3 trillion figure has been used regularly since late 2010, despite significant changes in world trade over the last five-plus years.

Over the past several years, the SCS has emerged as an arena of U.S.–China strategic competition. China's actions in the SCS—including extensive island-building and base construction activities at sites that it occupies in the Spratly Islands, as well as actions by its maritime forces to assert China's claims against competing claims by regional neighbors such as the Philippines and Vietnam—have heightened concerns among U.S. observers that China is gaining effective control of the SCS, an area of strategic, political, and economic importance to the United States and its allies and partners. Actions by China's maritime forces at the Japan-administered Senkaku Islands in the East China Sea (ECS) are another concern for U.S. observers. Chinese domination of China's near-seas region—meaning the SCS and ECS, along with the Yellow Sea—could substantially affect U.S. strategic, political, and economic interests in the Indo-Pacific region and elsewhere (Hsiung 2018).

China's sweeping claims of sovereignty over the sea—and the sea's estimated 11 billion barrels of untapped oil and 190 trillion cubic feet of natural gas—have antagonized competing claimants Brunei, Indonesia, Malaysia, the Philippines, Taiwan, and Vietnam. As early as the 1970s, countries began to claim islands and various zones in the SCS, such as the Spratly Islands, which possess rich natural resources and fishing areas (Firestein 2016).

China maintains that, under international law, foreign militaries are not allowed to conduct intelligence-gathering activities, such as recon-naissance flights, in its EEZ. According to the United States, claimant countries, under the UN Convention of the Law of the Sea (UNCLOS), should have freedom of navigation through EEZs in the sea and are not required to notify claimants of military activities. In July 2016, the Permanent Court of Arbitration at The Hague issued its ruling on a claim brought against China by the Philippines under UNCLOS, ruling in favor of the Philippines on almost every count. While China is a signatory to the treaty, which established the tribunal, it refuses to accept the court's authority (Raditio 2019).

In recent years, satellite imagery has shown China's increased efforts to reclaim land in the SCS by physically increasing the size of islands or creating new islands altogether. In addition to piling sand onto existing reefs, China has constructed ports, military installations, and airstrips—particularly in the Paracel and Spratly Islands, where it has 20 and 7 outposts, respectively. China has militarized Woody Island by deploying fighter jets, cruise missiles, and a radar system.

In July 2022, the U.S. Secretary of State Antony Blinken called on China to stick to its international law obligations and promised any attack on the Philippines would trigger a U.S. military response in the SCS. He warned that the United States will defend the Philippines against any attack on its ships or aircraft in the SCS. The statement was made on the sixth anniversary of a 2016 decision by an international arbitration tribunal that largely ruled in favor of the Philippines over the disputed maritime border. China did not participate in the arbitration. "We re-affirm that an armed attack on Philippine armed forces ... would invoke US mutual defense commitments," Blinken said. The mutual defense commitments stem from a 1951 treaty between the allies.

The development of the SCS tension corresponds to the security dilemma continuum. Mounting evidence shows that instead of premeditated actions, the development of the SCS security dilemma is a result of uncertainty and inadvertency between China and other claimant states. The same applies to the tension between China and the United States in the SCS. Uncertainty is one of the key concepts of defensive realism. In contrast, offensive realism suggests that all states aim at power maximization and regional hegemony, which create much less uncertainty. The offensive realism assumption suggests that China will pursue a hegemonic ambition to resolve its dispute with other claimants and it is the only strategy to guarantee a state's survival (Hamilton and Rathbun 2013).

# Metaverse

### Disruptive Innovation Revisited

Technology has long been acknowledged as a disruptive force that radically changed the nature of work, business, and society in general. In the 19th century, the Industrial Revolution altered the world and how organizations were being managed profoundly and permanently. Then came electrification, the automobile, and mass production, just to name a few massive technological changes that have reshaped the 20th century. In today's 21st century, powerful digital technologies and the rise of Internet connectivity have created a knowledge-driven digital economy that has revolutionized to a more significant extent and made a considerable impact on and profound changes in human history toward the way we work, live, and do business every day (Bawany 2019).

We have seen a vast range of ever-improving advanced technologies that are driving the disruptive innovation that will continue to change and redefine our world. Advanced technologies can simply be defined as emerging technologies that may enable new ways of doing business that result in more economical consumer trade-offs as well as improving employees' productivity and enhancing the organization's sustainability in the longer term.

When an innovation creates a new market or value that disrupts an existing market, it is known as "disruptive innovation." It is a process where an underrated product or service starts to grow in popularity and displace and eventually replace an established player or market leader. The term "disruptive innovation" was coined by the late Harvard Business School (HBS) professor Clayton Christensen, who describes it as "a process by which a product or service takes root initially in simple applications at the bottom of a market and then relentlessly moves upmarket, eventually displacing established competitors" (Christensen 1997).

Before Christensen, an illustrious Harvard economic professor in the 1940s, Joseph Schumpeter differentiated innovation from that less ground-breaking change, calling it "creative destruction." According to him, creative destruction refers to the constant product and process innovation mechanism by which new production units replace outdated ones. He considered it as "the essential fact about capitalism" (Schumpeter 1942).

Christensen discovered the reason why it is incredibly challenging for existing firms to capitalize on disruptive innovation is that their existing systems, processes, business model, and operating philosophy that make them competent or sound at the current business would make them ineffective at competing for disruption (Christensen 1997).

Disruptive innovators have smaller margins, niche markets, and simple product offerings. These products begin their journey from the bottom and slowly climb their way to the top and dethrone the market leader.

When a new player enters the market, whose primary objective is to disrupt the industry, the market leader is in a paralysis state and tends to ignore the progress it is making. Soon, the startup or market challenger starts to challenge the market leader's supremacy. This is when the latter will begin to react, but it will be likely that the leader is too late unless it transforms itself quickly to stay relevant; otherwise, it will be lost in oblivion.

Given how extensively the phrase "disruptive innovation" has been invoked for nearly 20 years, Christensen and his coauthors revisit his most famous innovative ideas in the *Harvard Business Review* article, "What Is Disruptive Innovation?" (Christensen et al. 2015). They assert that the concept of "disruptive innovation" has proven to be a powerful way of thinking about innovation-driven growth and say that "Many leaders of small, entrepreneurial companies praise it as their guiding star; so do many executives at large, well-established organizations, including Intel, Southern New Hampshire University, and Salesforce.com." Regrettably, they also believe that the disruption theory is in danger of becoming a victim of its success since they discovered that despite it being widely accepted and known, the core concepts have been widely misunderstood and frequently misapplied.

### The Metaverse: What Is It and Why Is It Important?

The metaverse is starting to take shape, and it's going to change everything. We're not talking about some far-off future; the metaverse is already here. Virtual reality (VR) and augmented reality (AR) are becoming more and more popular, and as they continue to evolve, the metaverse will become an increasingly important part of our lives. Business owners and marketers need to start paying attention now to be ready for when it takes off.

Metaverse is a term that was coined by Neal Stephenson in his 1992 science fiction novel *Snow Crash* (Stephenson 1992). Metaverse is a portmanteau of "meta" and "universe." It's VR—characterized by persistent virtual worlds that continue to exist even when you're not playing—and AR that combine aspects of the digital and physical worlds. Consumers can discover information about your brand and make digital purchases of your items/services from the comfort of their own homes.

The metaverse is still being defined, both literally and figuratively. Yet its potential to unleash the next wave of digital disruption seems increasingly clear, with real-life benefits already emerging for early adopting users and companies (McKinsey 2022a). As we saw in previous shifts in technology such as the emergence of the Internet followed by social media, mobile, and cloud, novel disruptive innovation strategies can quickly become table stakes.

The metaverse has the potential to impact everything from employee engagement to customer experience, omnichannel sales and marketing, product innovation, and community building. Examining its potential effect should be part of strategy discussions, with leaders accelerating their analysis of how the metaverse could drive a very different world within the next decade. Of course, many questions remain, including how virtual worlds will be balanced with the physical world to ensure the metaverse is built responsibly, how it can be a safe environment for consumers, how closely it will align with the "open" vision of the next iteration of the Internet, and whether technology can advance quickly enough to build the metaverse of our imagination.

Some people think the metaverse is just a pipe dream, but we believe it will be an inevitable part of how we seek out entertainment, communicate, do business, and so on. According to the consulting firm McKinsey & Co, businesses' and consumers' annual global spending related to the metaverse could reach $5 trillion by 2030, with almost half of it spent on e-commerce. In McKinsey's study, 95 percent of executives said they believe the metaverse will have a positive impact on their respective industries in 5 to 10 years, and 25 percent said they expect it to drive 15 percent of their organization's total margin growth in five years. And that's why business owners and marketers should pay attention to broadening their reach further from the physical world to avoid trying to catch up with competitors later (McKinsey 2022b).

The metaverse is reshaping digital commerce, enabling businesses to create more personalized, immersive, and seamless experiences for their customers. Different technologies including AR, VR, artificial intelligence (AI), and machine learning (ML) are powering the metaverse, allowing users to interact and shop in a highly customized, virtual landscape on a new, never-experienced level.

Expert forecasts offer a glimpse as to how the metaverse will grow, what opportunities may abound, and the economic impacts that will ripple throughout markets. The metaverse technology market alone is already projected to hit $224 billion by 2030 (Research and Markets 2022).

### The Business Challenge

The metaverse will impact every business that consumers interact with every day. According to Gartner, the metaverse is where a quarter of us will be working, studying, shopping, and socializing for at least an hour a day by 2026 (Gartner 2022).

There are significant challenges, however. While pioneers have shown the metaverse provides opportunities that echo or even improve those in the real world, their potential remains unclear—and most companies are proceeding carefully. There is also concern about brand dilution, especially within the luxury market, as companies contemplate association with digital items and how that may derail their image from the core, luxury brand positions. An additional consideration is the maturity of AR/VR technology, in which glitchy applications can undermine the user experience of luxury goods, presenting an image and consumer engagement threat. Brands should consider what is necessary to strike the right balance between testing and learning and ensure they are rigorous in thinking through potential outcomes of actions taken in this new, exciting, and seemingly limitless space.

There is also the issue of what a metaverse venture means organizationally. Generating sustainable revenue from virtual worlds will require entirely new capabilities and an almost diametrical talent shift in the creative design process as well as digital execution. Brands may need to review existing organizational structures and skills, update their recruiting strategies, likely establish innovative partnerships with metaverse platforms, and acquire startups in the space.

Yet, the level of connectivity in the metaverse for certain users already shows how the virtual world could have a significant influence on consumer habits and trends in the physical world, not to mention how this may inform which physical designs are ultimately produced and sold.

While the last several years have brought significant changes to e-commerce, the metaverse is poised to revolutionize shopping in ways we can only imagine—for now. Early makers and adopters of the technology powering the metaverse continue to unveil new products and build excitement for the virtual universe.

The metaverse will combine the best of in-person shopping and e-commerce. How? By interacting with customers within virtual shopping malls, companies will learn more about individualized shopping and product preferences. Based on shopping behaviors, companies can use data gathered from prior customer visits to the metaverse to customize shopping experiences. Additionally, personalization leads to product recommendations or discounts to help further customize shopper experiences.

Within the metaverse, consumers will be able to utilize their senses of sight and touch while shopping—from the comfort of their couch. As both are so integral to the buying process, the experience would rival the immersive feeling of being in a physical store.

Online shopping can be viewed as a relatively individual activity. However, the metaverse is changing this aspect by making it a more social activity as people can freely interact with one another. As immersive experiences will be the norm in the metaverse, brands can invite customers to actively participate in social activities.

Research indicates that AR increases shopping times and yields higher conversion rates among consumers. Research by Vertebrae, a company specializing in AR and 3D e-commerce, reports conversion rates for customers increase by 90 percent when engaging with AR versus those that don't. The increased capabilities for product visualization can help brands achieve higher profit margins (Mottl 2020).

Brands will know how much merchandise to produce based on customer use and interaction in the metaverse. According to Google, 66 percent of individuals would like to get help from AR when shopping. In the metaverse, improved customer interactions will enable companies to get a better sense of customers, allowing them to tap into buying emotion. Overall, the customer will be happier in their experience and buying journey (Google 2019).

### How Metaverse Will Benefit Businesses?

*Accelerated manufacturing*: A product's life cycle before it hits the shelf involves multiple-step prices including procurement of raw materials, prototyping, and test phase, which take a significant amount of time. With metaverse in play, this manufacturing process could be accelerated. To speed up the process, stages like trial production testing, operation management, marketing, and other operations can be verified within the virtual community.

*Immersive shopping experience*: Shopping today is not just about the need or the product but also about the story and experience of buying from a particular brand that resonates with you. With Q-commerce ("quick commerce," sometimes used interchangeably with "on-demand delivery" and "e-grocery," which delivers small quantities of goods to customers almost instantly for less than an hour typically, whenever and wherever they need them) and e-commerce on the rise, metaverse will be at the forefront of creating innovative and meaningful interactions. As an AR platform, it will help companies offer unique experiences to their customer base. The popularity and visible growth of virtual characters in retail sectors like gaming or fashion has pushed brands to enhance digital experiences for dissemination of information and building customer loyalty.

*Remote work*: The pandemic catapulted companies into remote work. In the postpandemic world, most businesses continue to operate in a remote working module or a hybrid work module. While remote work has its pros, it has led to lesser creative interactions and communication between colleagues. Metaverse could be a way to bring back the work culture in play without compromising the remote working or hybrid work module. Academic studies have found that collaborative work among colleagues suffers when they work remotely. The lack of real-time in-person conversations hampers communication, and metaverse could no doubt help with the same by creating persistent VR workplace environments to encourage corridor chat, employee interaction, collaborative activities, and so on.

*Optimized corporate learnings and training*: Metaverse with its hyperreality will provide a digital reality where skill training, operations, orientation sessions, and so on can be held without disrupting everyday processes. Businesses today are looking to increase time and cost optimization. These strategies often require reorganizing workflows that might lead to slight delays. This is where metaverse will step in. Testing new adjustments and layout and flows digitally will not hamper work in the physical world, thus increasing productivity.

*Better customer engagement and enhanced marketing*: Marketing and customer interaction have come a long way from print ads. Engagement today is about resonating with the customer, allowing them to step into your world and connect with your product. Metaverse will bring a new meaning to marketing and engagement. For what can be termed as a unique and lucrative space for brands to rightly communicate to their audience, the metaverse will further enhance the shopping experience. This change will also call for heightened analysis of digital insights and traffic. From refined SEO, advertisement stats, and deciphering virtual avatars and their purchase pattern, metaverse will call for businesses to have an innovative strategy in place and help reach a more niche target audience best suited for your business.

Metaverse will require businesses to be flexible and adopt a long-term digital transformation strategy that will help them stay ahead of the curve and unfurl a world of new possibilities.

### Embracing the Metaverse

Market dynamics, global connectivity, and technology have all impacted the ways retailers connect with consumers and vice versa. Changing customer expectations have been a driving force behind the transformations to e-commerce over the last several years. Retailers are chasing innovations that enable fast, seamless, and personalized experiences. Metaverse is the most recent innovation to impact the e-commerce industry. With it still emerging, we can only predict the impact of the metaverse on e-commerce, but we are excitedly anticipating the future.

### Retail

For brands and retailers in the medium to longer term, the metaverse will be about adding a new sales channel to the omnichannel mix. This is also critical to unlocking the metaverse's ultimate potential. It will succeed in the consumer sector if it further blurs the line between the concepts of "online" and "offline" to create a unified experience. And it may not only create rich, intense, and seamless customer experiences that can span the physical and digital worlds, but also collect valuable new data points for understanding customers in a cookie-less world.

The metaverse presents an opportunity for retailers to reimagine and personalize the store environment for individuals and groups of customers. For example, using VR technology, customers at a sporting-goods retailer could shop in settings matching the specific sport they are buying equipment for, such as shopping for ski equipment in a virtual version of the Alps and even trying skis in VR. Metaverse malls are also being created, featuring storefronts where users can interact through their avatars.

## Financial Services

The metaverse brings together online social networks, gaming, cryptocurrencies, and increasingly diverse digital assets to enable novel services and experiences. Financial services companies have joined peers across industries in exploring the potential opportunity in the metaverse, though few are yet attempting this at scale. The likely future extent of the impact of the metaverse on the sector depends on the evolution of the underlying technology (especially utilizing Web3) and on the degree to which platforms are adopted as part of our daily interactions.

There is no shortage of financial services companies exploring the utility of the latest evolution of the metaverse. As its function transitions from primarily consumer entertainment to more commercial applications, and niche social interactions become a social network, the opportunities for the sector will only expand. Institutions may create digital branches in the metaverse to build their brand and credibility with users, demonstrate their ability to innovate, and even offer client interactions in a hybrid way with more traditional digital or even physical channels. As cyber insurance for companies and similar services become more commonplace, insurers and cybersecurity companies are well positioned to capture parts of this emerging value pool, maybe even in novel collaborations and models.

## Societal Change

The metaverse may bring extensive societal change. People could be working in a virtual world, playing games together, owning virtual assets, consuming virtual land and goods, socializing in virtual spaces, and creating worlds and items. We are not suggesting holding back from experimenting in the metaverse until the road map seems clear—that could place organizations at a competitive disadvantage that might be hard to recover from. Rather, organizations should take care to develop products responsibly, taking the opportunity to embed and engender digital trust while the metaverse is still in its formative stage. We are already seeing allegations of disturbing behavior within metaverse worlds (Shen 2022), underscoring the need to address emerging issues before they potentially become systemic problems.

## ChatGPT—Generative AI Systems

ChatGPT, a new artificial intelligence (AI) chatbot developed by San Francisco-based research laboratory OpenAI, has taken the world by storm. Hailed as a milestone in the evolution of the so-called large language models (LLMs), the world's most famous generative AI raises important questions about who controls this nascent market and whether these powerful technologies serve the public interest.

OpenAI's release of ChatGPT in November 2022 quickly became a global sensation, attracting millions of users and allegedly killing the student essay. It can answer questions in conversational English (along with some other languages) and perform other tasks, such as writing computer code.

The answers that ChatGPT provides are fluent and compelling, but despite its facility for language, it can sometimes make mistakes or generate factual falsehoods, a phenomenon known among AI researchers as "hallucination" (Coyle 2023).

Generative AI describes algorithms (such as ChatGPT) that can be used to create new content, including audio, code, images, text, simulations, and videos. Recent breakthroughs in the field have the potential to drastically change the way we approach content creation.

While many have reacted to ChatGPT (and AI and machine learning more broadly) with fear, machine learning has the potential for good. In the years since its wide deployment, machine learning has impacted several industries, accomplishing things like medical imaging analysis and high-resolution weather forecasts.

A 2022 McKinsey survey shows that AI adoption has more than doubled over the past five years, and investment in AI is increasing apace. Generative AI tools like ChatGPT and DALL-E (a tool for AI-generated art) have the potential to change how a range of jobs are performed. The full scope of that impact, though, is still unknown—as are the risks.

But there are some questions we can answer—like how generative AI models are built, what kinds of problems they are best suited to solve, and how they fit into the broader category of machine learning. Read on to get the download (McKinsey 2023).

AI is pretty much just what it sounds like—the practice of getting machines to mimic human intelligence to perform tasks. You've probably interacted with AI even if you don't realize it—voice assistants like Siri and Alexa are founded on AI technology, as are customer service chatbots that pop up to help you navigate websites.

Machine learning is a type of AI. Through machine learning, practitioners develop AI through models that can "learn" from data patterns without human direction. The unmanageably huge volume and complexity of data (unmanageable by humans, anyway) that are now being generated have increased the potential of machine learning, as well as the need for it.

By expanding the use of LLMs, companies could improve efficiency and productivity. (Coyle 2023).

However, the massive, immensely costly, and rapidly increasing computing power needed to train and maintain generative AI tools represents a substantial barrier to entry that could lead to market concentration. The potential for monopolization, together with the risk of abuse, underscores the urgent need for policymakers to consider the implications of this technological breakthrough.

Fortunately, competition authorities in the United States and elsewhere seem to be aware of these risks. In late 2022, the British Office of Communications launched an investigation into the cloud-computing market, on which all large AI models rely, while the US Federal Trade Commission is investigating Amazon Web (McKinsey 2023).

Generative AI is also pushing technology into a realm, thought to be unique to the human mind: creativity. The technology leverages its inputs (the data it has ingested and a user prompt) and experiences (interactions with users that help it "learn" new information and what's correct/incorrect) to generate entirely new content. While dinner table debates will rage for the foreseeable future on whether this truly equates to creativity, most would likely agree that these tools stand to unleash more creativity into the world by prompting humans with starter ideas.

## How Will ChatGPT Benefit Businesses?

These models are in the early days of scaling, but we've started seeing the first batch of applications across functions, including the following (Chui, Roberts, and Yee 2023):

- Marketing and sales—crafting personalized marketing, social media, and technical sales content (including text, images, and video); creating assistants aligned to specific businesses, such as retail
- Operations—generating task lists for efficient execution of a given activity
- IT/engineering—writing, documenting, and reviewing code
- Risk and legal—answering complex questions, pulling from vast amounts of legal documentation, and drafting and reviewing annual reports
- R&D—accelerating drug discovery through a better understanding of diseases and discovery of chemical structures

## The Business Challenge

The awe-inspiring results of generative AI might make it seem like a ready–set–go technology, but that's not the case. Its nascency requires executives to proceed with an abundance of caution. Technologists are still working out the kinks, and plenty of practical and ethical issues remain open. According to McKinsey, here are just a few (Chui, Roberts, and Yee 2023):

1. Like humans, generative AI can be wrong. ChatGPT, for example, sometimes "hallucinates," meaning it confidently generates entirely inaccurate information in response to a user question and has no built-in mechanism to signal this to the user or challenge the result. For example, we have observed instances when the tool was asked to create a short bio and it generated several incorrect facts for the person, such as listing the wrong educational institution.
2. Filters are not yet effective enough to catch inappropriate content. Users of an image-generating application that can create avatars from

a person's photo received avatar options from the system that portrayed them nude, even though they had input appropriate photos of themselves.

3. Systemic biases still need to be addressed. These systems draw from massive amounts of data that might include unwanted biases.

4. Individual company norms and values aren't reflected. Companies will need to adapt the technology to incorporate their culture and values, an exercise that requires technical expertise and computing power beyond what some companies may have ready access to.

5. Intellectual-property questions are up for debate. When a generative AI model brings forward a new product design or idea based on a user prompt, who can lay claim to it? What happens when it plagiarizes a source based on its training data?

## Conclusion

In companies considering generative AI, executives will want to quickly identify the parts of their business where the technology could have the most immediate impact and implement a mechanism to monitor it, given that it is expected to evolve quickly. A no-regrets move is to assemble a cross-functional team, including data science practitioners, legal experts, and functional business leaders, to think through basic questions, such as these: Where might the technology aid or disrupt our industry and/or our business' value chain? What are our policies and posture? For example, are we watchfully waiting to see how the technology evolves, investing in pilots, or looking to build a new business? Should the posture vary across areas of the business? Given the limitations of the models, what are our criteria for selecting use cases to target? How do we pursue building an effective ecosystem of partners, communities, and platforms? What legal and community standards should these models adhere to so we can maintain trust with our stakeholders?

Meanwhile, it's essential to encourage thoughtful innovation across the organization, standing up guardrails along with sandboxed environments for experimentation, many of which are readily available via the cloud, with more likely on the horizon.

# Demographic Shifts

## *Transition Into an Aging Urban World*

A young world will evolve into an aging, urban world. The world is aging as never before as a result of declining fertility and rising life expectancy. This demographic shift is not confined to the west: It is set to become an Asian phenomenon, too. In China, for example, the working-age population is already falling, and the old-age dependency ratio is projected to surpass that of the United States in the next 15 years. Africa, conversely, will be the source of more than half of the global population growth in the coming decades. By the early 2030s, the continent is expected to have a larger working-age population than China or India and a median age of 20. As Africa, the young continent, continues to grow even as populations elsewhere shrink, could it finally enter into a sustained period of rising prosperity?

The world will continue to urbanize, too. In 2021, the world hit "peak rural"—all future population growth is projected to come from urban centers as rural populations decline. Again, urban growth will come from outside the west. Whereas Europe and North America are projected to gain 13 large cities by 2035, Africa and Asia are expected to gain about 50 and 100, respectively (United Nations 2018).

The majority of today's business leaders take abundant labor for granted. Their careers have spanned an era of rapidly expanding global labor pools—an anomaly that is now ending. Three temporary developments converged in the 1950s to create the fastest labor force growth in modern history: the coming of age of the baby boomer generation, women's entry into the workforce, and the integration of China and India into the global economy. But shifting demographics, combined with technological and social changes, point to dramatically different labor market conditions in the coming decade.

Labor force growth and labor productivity growth form the two halves of the equation that determine overall economic output growth. Labor productivity growth without the kicker from labor force growth can create an overall macroeconomic climate of stagnation—Japan's lost decades are a good example of this phenomenon.

Global life expectancy at birth has now topped 70 years for men and 75 years for women. And the population living up to 100 and older is predicted to grow to nearly 3.7 million by 2050, from just 95,000 in

1990 (Letzing 2021). According to a study published in 2021, the biological "hard limit" on our longevity—barring disease and disaster—is as high as 150 years (Willingham 2021).

The progress made on extending life spans thanks to vaccines and other breakthroughs has created complications, like difficulty funding retirement for growing elderly populations in some places. But it's also inspired people to imagine a future where they pursue multiple careers and effectively combine several lives into one.

### Aging Baby Boomers

The biggest force powering the decades-long expansion of labor pools was the entry of the baby boomer generation into the workforce. Born in the 19 years following the end of World War II (1946–1964), baby boomers came of age as the full effects of antibiotics and vaccinations led to plummeting childhood mortality rates but before the mass introduction of birth control led to the declining birth rates now prevalent in developed and developing countries.

As baby boomers entered the workforce in the 1970s, nations around the world benefited from a demographic dividend. The U.S. labor force growth in the 1970s was 2.6 percent per year versus 1.5 percent just one decade earlier. Advanced economies' growth rates rose to 1.2 percent per year in the 1970s and 1980s. China saw a near trebling of labor force growth rates, to 2.8 percent per year, in the 1970s and 1980s compared with 1.1 percent per year for the prior decades (Harris 2018).

However, the sheer number of baby boomers around the world entering the workforce at the same time started a dramatic swelling of the labor pool that is now ebbing as baby boomers age into retirement. Only parts of South/Southeast Asia and Africa don't share this generational pattern. But these regions face other challenges in attracting large inflows of foreign investment and are unlikely to cushion the coming demographic debt.

### The Business Challenge

Demographic and social trends will have a significant impact on the workforce in the coming years. In today's struggling global economy, it is more important than ever for organizations to leverage the knowledge, skills, and abilities of all workers, from all generations. By capitalizing on the strengths and values of different generations, business leaders can create a sustainable competitive advantage for their organizations. For managers who have five generations of employees sitting in a meeting or working on a project, it can seem like each generation has its worldviews, priorities, career models, motives, and values (Bawany 2013a).

## The Multigenerational Workforce—Challenge and Opportunities

The 2015 research report entitled "Inspiring Your Future Workforce: How to Lead and Engage Gen Y and Z Effectively" interviewed both Gen Y and Z respondents who confirmed and dispelled stereotypes about Gen Y (who are also known as the millennials) who increasingly are making up a larger part of today's workforce and shed new insights on Gen Z who had started joining the corporate world then (Centre for Executive Education 2015).

The longitudinal research by Centre for Executive Education (CEE) discovered five generations of employees working side by side at the workplace, with the generational classification as follows:

1. The traditionalists (born from 1925 to 1945)
2. Baby boomers (born from 1946 to 1964)
3. Generation X (born from 1965 to 1980)
4. Generation Y/millennials (born from 1981 to 2000)
5. Generation Z/digital natives (born from 2001 to 2020)

In December 2021, CEE embarked on the research "Leading and Engaging Your Multigenerational Talent in the Post-Pandemic 'New Normal' Workplace" and it was discovered regrettably that many leaders at the workplace are still relying on stereotypes about communication styles, personal values, work ethics, and technological abilities, resulting in certain assumptions about supervising such a diverse group of employees (Centre for Executive Education 2021) and unfortunately this sometimes resulted in workplace conflicts.

Although there is some relevance in segmenting the workforce in such a way by generational differences, this latest research during the recent COVID-19 pandemic unveiled that successful leaders adopted a more individualistic focus on each employee, which is the best practice among many corporations that do not only survive but thrive during the pandemic.

All the different generations of employees share the common experience of navigating through recent disruptive challenges to their lives and livelihoods as well as at home and the workplace, displaying resilience and quickly adapting to a different type of workplace (remote, in-office, or hybrid model). This has caused a significant shift in the way workers view their jobs, with many re-evaluating their purpose and employment situations. Ideas that may have caused friction in the past, such as differing opinions on professionalism, more relaxed working conditions, casual attire, and flexible schedules, may be nonissues in today's business landscape.

These successful leaders adopted the following approaches in managing a multigenerational team in the postpandemic era of the "new normal" workplace.

### Adopt Emphatic Listening and Flex the Communication Styles

When you focus on the person and engage with their message, you move from recognizing words to understanding the feelings and motivations behind them. This includes following up with questions if needed. It's also about knowing when to stay silent.

Empathic listening is a dynamic and compassionate process that calls for more than taking in someone else's words. You're communicating with that person as well. You're showing that you care about them, their thoughts, and feelings and are willing to take the time to hear them out. Empathic listening helps us to listen and understand how others feel. It's one of the most important emotional and social intelligence skills that we need to maintain healthy or positive relationships with others.

Empathic listening helps us to relate to those around us more healthily and effectively. It helps us to deal with the people closest to us and also to realize our mistakes in the way we relate to other people in society. As a result, we start to rethink our points of view and improve as people.

The leader needs to be mindful and aware of each team member's values, motives, and interests to engage them effectively. Successful leaders also take the time to understand the types of communication that work best with the various generations of employees.

They should flex their communication styles and practice clear and concise communication through different channels that drive employee performance and enhance workplace productivity. This requires being in tune with employees to recognize the general methods that lead to success, whether team e-mails, one-on-one chats, or direct/text messaging.

Flexing and adapting one's style of communication to suit the other team members is a critical element of the best practice SCORE™ Framework for Developing High Performance Teams, which can be found in Chapter 9 of this book.

### Have a Flexible Workplace Arrangement

We have seen how the evolution of a flexible workplace quickly accelerated during the pandemic when employees had been provided with the ability and experience to work remotely. While the long-term trend may be hybrid work (with part of the workforce in the office and the remaining working remotely from home), leaders should carefully balance the company's needs with the desires of their employees.

There is a need for a clear "hybrid workplace" policy to be instituted to ensure that both organizational justice (fairness to all generations of employees in the organization) and procedural justice (fairness in the manner the policy is being implemented without bias to any generation of employees) are strictly adhered to. For example, employees in the younger and older generations may need more remote days for very different reasons, such as daycare issues or concerns about workplace health and safety. Business leaders who remain flexible should experience increased employee morale and engagement. The hybrid workplace is one of the key best practices adopted by leading organizations globally in preparation for the postpandemic era of the "new normal" workplace.

### Adopt "Reverse Mentoring" and/or "Cross-Generational Mentoring"

In a multigenerational workplace, it is expected that there are differences in experience levels and the range of skill sets of the different generations. Leaders from the best-in-class organizations leverage the strengths of each generation by encouraging "reverse mentoring" or "cross-generational mentoring."

It is a well-known fact that both Generation Y/millennials and Generation Z/digital natives tend to be more tech-savvy than Generation X and baby boomers. The millennials have an innate ability to help older co-workers or even senior older leaders ("reverse mentoring") who may be less proficient in technology to feel more comfortable and knowledgeable. Conversely, more seasoned workers have years of experience and institutional/process-related knowledge to share with new hires and younger workers.

When leaders support ongoing cross-generational mentoring via Zoom or in person, employees expand their skill sets, team building is nurtured, and camaraderie increases. As the lines between generations blur and their relevance diminishes, leaders realize that most employees are seeking many of the same things, which is a great corporate culture that is based on trust-based partnership, promotes work–life balance, and aligns with the purposes of an organization that gives meaning to their careers, professional development opportunities, and flexible schedules. The details on "reverse mentoring" in a multigenerational workplace can be found in Chapter 8 of this book.

### Adopt a "Managerial Coaching" Approach at the Workplace

Managerial coaching is about developing and maximizing an individual employee's potential, which will consequently impact positively on the organization's performance. It is about more inquiry (ask) and less advocacy (tell), which means helping that individual to learn rather than teaching.

Coaching sets out to embrace the employee as an individual and understands the organizational context in which the employee operates. It seeks to achieve alignment between the individual employee, team, and organizational goals. It is a proven and highly effective strategy where leaders can develop the skills about how to request and provide performance feedback and help their team members to discover opportunities for growth within the organization by leveraging individual or team coaching.

In their role as a managerial coach, the leaders can provide insights to team members on what they need, to reach the next level of their careers. They could also assist their team members to know what skills they need so that they can perform at a better level and how they can attain those skills. They could also guide their team members on how to handle difficult conversations and conflicts with internal and external stakeholders. The details on "managerial coaching" and "developing a corporate-wide coaching culture" can be found in Chapter 8 of this book.

### Conclusion

There are ways to bridge the generational gaps. It begins with communication, humility, and deeper curiosity about the strengths and limitations of our team members and ourselves. It begins with the acceptance that we are fundamentally different people with equally valuable insights to offer.

Successfully managing a multiple-generation workforce and attracting younger employees requires an awareness of changing needs, a willingness to embrace new ways of managing staff, and attracting the best talent. Now is the time to make these investments to lay the foundation for long-term success.

### The Rise of Generation Z (Digital Natives)

They need to enhance their understanding of generational characteristics and the impact of their management practices on each of these groups so that they can leverage the strengths of each generation. Taking full advantage of the multigenerational workforce will enable employers to effectively attract and retain employees, build teams, deal with change, and increase employee engagement (Bawany 2015c).

Organizations struggle with the challenges of effectively managing a more diverse workforce. These challenges often relate to variations in perspective, values, and belief systems as a result of generational differences and are further complicated due to the age differences between managers and employees. The assumption that people of varying ages will understand each other or have the same perspective and goals is far from true. To be successful, managers need to understand and value the diversity resulting from generational differences, varying perspectives, and differing goals.

Each generation brings different experiences, perspectives, expectations, work styles, and strengths to the workplace. Despite the perceived "generation gap" from differing views and potential conflict, organizations have the opportunity to capitalize on the assets of each generation to achieve a competitive advantage. Each brings unique assumptions to the job. As a result, events in the workplace are often interpreted differently by individuals of different generations' values (Bawany 2013b).

## Intergenerational Conflicts

Intergenerational conflicts will potentially rise, drawing in businesses. As retirees and the working-age population battle for resources, businesses may become indirectly involved. Businesses, management teams, and even shareholders may add their voices to the conversation about government transfers as they grapple with existing pension obligations, the scarcity of highly skilled workers, social pressure to address job losses, and declining incomes among mid to low-skilled workers.

What may seem like good news to a boomer might well be an unsettling and unwelcome development to a member of Generation X. Things that members of Gen Y love often seem unappealing or frivolous to those in older generations. Like any other generation, Gen Z or the linksters bring their mindset into the workforce. They are called linksters because no other generation has ever been so linked to each other and the world through technology. Their struggles in the work environment are tied to their youth and inexperience. They are complete digital natives and cannot function without communicating through social media. They desire change, stimulation, learning, and promotion that will conflict with traditional organizational hierarchies' values (Bawany 2013a).

Leaders today are facing a critical challenge: how to adapt their leadership practices and style to get the best out of the next generation of employees. They can't do so alone. Organizations have a responsibility to help managers understand how workers' expectations have changed and how they can adapt their leadership style to these new conditions. More importantly, organizations need to provide leaders with the tools and processes which allow leaders to reward and recognize, train and develop, and empower Generation Y employees more effectively (Bawany 2014).

Flexibility is vital to managing Gen Y and Z, especially if your organization comprises a multigenerational workforce. By understanding Gen Y and Z and adapting your management styles accordingly, you can effectively harness the potential of future generations of employees while maintaining the loyalty of other staff, thus effectively attracting and retaining employees, building teams, dealing with change, and increasing employee engagement.

## Wealth Inequality

Aging populations typically increase wealth inequality because older households tend to have higher levels of accumulated wealth relative to younger households at a similar socioeconomic level. The bulge of baby boomers in high-wealth and high-income years versus millennials in low-wealth and low-income years creates the case for rising inequality. By itself, it does not stem from a lack of social mobility, and it should pass over time. But other causes of rising income inequality can be problematic. People with higher incomes enjoy a longer period of wealth accumulation because they tend to live longer and healthier lives.

The trend toward longer, healthier lives is likely to continue to benefit higher-income individuals disproportionately since it extends the span of earning years and time to accumulate assets. While we can only speculate on the magnitude of those gains, ongoing medical advances are likely to continue increasing the life span of higher-income individuals faster than those at the lower end at least through the next decade, which in the short run could increase inequality.

Managing the transition to an older society will require investment in, and supporting structures for, an equitable balance. There are choices to be made, for example, about the extent to which society prioritizes adding years to life and life to years—taking the view of health as an investment—rather than investing in other demands on expenditure. In other words, the world could age gracefully, with healthy, productive later years becoming the norm, or old-age dependency could impose heavy social and economic costs on the young. Moreover, it is unknown how shrinking working-age populations, in China and Europe, for example, and growing ones in Africa and India will affect their economies (McKinsey 2020).

There is no set formula for managing through significant macroeconomic upheaval. But there are many practical steps companies can take to assess how a vastly changed macroeconomic landscape might affect their business and how to position themselves for change. In our view, the most important one is building resilience. Organizations that can absorb shocks and change course quickly will have the best chance of thriving in the turbulent 2020s and beyond.

## The Next Global Pandemic

Before COVID-19 emerged as a global threat in 2020, institutions around the world had been trying to tackle the issue of pandemic preparedness. But those groups were underfunded, did not have clear-cut roles, and—importantly—were not working together. Now, as public health researchers and officials look ahead to future pandemics, the situation remains largely the same.

The COVID-19 pandemic has highlighted how various spheres of life, such as public health, economics, employment, community, and even mental health, are closely intertwined. With tens of millions infected and thousands dying from the virus worldwide, COVID-19 has not only put pressure on the healthcare systems around the world, but it has also affected many aspects of contemporary life. These include the contraction of the global economy, the disruption of communal harmony, the negative impact on the psychological well-being of members of the public, and difficulties in keeping the public updated on the evolving pandemic situation.

To better prepare for future pandemics, the Group of 7, or G7—the countries of Canada, France, Germany, Italy, Japan, the United Kingdom, and the United States—announced the Pact for Pandemic Readiness at its annual summit in June. The initiative aims to train scientists and healthcare workers from around the world with a standard set of pandemic response skills, creating a global network that can collaborate on outbreak detection and control (Lau 2022).

The G7 announcement comes at a time when climate change is increasing the threat of infectious disease outbreaks. As wildlife habitats disappear, animals are moving closer to each other and to humans, interacting in new ways that create more opportunities for viruses to jump between species.

### Update on the COVID-19 Pandemic

The World Health Organization (WHO) reported that as of October 17, 2022, there have been 621,797,133 confirmed cases of COVID-19, including 6,545,561 deaths. As of October 11, 2022, a total of 12,782,955,639 vaccine doses have been administered (World Health Organization 2022a).

The world has never been in a better position to end the COVID-19 pandemic, the head of the WHO said on October 14, 2022, during his regular weekly press conference. That was his most optimistic outlook yet on the years-long health crisis which has killed over 6.5 million people (United Nations 2022b).

"We are not there yet. But the end is in sight," WHO Director-General Tedros Adhanom Ghebreyesus told reporters at a virtual press conference. That was the most upbeat assessment from the UN agency since it declared an international emergency in January 2020 and started describing COVID-19 as a pandemic three months later (United Nations 2020).

In the wake of COVID-19, there have been calls for the world to be better prepared for the next pandemic. These calls are driven by a sense that the outbreak could have been foreseen and prevented or that the spread could have been more effectively contained causing less social and economic disruption and averting deaths. Such calls have been made in the past and have resulted in meaningful action. Yet, the world tends to move on quickly, with new crises taking center stage, resulting in the now familiar cycle of "panic and neglect." This is a concern: Although the timing and nature of the next pandemic spark are unknowable, it is certain to happen.

### The Next Global Pandemic—How, When, and Where?

The emergence of a new pandemic would potentially be a devastating disruptive event. First, it's useful to understand some key terminology:

1. An *epidemic* is an outbreak of a disease in a particular location.
2. A *pandemic* is an outbreak of a disease which spreads to and occurs in many different geographic areas at the same time.
3. *Endemic* diseases are established and circulating regularly in populations. Some endemic diseases such as influenza can have surged in transmission or have epidemics at certain times.
4. A *pathogen* is an organism that causes a disease to its host, including but not limited to viruses.

Pandemics may end in one of two ways:

1. Zero transmissions where health authorities close off all chains of transmission and drive cases to zero, as we have seen with all Ebola epidemics to date, or
2. The disease becomes "endemic," which is an ongoing part of the infectious disease landscape, as we have seen with tuberculosis today.

As in the case of the COVID-19 pandemic, Yonatan Grad, Melvin J. and Geraldine L. Glimcher associate professor of Immunology and Infectious Diseases of Harvard T.H. Chan School of Public Health, said that it is difficult to predict the timeline for the new normal as the duration of vaccine protection, social contact, and the virus mutations and transmissibility play key roles (Feldscher 2021). This can be seen in the devastating impact of the Delta and Omicron variants globally.

Professor Grad asserts that the expectation that COVID-19 will become endemic essentially means that the pandemic will not end with the virus disappearing; instead, the optimistic view is that enough people will gain immune protection from vaccination and from natural infection such that there will be less transmission and much less COVID-19-related hospitalization and death, even as the virus continues to circulate.

He further adds:

> The expected continued circulation of SARS-CoV-2 stands in contrast with the first round of SARS in 2003 and with the Ebola virus outbreak in West Africa in 2014 when public health measures ultimately stopped spreading and brought both outbreaks to an end. While there are important differences among the viruses and the contexts, this comparison underscores the critical need to improve our global public health infrastructure and surveillance systems to monitor for and help respond to the inevitable next potential pandemic virus.

### *Future of Pandemic Preparedness and Response*

Maintaining, enhancing, and adapting the global COVID-19 response is vital to end the acute phase of the pandemic. We must work to optimize and maintain the gains of the past two years so that the world can face the future readily for any health threat. Pathogens will continue to emerge and re-emerge with the potential to cause epidemics and pandemics of disease, death, and disruption of a magnitude equal to or greater than SARS-CoV-2.

Outbreaks of infectious pathogens have been a defining feature of human history, and any analysis of prevailing trends strongly suggests that outbreaks of pathogens of pandemic potential are set to continue to increase in frequency in the foreseeable future. COVID-19 was disease X, and the next disease X is out there. SARS-CoV-2 will continue to circulate in the foreseeable future. The gains made since 2020 in surveillance and public health response capacity for COVID-19, including new technological advancements in diagnostics and genomic surveillance and the strengthening of established networks and partnerships, must not be lost as authorities reallocate public health resources to other pressing needs. We must retain the agility and the public health intelligence necessary to rapidly scale up and relax response efforts in response to dynamic changes like the pandemic threat.

Each country has a unique risk profile—enhanced preparedness for future health emergencies requires national operational plans that are tailored and responsive and that incorporate the lessons learned from COVID-19. In addition to national plans, WHO must support member states to negotiate, develop, and implement global mechanisms and systems for pandemic preparedness.

It is impossible to predict when the next pandemic will occur as they are random events. They can begin anywhere in the world where animals and humans are in close proximity as pandemics most often originate when a pathogen transfers from an animal in which it lives to a human never before infected with that pathogen.

The biggest risk comes from pathogens that circulate in animals making the jump into humans. As COVID-19 has demonstrated, once someone is infected in one part of the world, trade and travel will rapidly carry the virus nearly everywhere else. Assessing which pathogens are most likely to make the jump enables us to prepare vaccines and treatments. The World Health Organization has identified several priority diseases with pandemic potential, including Crimean–Congo hemorrhagic fever, Ebola, Marburg, Lassa fever, MERS, SARS, Nipah virus infection, and Zika (Sridhar 2022).

However, there are many pathogens with pandemic potential circulating in animals that we do not know about. It is crucial to identify hotspots where humans and animals come into contact and take steps to reduce risk. For example, hygiene standards at markets where animals are slaughtered and sold could be more closely regulated.

### The Challenge to Public Health Systems

When COVID-19 was declared a pandemic, many nations—including highly resourced ones—found themselves unprepared to deal with the rapidly unfolding public health crisis. Underlying vulnerabilities that had long predated the pandemic—such as health inequalities and flawed communication between public health and healthcare delivery systems—were brought to the fore. Many response plans that had looked good on paper now failed to deliver in practice. The upshot was that public health systems were not as resilient to acute threats as had been assumed. Indeed, criticism surrounding the initial response by some national public health authorities to "monkeypox," which the World Health Organization declared a Public Health Emergency of International Concern on July 23, 2022, suggests there is more work to be done (World Health Organization 2022b).

Many governments are investing in strengthening their pandemic preparedness. But how will they know if those investments will prove effective when the next crisis strikes?

As COVID-19 demonstrated, pandemics touch all of society. Therefore, mounting an effective response calls for specialized capabilities and enablers within and beyond public health systems. Participants in the Geneva Preparedness Forum 2022: Measuring Pandemic Preparedness, held on the sidelines of the World Health Assembly in May 2022, noted the importance of a holistic response involving every part of the government to counter pandemics (World Health Organization 2022c).

### What Could Be the Next Pandemic?

There are a few known pathogens, either viruses or bacteria, that can cause pandemic- or epidemic-prone diseases.

Most influenza viruses originate in wild waterfowl. The H1N1 swine flu virus had its origins in bird populations, which were thought to have then transferred the infection to pigs where it mutated in such a way that it could transmit easily from human to human—once humans had been infected directly by pigs.

Respiratory infections represent one of the highest risks of an epidemic or pandemic after emergence and human-to-human spread, as infected humans often create aerosols when they cough, sneeze, or speak loudly.

Influenza

The influenza virus is an unstable virus that originates in wild waterfowl, which transmits the infection to domestic birds and poultry, and they then pass it on to animals and/or humans. Sometimes, the influenza virus mutates into a form that can spread easily in humans. In those circumstances, a pandemic can occur.

We know there will be another influenza pandemic at some point. In 1918, we had the most devastating infectious disease event in recorded history: the 1918 influenza pandemic. Since 1918, three influenza pandemics have occurred: in 1957, 1968, and 2009 (H1N1). The risk of a new influenza virus transmitting from animals to humans and potentially causing a pandemic is real and serves as a warning that we must continue to be prepared for the next pandemic (World Health Organization 2019).

Before the COVID-19 pandemic, advance plans in most countries anticipated a pandemic strain of the influenza virus. But countries in Asia, which had experienced outbreaks of SARS coronavirus in 2003, tended also to consider coronaviruses.

Avian Influenza

Avian influenza (AI), most commonly known as "bird flu," is a highly contagious viral disease that affects both domestic and wild birds. AI viruses have also been isolated, although less frequently, from mammalian species, including humans. This complex disease is caused by viruses divided into multiple subtypes (i.e., H5N1, H5N3, H5N8, etc.) whose genetic characteristics rapidly evolve. The disease occurs worldwide but different subtypes are more prevalent in certain regions than others.

Birds are the natural hosts for AI viruses. After an outbreak of the H5N1 virus in 1997 in poultry in Hong Kong SAR, China, since 2003, this avian and other influenza viruses have spread from Asia to Europe and Africa. In 2013, human infections with the influenza A (H7N9) virus were reported in China (Centers for Disease Control and Prevention 2022a).

The many strains of AI viruses can generally be classified into two categories according to the severity of the disease in poultry:

1. Low-pathogenicity AI (LPAI) that typically causes little or no clinical signs
2. High-pathogenicity AI (HPAI) that can cause severe clinical signs and possible high mortality rates

With devastating consequences for the poultry industry, farmers' livelihoods, international trade, and the health of wild birds, AI has captured the attention of the international community over the years.

Where outbreaks occur, it is often the policy to cull all poultry, whether infected or healthy, to contain the spread of AI. This represents heavy economic losses for farmers and a long-lasting impact on their livelihoods.

But poultry is not the only one impacted. While they play a major role in the spread of the disease, wild birds also become victims of bird flu viruses.

AI is also a major concern for public health. Whenever AI viruses circulate in poultry, sporadic cases of AI in humans are sometimes identified.

In February 2022, the United States uncovered the highly pathogenic AI (HPAI) Asian (H5N1) virus outbreak among poultry (epizootic) in some countries, which is not expected to diminish significantly in the short term. Thus, sporadic human infections with HPAI Asian H5N1 virus resulting from direct or close contact with infected sick or dead poultry are expected to continue to occur and some of those cases will likely be fatal (Centers for Disease Control and Prevention 2022a).

As bird flu outbreaks in wild birds and poultry continue across the United States, the country approaches a record number of birds affected compared to previous bird flu outbreaks. Since early 2022, more than 49 million birds in 46 states have either died as a result of bird flu virus infection or have been culled (killed) due to exposure to infected birds. This number is nearing the 50.5 million birds in 21 states that were affected by the largest bird flu outbreak that occurred in 2015. Even so, the number of states affected in 2022 is already more than double the number of states that were affected in 2015 (Centers for Disease Control and Prevention 2022b).

Because HPAI H5N1 viruses are always changing, CDC and other public health agencies look for genetic changes in HPAI H5N1 viruses that may impact how HPAI H5N1 viruses spread from person to person or their susceptibility to influenza antiviral drugs.

Coronavirus

There have been three outbreaks caused by coronaviruses in humans during the past 20 years. Each originated among wild animals and one of these viruses, SARS-CoV-2, is the cause of the COVID-19 pandemic.

In addition, four coronavirus strains are endemic in humans, causing the common cold. These are thought to have emerged from animals at some time in the past. SARS-CoV-2 is emerging to be the fifth endemic strain.

Ebola

Highly lethal infections with a short incubation period, such as the Ebola virus disease, are much less likely to become pandemic.

They cause severe illness early in infection that incapacitates and kills those infected, giving the virus little time to be transmitted to others.

By contrast, HIV has a long period when it does not cause signs and symptoms but can transmit from human to human, making it well adapted to becoming endemic.

SARS-CoV-2 has a relatively low level of mortality compared to the Ebola virus. In the future, it is possible, but not predictable, that a more lethal coronavirus strain could emerge.

## Implications of the Megatrends Disruptive Forces

Recovering from the economic shock resulting from the COVID-19 pandemic, the big question dominating global economic headlines in the second half of 2022 is "Are we headed toward a global recession?"

Policy makers, from U.S. Federal Reserve Chair Jerome Powell to International Monetary Fund (IMF) managing director Kristalina Georgieva, have suggested that a recession in key economies, and potentially at the global scale, is possible. The United States is already in a technical recession, given consecutive contractions in the first two quarters of 2022, but there is debate over the scope and implications of the economic slowdown (Needham 2022).

On October 11, 2022, the IMF warned of a worsening outlook for the global economy in its World Economic Outlook report, highlighting that efforts to manage the hottest inflation in decades may add to the damage from the war in Ukraine and China's slowdown. The IMF cut its forecast for global growth in 2023 to 2.7 percent, from 2.9 percent seen in July 2022 and 3.8 percent in January 2022. The risk of policy miscalculation has risen sharply as growth remains fragile and markets show signs of stress, and about one-third of the global economy risks contracting next year, it said, with the United States, European Union, and China all continuing to stall (International Monetary Fund 2022a).

Global economic activity is experiencing a broad-based and sharper-than-expected slowdown, with inflation higher than seen in several decades. The cost-of-living crisis, tightening financial conditions in most regions, Russia's invasion of Ukraine, and the lingering COVID-19 pandemic all weigh heavily on the outlook. Global growth is forecast to slow from 6.0 percent in 2021 to 3.2 percent in 2022 and 2.7 percent in 2023. This is the weakest growth profile since 2001 except for the global financial crisis and the acute phase of the COVID-19 pandemic. Global inflation is forecast to rise from 4.7 percent in 2021 to 8.8 percent in 2022 but to decline to 6.5 percent in 2023 and to 4.1 percent by 2024. Monetary policy should stay the course to restore price stability, and fiscal policy should aim to alleviate the cost-of-living pressures while maintaining a sufficiently tight stance aligned with monetary policy. Structural reforms can further support the fight against inflation by improving productivity and easing supply constraints, while multilateral cooperation is necessary for fast-tracking the green energy transition and preventing fragmentation (International Monetary Fund 2022b).

Several factors will decisively shape the economic outlook: the course of the Russo-Ukrainian war; disruptions from endemic COVID, especially in emerging markets; U.S.-China relations and their impact on international trade and cooperation; rising protectionism; and the availability of technology and scale of innovation.

These factors will determine whether we can avoid a recession and influence the course of inflation, supply chain dynamics, and international trade.

Each of the mega-disruptive forces highlighted above would be challenging on its own; taken together, they can seem daunting. Yet the opportunities for the economy, business, and society that these global forces generate are equally compelling and there is indeed new prosperity for those quick to embrace them. We cannot ignore the potential challenges, chief among them the growing social inequalities that could arise as a result. As societies, we will face challenges related to the future of work as well as inclusive growth; the two are closely linked. Embracing the trends while mitigating their negative impact on those who cannot keep up and our environment is the new imperative of our era.

Taking advantage of the opportunities that these trends offer—and avoiding or taming the challenges—will require big adjustments. In the subsequent chapters, we sketch out the impact of these mega-disruptive forces and what businesses can consider in achieving a balancing act toward how a more sustainable society might look like. These ideas do not amount to a comprehensive action plan and are not meant to be exhaustive.

## Conclusion

In today's world, one thing is certain: uncertainty, a status that has emerged as the defining characteristic of our age.

For decades, much of the world enjoyed relatively steady economic and social gains. As a global collective, we have experienced better standards of living, improved transport and communication, improved civil liberties for more of the world than before, and improved life expectancies and public health. New technologies and a movement toward freer trade brought a record number of people into the global economy, creating expanded and robust economic flows.

But today, much of this economic logic is being upended. First, the pandemic and then the invasion of Ukraine presented the world with the most significant set of challenges since World War II. And now, in part on the back of these two crises but also driven by longer-term trends, the world faces strong headwinds, which will likely slow growth and create significant challenges for leaders around the globe.

Bold new approaches to productivity, supply, consumption, and leisure are required—and are being adopted at surprising speed as an array of other disruptive forces accelerate and become increasingly apparent.

While some indicators now suggest that the worst-case outcomes of these potential crises may have been averted, particularly regarding energy and food supply disruptions at the global level, volatility persists. The implications for the global economy over the next few years remain uncertain at best.

# CHAPTER 3

# The VUCA-Driven Disruptive World

## Introduction: Demystifying VUCA—What It Means and Why It Matters

In today's highly disruptive and digital-driven world, organizations continue to be impacted by a multitude of changes and it influences the way they operate. With increasing volatility in the markets, ever-changing customer needs, and continuous technology-led disruptions to business models, an organization's agility is what can help it wither the storm of changes that hit it every day (Bawany 2016a).

On the other hand, the complexity and disruptions in the business environment today continuously decrease the visibility of businesses beyond a quarter, impeding organizations' ability to build long-term plans and requiring them to reinvent continually.

Responding to these external changes through continuous internal transformations is required for businesses to be relevant in the increasingly volatile, uncertain, complex, and ambiguous (VUCA) world. Leaders will have to visualize and anticipate these changes even before they occur, and it has to be reflective of the strategies they create. The speed with which the changes are occurring would also mean that they must bring a high degree of rigor in execution, have strong self-belief and confidence, and build a high-performance culture comfortable with change and capable of driving change across all levels (Bawany 2018c).

Why is it that some organizations continue to thrive in this new world while others fritter away with the first whiffs of change? Why is it that those specific organizations that manage to navigate through the complexity of interconnected economies and the downturns of volatile markets would be able to continue to build new products, transcend new geographies, and experiment with new technology platforms with outstanding results? In contrast, what makes others fail miserably even at the slightest changes in their business models or external environment?

In short, the answer lies in the fact that these successful organizations and their leaders thrive in the disruptive VUCA-driven world. The term "VUCA" has its genesis back at the end of the Cold War and was first coined by the U.S. Army War College (Whiteman 1998) to ring in an era marked by increasingly ambiguous, multilateral, and multifaceted challenges in conditions that are volatile, uncertain, complex, and ambiguous (Stiehm and Townsend 2002).

The acronym itself was not created until the late 1990s, and it was not until the terrorist attacks of September 11, 2001, that the notion and acronym took hold and gained prominence. VUCA was subsequently adopted by strategic business leaders to describe the chaotic, turbulent, and rapidly changing business environment that has become the "new normal." By all accounts, the chaotic "new normal" in business is real.

The Global Financial Crisis (GFC) of 2008–2009, for example, rendered many business models obsolete, as organizations throughout the world were plunged into turbulent environments like those faced by the military. At the same time, rapid changes as a result of technological developments like social media exploded; the demographic changes where the world's population continued to grow and age simultaneously; and global disasters and pandemics such as COVID-19 disrupted lives, economies, and businesses (World Health Organization 2020a).

It is a challenging, rapidly changing, and evolving business environment where not all the facts or interrelationships can be known or identified. Leaders will often have to operate or make decisions without having all the relevant facts on hand or fully understanding the forces that may be influencing a particular situation or a business problem. Hence, there is a need for leaders to develop and demonstrate relevant skills and competencies to operate in this "new normal" and embrace this ambiguity to lead their organization to success with the right strategy and vision despite the chaotic environment that they are operating in (Bawany 2018a).

Today, we have to acknowledge that no matter where we live, work, or manage our businesses, there are lots of uncertainties around us, and these could be a result of political, economic, societal-cultural, and

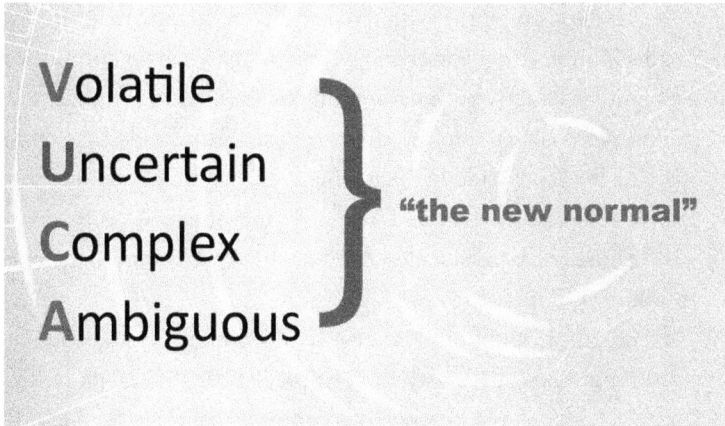

*Figure 3.1  The four elements of the VUCA business environment*

political forces. Across many industries, a rising tide of volatility, risk, and business complexity is disrupting markets and changing the nature of competition (Doheny, Nagali, and Weig 2012).

The four elements of VUCA (see Figure 3.1) describe the "fog of war"—the chaotic conditions that are encountered on a modern battle-field. Its relevance to leaders in business is clear, as these conditions are highly descriptive of the environment in which business is conducted every day (Bawany 2019).

Leaders would need to understand the following implications of the characteristics of VUCA on their organization and its relevance to today's workplace is clear, as these conditions are highly descriptive of the environment in which business is conducted every day (Bennett and Lemoine 2014).

1. **Volatility**

   *What is it?* Volatility refers to the rate of change of information and the pace of change in the situation. Things can change unpredictably, suddenly, and incredibly, especially for the worse. There is a brutal increase in four dimensions of changes we face today: type, speed, volume, and impact. Given the lack of predictability in issues and events, these volatile times make it difficult for leaders to use experience and events as predictors of future outcomes, making forecasting extremely difficult and decision making a real challenge (Bawany 2020).

A rapidly changing environment calls for adaptive and innovative decision making. Power and wealth set the stage for competition over finite resources. Both nature and how businesses compete in the market place change rapidly, driven on the "hard" side by technology and the "soft" side by increasingly easy communication. Some change seems short term and explosive, but often that is because it was unanticipated. Challenges faced are unexpected and most likely of unknown duration.

*Examples*: Commodity pricing is often quite volatile; jet fuel costs, for instance, have been quite unpredictable in the 21st century. Crude oil is the base for lots of products, including jet fuel. The Organization of Petroleum Exporting Countries (OPEC) is the primary influencer of fluctuations in crude oil prices. OPEC is widely seen as the most influential player in oil price fluctuations. Still, primary supply and demand factors, production costs, political turmoil, and even interest rates can play a significant role in the price of oil (Lioudis 2020).

*How do we address it?* Agility is key to coping with volatility. We need to develop a better way of anticipating the Future. We can overcome this challenge by gaining knowledge and being well-prepared with the information and resources necessary to envision the Future, anticipate and plan to mitigate the risk of potentially disruptive events. Funds should be aggressively directed toward building slack and creating the potential for future flexibility, for instance, stockpile inventory, which could typically be expensive; hence the organization's investment should match the risk.

2. **Uncertainty**
*What is it?* Uncertainty is a result of volatility as we are unable to predict future events. Important information is not known or definite; doubtful, unclear about the present situation and future outcomes; and not able to be relied upon. The uncertainty stems from the inability to know everything about the current situation and the difficulty of predicting what the effects of a proposed change today will be in the future. It can also arise because decision makers do not have proper "intelligence"-gathering operations, including competitors or market intelligence. It can result in deception where competitors

seek to gain an advantage by surprising the organization with their pre-empted marketing actions (Bawany 2020).

*Examples*: A competitor's pending product launch muddies the future of the business and the market that the organization similarly serves. As we have seen in the Netflix versus Blockbuster case study in Chapter 1, Blockbuster remained the same for years while their competitor, Netflix, disrupted the TV and movie rental industry by creating a sustainable competitive advantage where they upset the entire industry by launching online video streaming. It didn't turn out so well for Blockbuster, which eventually filed for bankruptcy (Chapter 11) in 2010 (Bernstein 2014).

Another example would be antiterrorism initiatives that are generally plagued with uncertainty: While we may understand the many causes of terrorism, we do not know exactly when and how they could spur attacks.

*How do we address it?* Given that today's business environment is continuously changing, especially in the era of digital technology, there is a need to keep up with the times and stay relevant. We, therefore, need to invest in information, big data analytics, and knowledge management systems and this works best in conjunction with structural changes allowing organizations to reduce uncertainty. With uncertainty, strategic leaders must be willing to take measured and prudent risks, be able to assess risk accurately, and develop risk management strategies.

3. **Complexity**

*What is it?* Complexity differs from uncertainty, though its effects may sometimes be similar. There are many different and connected parts, such as multiple key decision factors, the interaction between diverse agents, emergence, adaptation, coevolution, and weak signals. There are often numerous and difficult-to-understand causes and mitigating factors (both inside and outside the organization) involved in a problem (Bawany 2020).

Many situations consist of various interconnected parts and variables. Being well informed of all these different parts can be extremely overwhelming and more often than not technical too. This layer of complexity, added to the turbulence of change and the absence of past predictors, adds to the difficulty of decision making. It also leads to confusion, which can cause ambiguity, the last letter in the acronym of VUCA.

*Examples*: It can be seen when an organization decides to launch products outside its core competencies or move into foreign markets. Doing business in new countries often involves navigating a complex web of tariffs, laws, regulations, logistics, societal-cultural values, as well as marketing and consumer behavior-related issues.

The U.S. big-box retailer Walmart failed to take into account cultural nuances, in particular personal space, when it opened up shop in Germany in 1997. The chain opened 85 stores in an attempt to tap into the frugal country's lucrative discount department market. But with intricate labor laws, restricted business hours, and rows upon rows of regulatory red tape, the market was harder to crack than the American retail giant anticipated. The icing on the cake was that the customers were a tad bit freaked out by Walmart greeters and their propensity to bag customers' groceries for them, both unusual practices in Germany. In 2006, Walmart pulled out at the cost of U.S.$1 billion (Clark 2006).

*How do we address it?* Organizations should develop specialists that are better able to deal with such complex issues. Additionally, building upon resources that are adequate to address complexity can go far in the success of an organization as well.

At the strategic level, there are an enormous number of factors that may have a causal bearing on a given situation. The effects have become more sophisticated in our globalized, technologically connected world.

The temptation to reach for short-term solutions and the pressure to address symptoms quickly are compelling. Competing demands of various constituencies with strategic influence further add to the complexity facing the disruptive leader. So, system complexity affects the ability of the leader to formulate and execute effective strategies. Determination of cause and effect relationships is made more difficult because of the lag time between cause and effect in large, complex, and unfamiliar systems. Often, things get worse in the short term before they get better in the long run.

4. **Ambiguity**

*What is it?* Ambiguity exists when a decision maker does not understand the significance of a given event or situation—doesn't know what is happening. The situation could be open to more than one interpretation; the meaning of an event can be understood in different ways. Casual relationships are utterly unclear as no precedent exists, forcing the leader to face unknown factors. It can occur when leaders do not have the right mental models and breakthrough mindsets, thereby observing events that "don't make sense" (Bawany 2020).

Ambiguity can also happen when an event or situation can legitimately be interpreted in more than one way. Vulnerability to misinterpretation of events in complex cases is high when decisions are centralized, decision pressure is high, the decision maker is powerful, and the decision maker acts alone. As a result, this would be a recipe for disaster.

*Examples*: It can be found in situations when a business needs to consider multiple perspectives and considerations, with little information available, when they decide to move into immature or emerging, or unknown markets. The other scenario would be when the organization launches products outside its core competencies. Another case in point is the transition from print to digital media has been very ambiguous when it was first introduced; some companies are still learning how customers will access and experience data and entertainment given new digital technologies in the era of Industry 4.0.

In the engineering and construction industry, macro- and micro-economic trends continuously influence and shape the business environment, requiring leaders to approach both opportunities and challenges from multiple perspectives without falling subject to their viewpoint. Among the challenges the industry faces are sustained cost pressures, ongoing labor shortages that affect productivity, and trends toward fixed-bid projects that often demand a level of pricing and operations precision that is difficult to obtain with traditional systems (Deloitte 2020b). There is no shortage of data to process, interpret, and analyze, which would assist in resolving these challenges. With a few clicks of a mouse, a leader can collect benchmark data or information such as industry productivity rates, GDP or market growth, and relevant suppliers' costs. However, without the clarity of strategic thinking, this information is ambiguous at best and can mislead the leader or only confirm what he or she wants to see (confirmation bias). The typical human response to ambiguity is to look for incremental problems to solve but fail to grasp the broader root issues.

*How do we address it?* The likelihood of making the right strategic decisions is more probable when the leader shifts his or her mental model and creates a climate that promotes a questioning attitude toward the obvious and encourages multiple perspectives that differ from his or her own. To tackle the issue of ambiguity, organizations should experiment and take calculated risks and leaders need to adopt a suite of cognitive readiness and critical thinking skills which would assist in complex problem solving and decision making.

Experimentation is necessary for reducing ambiguity. Only through intelligent experimentation can business leaders determine what strategies are and are not beneficial in situations where the previous rules of business no longer apply. This would involve a good understanding of cause and effect, which requires generating hypotheses and testing them. Leaders need to design the experiments so that lessons learned can be broadly applied throughout the organization.

## Case Study: The VUCA Impact of the COVID-19 Pandemic

### 1. Volatility

Oil demand has plummeted since the onset of the coronavirus pandemic in early 2020. Oil prices have become volatile thanks to unexpected swings in the various factors affecting the global oil supply and demand (Bawany 2020). The COVID-19 pandemic and economic slowdown have sent the demand for oil plummeting. That has offset the three other factors affecting oil prices: rising U.S. oil production, the diminished clout of OPEC, and the strengthening of the U.S. dollar (Amadeo 2020).

Another example is when prices fluctuate after a natural disaster takes a supplier off-line, as we had seen in the COVID-19 pandemic when the outbreak started in Wuhan, the capital of central China's Hubei province. Given China's dominant role as the "world's factory" means that any significant disruption puts global supply chains at risk (Deloitte 2020a). The global economic and financial ramifications of the pandemic have been felt through global supply chains, from raw materials to finished products.

Furthermore, as we have seen in the daily situation report by the World Health Organization (WHO), the volatility of the COVID-19 pandemic is seen through the brutal increase in the confirmed cases and the resulting deaths. No one can predict when the pandemic will end (World Health Organization 2020b).

2. **Uncertainty**

COVID-19's trajectory is defined by uncertainty: Estimates of severity suffer from an uncertain denominator making accurate mortality figures hard to quantify; uncertainty abounds in individuals' reactions, and change is rife concerning capacity estimates and sustainability of interventions and also when the safe distancing measures and travel restrictions could be lifted so that economies could be opened and business could return to normalcy (Bawany 2020).

At the onset of the pandemic, scientists were then racing to model the next moves of the coronavirus, which was then hard to predict, and also as to when the vaccine will be available. Today, SARS-CoV-2, the virus that causes COVID-19, change over time. Some changes may affect the virus's properties, such as how easily it spreads, the associated disease severity, or the performance of vaccines, therapeutic medicines, diagnostic tools, or other public health and social measures.

There is much uncertainty then about the extent of the devastating damage and the huge impact the pandemic will have on economies, markets, jobs, people's lives, families, and communities (United Nations 2020).

The travel and tourism industry is one of the hardest-hit sectors and currently accounts for 10 percent of the global GDP. The World Travel and Tourism Council (WTTC) has warned the COVID-19 pandemic could cut 50 million jobs worldwide in the travel and tourism industry with Asia expected to be the worst affected. The WTTC projected that once the outbreak is over, it could take up to 10 months for the industry to recover (Faus 2020).

3. **Complexity**

From the initial outbreak in China in December 2019, COVID-19 has now spread to more than 210 countries at the time of writing in April 2020 (World Health Organization 2020b).

COVID-19 (its scientific name SARS-CoV-2) is a new strain that was discovered in 2019 and has not been previously identified in humans (Bawany 2020). It has presented health experts with a rapidly evolving and complex challenge. Scientists do not yet know fully how lethal the new coronavirus is, and in the early days, there was uncertainty as to whether it would evolve into another strain. This has been answered in April 2020, when scientists in China found 33 mutations of COVID-19, which is a crucial development for the vaccine developers so that they could avoid potential pitfalls (Mercer 2020).

4. **Ambiguity**

A mystery remains: How and when did the virus cross over to humans? Doubt has been cast on the idea that it happened in the Huanan Seafood Market in Wuhan, China, in December 2019 (Lu 2020) or possibly elsewhere, including Wuhan's Institute of Virology. Researchers are trying to identify the real source of the infection with the hope that this knowledge could help prevent future pandemics of other new coronaviruses (Bawany 2020).

There are also conspiracy theories on whether the virus was an American bioweapon aimed at China (Fisher 2020).

There are also ethical questions about the level of transparency of some governments' responses to the pandemic to their people. In Wuhan, China, the epicenter of the pandemic, a healthcare professional and whistle-blower, Dr. Li Wenliang, tried to raise early warnings about the severity of the pandemic but was silenced by government officials (Graham-Harrison 2020).

In the United States, a political back-and-forth over messaging was playing out between the then President Donald Trump, Vice President Mike Pence who was in charge of the U.S. government's response to COVID-19, and their top health experts, including career professionals like Dr. Anthony Fauci, physician, immunologist, and leading expert on infectious diseases currently serving as the director of the National Institute of Allergy and Infectious Disease (NIAID) (Shear and Haberman 2020).

Mixed messaging can result in low levels of trust in governments and the spread of fake news, a development the WHO labeled as an "infodemic" (Thomas 2020). Governments must act openly and transparently to build and maintain the trust of citizens.

## Meeting the Leadership Challenges of VUCA

Leading in a world that is VUCA not only provides a challenging environment for leaders to operate and for executive development programs to have an impact, but also offers a much-needed range of new competencies. The new reality is that organizations begin to acknowledge that new and different capabilities are needed to succeed in this *new* normal (Bawany 2016a, 2019).

In Deloitte's "2019 Global Human Capital Trends" survey, 80 percent of respondents agreed that the 21st century had imposed new requirements on business leaders. Among these respondents, 81 percent cited the ability to lead through more complexity and ambiguity, followed by leading through influence, managing remotely, managing a workforce that combines humans and machines, and leading more quickly (Volini et al. 2019).

Each of these requirements reflects elements of our connected and digital lives. Together, they point to a disruptive and digital-driven "VUCA" world that directly challenges the leaders' ability to develop stability and direction for their businesses (Bawany 2020).

### The VUCA Prime Model

The four elements of VUCA identify the internal and external conditions affecting organizations today (Volini et al. 2019).

The VUCA Prime model (see Figure 3.2) was developed by Robert Johansen, a distinguished fellow at the Institute for the Future and

**VOLATILITY = V    V = VISION**
**UNCERTAINTY = U    U= UNDERSTANDING**
**COMPLEXITY = C    C = CLARITY**
**AMBIGUITY = A    A = AGILITY**

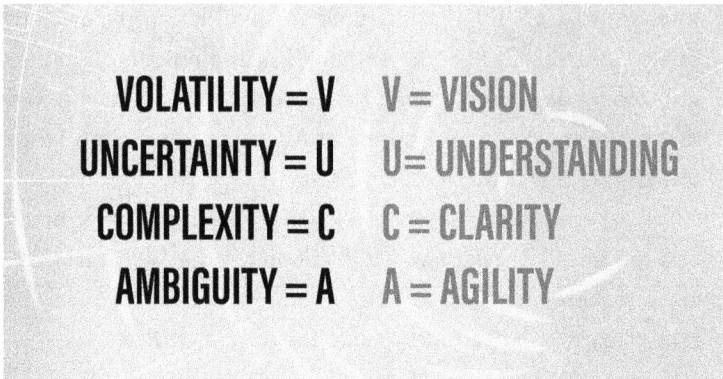

*Figure 3.2  The VUCA Prime model*

the author of *Leaders Make the Future: Ten New Leadership Skills for an Uncertain World*. Johansen flips the VUCA model and focuses on the characteristics and skills business leaders must develop to counter the effects of a VUCA environment. Johansen proposes that the best VUCA-driven disruptive leaders have a vision, understanding, clarity, and agility (Johansen 2012).

In the VUCA Prime model, *volatility* can be countered with *vision* because vision is even more vital in turbulent times. Leaders with a clear vision of where they want their organizations to be can better weather disruptive environmental changes such as economic downturns or new competition. They can make business decisions to counter the turbulence while keeping the organization's vision in mind (Bawany 2020).

*Uncertainty* can be countered with *understanding* and the ability to stop, look, and listen. To be successful in a VUCA environment, leaders must learn to look and listen beyond their functional areas to make sense of the volatility and to lead with vision. Leaders would be required to communicate with all levels of employees in their organization and to develop and demonstrate teamwork and collaboration skills leveraging the SCORE™ high-performance team framework (Bawany 2019, 2020).

*Complexity* can be countered with *clarity*, which is the process of trying to make sense of chaos. In a VUCA world, chaos comes swiftly and hard. Leaders who can quickly tune into all of the specifics associated with the chaos can make better, more informed business decisions.

Finally, *ambiguity* can be countered with *agility*, the ability to communicate across the organization and to move quickly to apply appropriate solutions to the pressing challenges on hand. Vision, understanding, clarity, and agility are not mutually exclusive in the VUCA Prime. Instead, they are intertwined elements that help managers become more influential VUCA leaders.

The VUCA Prime model can be seen as the continuum of skills leaders can develop to help make sense of leading in a VUCA world. HR and talent management professionals can use the VUCA Prime as a "skills and abilities" blueprint when creating leadership development plans (Bawany 2020).

VUCA leaders must have the foresight to see where they are going but must also remain flexible about how they get there. They must demonstrate a high level of self-awareness of their strengths and weaknesses as leaders, cognitive readiness and critical thinking skills, and mental and learning agility to learn fast because change is constant. Resilience, adaptability, openness to change, working collaboratively, and being excellent communicators are essential traits to thrive in a complex VUCA environment.

These skills and abilities are a far cry from the more function-specific skills and abilities leaders needed in the past to succeed. HR and talent management professionals must refocus their leadership development efforts to hone these more strategic, complex critical-thinking skills.

## The "LEAP" Framework—Navigating Through the "Fog" of VUCA

To lead and manage the managerial challenges successfully in the VUCA-driven disruptive business environment, leaders need to "LEAP" through the fog (Bawany 2016a) and demonstrate the relevant leadership competencies and skills to navigate through the "fog" (see Figure 3.3).

### Liberal

A leader needs to exhibit liberal thinking with a breakthrough mindset where he or she is open to developing new behaviors, skills, or opinions,

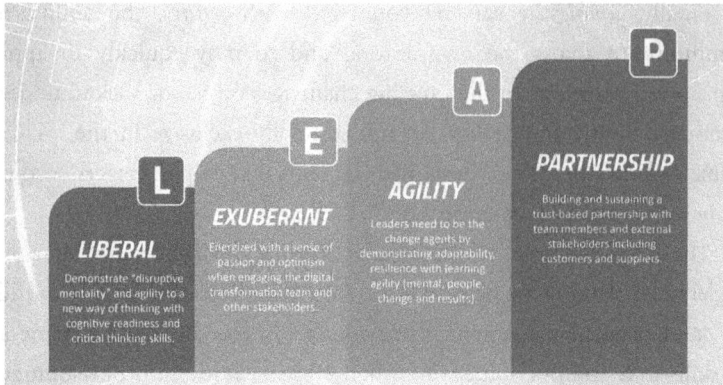

*Figure 3.3  The "LEAP" framework—navigating through the "fog" of VUCA*

and willing to adapt or discard existing values if and when necessary to survive in the *new* normal.

Leading in a disruptive environment means getting used to incredible levels of uncertainty. A leader will never know how something will work until he or she tries it. Modifying their assumptions and adapting or revising the plans depending on the desired results is the standard practice of the most highly effective disruptive leaders.

A leader's mindset is the most powerful tool he or she has. It informs what a leader believes is possible, or impossible, and how he or she builds a path to achieve it. A leader's experiences inherently inform his or her mindset, and sometimes that information can stifle or impede the ability to resolve business challenges. Mindsets are critical to creating any new reality (Bawany 2020).

### Exuberant

Leaders that thrive in a disruptive environment are energized and demonstrate a sense of passion and optimism, while at the same being grounded in reality, in engaging the team and other stakeholders. They are optimistic and consistently look for the good in all successes, failures, and challenges.

Optimism refers to having a positive outlook or thinking positively. Optimistic leaders tend to see the good in people and organizations and believe in favorable results. They are simply able to see possibilities and seek opportunities.

Passion is a sense of energy for something. Leaders' passion and purpose are their internal energy source, the fire or determination they have for reaching some destination up ahead. They tell a leader why he or she is on this journey and what they want from life. Passion and optimism can lift others beyond self-perceived limitations, which can then lead to team success during times of challenge, change, and even disappointment (Bawany 2020).

## Agility

Organizational agility has consistently been found in research to be critical to business success in a turbulent business environment. It results in faster time to market, improved operating efficiency, more satisfied customers and employees, as well as higher revenues.

Leaders need to be change agents by demonstrating resilience with mental and learning agility. Learning agility is the ability and willingness to learn from every situation a leader goes through in life—including the ones where they have no idea what to do—and to find solutions by leveraging cognitive readiness and critical thinking skills. The inability to adapt proficiently has often been cited as the reason for leadership derailers.

Disruptive leaders know that the key to organizational success lies in using the insights from experimenting to chart a new direction. It doesn't matter if the leader doesn't understand what's happened the first time his or her organization tries something new. If the leader keeps his or her eyes and ears open, he or she will be better informed the second time. That's the hallmark of a disruptive leader (Bawany 2020).

## Partnership

Building and sustaining a trust-based partnership with employees, team members, and external stakeholders, including customers and suppliers, is crucial, especially during disruptive times. When people trust a leader, they have confidence in that leader's decisions. Even in times of uncertainty, they will be influenced by and support the leaders. That is because they expect their leaders to do what the leaders say will do.

As disruptive leaders, aligning their words and actions is a crucial pillar for building trust in the workplace and, ultimately, for an organization's success. The reality is that what leaders say and do has the most impact on their team member's perception of an organization. When the leader's words and actions are not congruent, team members are less likely to become engaged and committed to the organization.

It is also crucial to remove "silos" within organizations to ensure effective collaboration and involvement at every level (intra- and inter-team) to create a trust-based organizational climate that is needed to make the organization successful.

The leader should continuously develop these trust-based relationships by demonstrating his or her emotional and social intelligence competence and reliability by ensuring commitments or promises made are being honored or fulfilled as well as communicating key agreements and decisions. When leaders treat stakeholders like they would a valued client and take time to have one-to-one conversations and engage with them regularly, the leaders will earn respect and ultimately build robust and meaningful stakeholder relationships.

## Conclusion

We are operating in a hypercompetitive, disruptive, digital, and VUCA-driven business environment. The world moves faster today when compared to 20 to 30 years ago. Businesses feel the pressure to decrease time to market and improve the quality of products while delivering on ever-changing customer expectations to maintain competitive posture, that is, be adaptive and agile. Driving and achieving sustainable results in this new normal is incredibly challenging even for organizations that have the benefit of leveraging upon dedicated and knowledgeable employees and business leaders (Bawany 2020).

Today, research by the Centre for Executive Education (CEE), Executive Development Associates (EDA), and others has shown that disruptive leaders need to demonstrate a suite of leadership competencies including cognitive readiness (critical and strategic thinking skills), emotional and social intelligence, resilience, managerial coaching, and leading team for performance among others effectively, in driving results and achieving success in a high-performance organization (Bawany 2019).

# CHAPTER 4

# "C.R.I.S.I.S." Leader

## Lessons From the Frontlines

### Introduction

The level of disruption that leaders are facing in recent years is unprecedented. The complexity and scale of the disruptive challenges they are navigating have left many leaders feeling overwhelmed. However, recent research by the Disruptive Leadership Institute (DLI) involving 529 C-suite leaders (CEOs and direct reports to CEOs) has unveiled that not all leaders are struggling (Disruptive Leadership Institute 2022). Some do thrive in times of crisis and chaos. These leaders who are thriving are not doing so by chance. They are proactively demonstrating specific leadership practices and skills resulting in success for their respective teams and organizations, which will be further elaborated on later.

A crisis also tends to bring a high degree of chaos and confusion into an organization. Typically, there is a lack of information precisely when virtually everyone in the organization has a huge emotional need for it. Those involved need to know and understand what happened, why it happened, and how it will impact their futures. Ambiguity is especially potent.

### Leadership

It has been argued that the term "leadership" is ambiguous due to its origins in the common vocabulary (Janda 1960; Yukl 1989). The earliest written evidence of this originates from Egyptian hieroglyphics dating back to 2300 BC. Most character-based languages have unique symbols for "leader" and "leadership" and do not spell them out. According to one Egyptian scholar, the Pharaoh possessed the quality of a perceptive heart and was endowed with a speech that was characterized by authority and justice (Lichtheim 1973). Similar qualities were enounced by Sun Tzu in 512 BC, who wrote that a leader stands for the virtues of wisdom, sincerity, benevolence, courage, and strictness (Tzu 2005).

Attempts to produce a single unifying definition have repeatedly fallen short of acceptance. Leadership authors like to quote Stogdill who said, "there are almost as many definitions of leadership as there are persons who have attempted to define the concept," but this just states the obvious. The efforts of writers on the ingredients of effective leadership have produced conclusions about what leaders do that are often confusing and even conflicting (Bass and Stogdill 1990). In this climate of disagreement, several descriptions of what makes for effective leadership have gained more favor than others. Among the more widely accepted factors are traits, behavior, information processing, relationships, and follower perceptions (Kets de Vries 2004).

From this author's perspective, leadership can be defined as:

> The ability of an individual to envision the future and impact and influence the followers toward achieving it by giving purpose (meaningful direction) to the collective effort and embodying values, and creating the organizational climate where the purpose can be accomplished.

Influence is the ability to persuade, convince, motivate, inspire, and judiciously use power to affect others positively. Generally speaking, it's not the kind of authority that comes from leveraging title, position, or regulations. But exactly how is this different from other methods of leadership that managers carry out every single day? After all, the ability to influence others is an important part of leadership in good circumstances as well as bad. The power of influence would seem to be a useful leadership skill no matter what the managerial style of the individual leader, where some managers are more participative and coaching than others and some are more coercive or autocratic and pacesetting, for example, in the way they approach their work (Bawany 2020).

The difference lies not in the importance of influence as a leadership capacity but rather in the particular context of the crisis itself, an emotional cauldron (a situation characterized by instability and strong emotions) that distills the components of influence into a potent concentrate of empathy, caring, and empathetic listening and communication. Crisis leadership is a special case in which these specific tools of influence perform a critical role. In a crisis, timelines are more critical. There isn't as much time for reflection. Rapid decision making and a higher call to action become the norm (Bawany 2015a).

## Crisis

The problem with the term "crisis" is that it is used in different ways by different professions. In a general sense, the term implies an undesirable and unexpected situation that possesses latent harm to people, organizations, or society and could be viewed as an abnormal event (Almond et al. 1973).

Although crises typically engender a sense of urgency, countless chronic crises pose long-term risks which are not urgent in that they do not pose an immediate danger. Climate change, for one, dismisses this definition.

The Harvard Business School definition states that a crisis is:

a change—either sudden or evolving—that results in an urgent problem that must be addressed immediately. (Luecke and Barton 2004)

The word itself originates from the Greek *krisis,* which means "to sift or separate" (Klann 2003). A crisis has the potential to divide an organization's past from its future, to replace security with insecurity, and to separate effective leaders from ineffective ones. A crisis also has the potential to swap routine for creativity and to shift an organization from "business as usual" into significant change.

Like leadership, this term has ancient roots and was well understood. The Chinese defined it in the way they wrote it. Many crisis authors have spoken of how the word "crisis" is composed of two characters (危机wēi jī), one meaning "danger" and the other "opportunity." But, it has been convincingly argued that the meaning of wēi jī may not be construed from a strict dictionary interpretation due to the complex nature of interpreting different combinations of Chinese characters (Mair 2007). Although simple Chinese dictionaries show that the word jī has only a couple of meanings, it can acquire hundreds of meanings when it is used in combination with other characters. Thus, the only possible interpretation of wēi jī is "danger" + "incipient moment/crucial point." In other words, wēi jī refers to a potentially dangerous situation when something begins or changes.

Despite the failure to associate the word "opportunity" with wēi jī, the fact remains that crises can produce remarkably positive outcomes. It has been said that virtually every crisis contains the seeds of success as well as the roots of failure and that crises contain an element of duality (Drennan and McConnell 2007). The basic physics concept that every force has an equal and opposing force appears to apply here since some people always manage to benefit from the sufferings of others. Potential opportunities that can arise from a crisis extend far beyond the simple dictionary definition of opportunity (Drennan and McConnell 2007) and demonstrate that failure to consider this aspect of crises is not advisable. It is thus telling and disappointing that the crisis gurus quoted above have elected to focus solely on danger and have failed to include opportunity in their definitions.

Effective crisis leadership can rescue an organization from chaos and deliver opportunities where before there were only disadvantages. Organizations that successfully handle crises can come out of them stronger and with greater employee, customer, and community loyalty than existed before the crisis. Leaders must look deep into the crisis for such opportunities that not only benefit the organization but also raise the potential for individual achievement among the organization's employees. In their search, they should look to human elements—the emotions, the behaviors, and the reactions that affect and are affected by the crisis and can influence its outcome.

From this author's perspective, a crisis can be defined as:

A damaging event or series of events that are generally characterized by a profound change with a high degree of instability and carries the potential for extreme impact on the organization's sustainability and continuity. It's significant because the damage that can be caused can be physical, financial, or reputational in its scope, and as a consequence, it will be decisive in determining the future of the organization.

## Crisis Leadership

Leading in a crisis can be challenging. Managers who have led in such circumstances describe the experience as highly developmental—a benchmark in their professional careers. But what does effective leadership during a crisis look like? There may be as many descriptions of leadership and crisis leadership; however, this author would define crisis leadership as:

The ability of an individual to recognize uncertain situations or potentially damaging events or series of events that possess latent risks and opportunities to ensure organization preparedness and make and implement critical decisions through influencing followers resulting in successfully eliminating or reducing the threats or negative impact of the said situation or event.

## The "C.R.I.S.I.S." Leader: Effective Leadership Practices in Crisis Response

A crisis creates a series of conditions that test the limits of teams and organizations, often forcing leaders to re-examine their core values. The word "crisis" broadly describes a low-probability event that has a high potential for serious consequences. Crises are time sensitive, and as the clock ticks, the window to achieve a successful outcome closes. To make matters more challenging, the unexpected and often unprecedented nature of a crisis means that reliable information to assist decision making is scarce. Leaders must grapple with uncertainty surrounding the cause and the solution to the crisis. Considered together, these elements create a tumultuous storm through which leaders must navigate.

To lead effectively during a crisis, it is beneficial to examine how a crisis impacts team dynamics. Given the high degree of uncertainty surrounding a crisis, leaders may feel that they are losing control. Therefore, some may reflexively overcompensate for this loss and attempt to control as many facets of the team as possible. However, this overreliance on centralizing decisions and tasks, instead of delegating, can produce massive inefficiencies in crisis response. Simply put, micromanaging may restore the leader's sense of control at the expense of the team's efficiency, which delays the implementation of effective strategies.

Leaders may also be tempted to switch to a survival mode. In this scenario, all energy and focus are directed toward minimizing the immediate threat, protecting reputation, and cutting costs. Although this leadership mentality can be necessary for the short-term response to a crisis, it may marginalize the emotional needs of the team and the public, who are experiencing panic, isolation, anxiety, and helplessness. In addition, a persistent survival mentality can undermine the team's sense of purpose and long-term mission.

Effective crisis leadership boils down to responding to the human needs, emotions, and behaviors caused by the crisis. Effective leaders respond to those emotional needs as those needs are perceived by those experiencing the crisis, not just to their perception of what those emotional needs are, might be, or should be. The crisis will affect employee morale, attitudes, productivity, ability to focus, stress levels, relationships, and more. People are more apt to follow a leader who is reassuring and who can meet their primary needs—those needs they least want to give up.

The military's single peacetime focus is preparing for combat, the ultimate crisis, because it involves life and death. A major element of the military's training teaches soldiers how to deal with the range of emotions they will experience before, during, and after combat (Klann 2003). These emotions generally include horror, apprehension, grief, rage, revenge, loneliness, sadness, repulsion, vigilance, anguish, and guilt. Military leaders know these emotions will be experienced and must be controlled or the soldiers will not be able to function on the battlefield. Combat leaders must learn to deal with their own emotions as well as with the emotions of the soldiers under their charge. This is the same challenge civilian leaders face during a crisis, and they can expect the same kinds of emotional chaos to flow over the people in their organization and themselves.

Modern crises unfold in front of a worldwide audience because of the rise in the 24-hour news cycle and increased access to media. Therefore, today's leaders must not only contend with the crisis itself but also navigate scrutiny in real time; minute-to-minute updates can make or break public trust. This intense spotlight might tempt leaders to avoid blame and escape accountability for a crisis. These self-interested tendencies can foster an "every man for himself" mentality that sows mistrust among team members. Consequently, the leader's communication style and degree of consistency shape the team's morale and guide public perception of the leader's response.

Crisis researchers recognize that leaders who routinely deliver honest and empathetic communication are most effective during a crisis. Although it is challenging to remain transparent about bad news and setbacks as a crisis develops, the payoff is that the team and the public perceive the leader as authentic. Thus, it is necessary that leaders avoid downplaying credible threats and overpromising positive outcomes that they know to be unrealistic. In addition, displays of genuine empathy for those affected by the crisis reflect self-awareness and acknowledgment of peripheral stakeholders, not just their immediate organization.

Recognizing that a company faces a crisis is the first thing leaders must do. It is a difficult step, especially during the onset of crises that do not arrive suddenly but grow out of familiar circumstances that mask their nature. Examples of such crises include the SARS outbreak of 2002–2003 and now the coronavirus pandemic. Seeing a slow-developing crisis for what it might become requires leaders to overcome the normalcy bias, which can cause them to underestimate both the possibility of a crisis and the impact that it could have.

Corporate crises can be highly damaging. They erode trust, destroy company value, and, for some, can ultimately lead to the organization's failure. However, these impacts are not inevitable outcomes; some organizations and leaders do thrive during a crisis. The DLI set out to understand why this was the case with a research project delivered in partnership with the Centre for Executive Education (CEE), a global executive development organization headquartered out of Singapore (Disruptive Leadership Institute 2022).

The data collection included both qualitative and quantitative analyses conducted in the second half of 2022. In-depth interviews were conducted with over 529 C-suite executives (CEOs and their direct reports)

**C**ommunicate: Empathetic Listening, Be Purposeful

**R**esilience: Be Calm, Compassion, Be Reflective

**I**ntelligence: Use Big Data and AI for Decision Making

**S**hift Mental Model: Adopt Growth Mindset

**I**nspiring: Be Courageous, Persevere, and Build Trust

**S**et the Recovery Path: "Where We Were" and "Where We Want to Go"

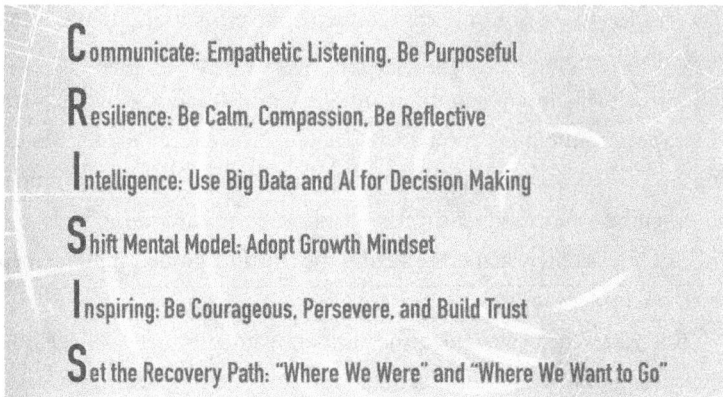

*Figure 4.1 The "C.R.I.S.I.S." leadership model*

around the world (North America, EMEA (Europe, Middle East, and Africa), and APAC (Asia-Pacific)). The respondents identified the mega-trends of disruptive forces that are expected to impact their organizations in the coming years.

The research also uncovered exemplary leaders who have been able to navigate successfully the organizational and leadership challenges resulting from the COVID-19 pandemic and the past disruptive events including the Global Finance Crisis (GFC) in 2018–2019. These leaders have demonstrated the competencies, behaviors, and traits of a "C.R.I.S.I.S." leader.

The "C.R.I.S.I.S." model (see Figure 4.1) offers a summary of the contemporary research-based leadership practices that are linked with successful crisis response (Disruptive Leadership Institute 2022). Each skill, trait, and perspective is a useful tool for leading during a crisis. But they are even more effective when integrated into a single crisis leadership strategy. Consider how the following skills, traits, and perspectives might add to a leader's ability to get results through others even during times of crisis.

## The "C.R.I.S.I.S." Leadership Model

### Communicate

Particularly during a crisis, the ability to genuinely and effectively empathize with the people affected can make all the difference regarding whether a leader will succeed or fail. Never before have leaders been under such intense scrutiny from their stakeholders aimed at assessing whether they demonstrate the care, authenticity, purpose, and values that organizations profess to subscribe to.

Crisis communications from leaders often hit the wrong notes. Time and again, we see leaders taking an overconfident, upbeat tone in the early stages of a crisis—and raising stakeholders' suspicions about what leaders know and how well they are handling the crisis. Authority figures are also prone to suspend announcements for long stretches while they wait for more facts to emerge and decisions to be made.

Neither approach is reassuring. As Amy Edmondson recently wrote,

> Transparency is "job one" for leaders in a crisis. Be clear about what you know, what you don't know, and what you are doing to learn more. (Edmondson 2020)

Thoughtful, frequent communication shows that leaders are following the situation and adjusting their responses as they learn more. This helps them reassure stakeholders that they are confronting the crisis. Leaders should take special care to see that each audience's concerns, questions, and interests are addressed. Having members of the crisis response team speak firsthand about what they are doing can be particularly effective.

Communications shouldn't stop once the crisis has passed. Offering an optimistic, realistic outlook can have a powerful effect on employees and other stakeholders, inspiring them to support the company's recovery.

The DLI research has found that inspiring and transformational leaders during times of crisis tend to seek out and act on the counsel or advice of others. They also have a team of advisors that can offer as many perspectives as possible on their situation, be it organizational or leadership challenges.

It is never easy to communicate bad news with the inherent risk of unsettling key stakeholders. In the context of a crisis such as COVID, it is tempting to talk down the threat to the organization. However, these leaders owe it to their stakeholders to provide honest depictions of reality and to be as clear as possible about known facts as well as "known unknowns." Attempts to underplay the threat will undermine the credibility of future communications, as well as the trust that is integral to successful organizational culture.

Aside from dealing with bad news, communication more broadly is a critical aspect of leading during a crisis. It is important to communicate early and frequently, even with incomplete information. Strong public speaking and motivational skills are a vital part of a leader's skill set but these are particularly important in a crisis. Communications must also have some positivity and hope for the future to motivate stakeholders and direct their energy. This may be viewed as bounded optimism.

After seeing Marriott's revenue fall by nearly 75 percent in most markets because of COVID-19, CEO Arne Sorenson wanted to deliver a video message to employees. His team advised against it because of his appearance: He had been undergoing treatment for pancreatic cancer, and chemotherapy had left him bald. Sorenson made the video nonetheless. In it, he announced that he and the company's chairman would forgo their salaries in 2020 and that the executive team's compensation would be halved. He choked up at the end while talking about supporting Marriott associates around the world (Aten 2020). The video has inspired other leaders to give up their salaries too (Sundheim 2020).

Communicating clearly and often during a crisis is essential, but can be difficult. A leader has some advantage if the organization's crisis management action plan (CMAP) has set up some communication guidelines. With or without a guide, however, the bottom line is simple: Keep internal and external communication lines open and working so that everyone is informed and they don't have to make up their own stories about the crisis.

Based on the seriousness of the crisis (i.e., the perceived level of the crisis), the organization's senior leaders must also decide who should be informed, when, and how. These stakeholders might include the organization's employees, community groups, local government leaders and officials, government regulators, stockholders, customers, suppliers, the local neighborhood, and the news media.

From the outset of the crisis, senior leaders should be out among the employees sharing what they know has occurred, explaining what is being done about it now (and what steps are being taken so it won't happen again), and, when possible, describing implications for the future. Leaving employees out of the information loop during a crisis can be a major mistake. An organization's employees are a loud voice for the organization. They will undoubtedly tell their immediate circle of influence what they think happened, based on what they know. Their knowledge can be the truth that they heard from their leaders or it can be the rumors and gossip they heard in the hallway. If they are not told what is going on, their fears and anxieties about the crisis can turn into anger, distrust, and even revenge. And the organization will become the target of these emotions and possibly destructive behavior.

Many consider New Zealand a success story in its handling of COVID-19. Prime Minister Arden's communication concerning COVID-19 has been exemplary. In the context of the early lockdown, by directing people to "stay home to save lives," the prime minister succinctly offered real purpose to her direction. While giving direction, this early communication also involved meaning, as Arden was creating a narrative around how New Zealand would work together to overcome the threat of COVID (Friedman 2020). Similarly, the way Arden addressed the nation from home—wearing casual clothes and with a child's toys in plain sight—at a time of national lockdown was a great example of showing empathy and identifying with her citizens (Ardern 2020).

What the organization's leadership initially communicates to the organization's internal and external stakeholders should include (and generally be limited to) the known details of the situation, what went wrong and why, what is being done to deal with the immediate situation, and the actions that are and will be taken to ensure the situation does not happen again. Leaders should stick to the facts and avoid conjecture. In the early stages of the crisis, it is also wise to avoid speculating about the future implications of the crisis. If pressed, leaders can say that the greater implications are unknown at present but will be analyzed. Under no circumstances should leaders fabricate or change information with the intent to deceive. Such actions will certainly be found and exacerbate the crisis.

There are immediate and specific communication actions that leaders can take to reduce the negative impact of the crisis and also sustain (and perhaps even improve) relationships with stakeholders. Some of the most important external stakeholders during a crisis are the media; and clear, consistent communication with them is critical during a crisis. The news media can extend the leader's communication resources. If handled correctly, a leader can use the media to exert a powerful, positive, emotional impact on all stakeholders, and in particular on the organization's employees.

The best practices adopted by these leaders include asking themselves the following questions:

- "Do I have access to diverse voices and sources of information?": They adopt scenario planning to determine whose knowledge or expertise they might need in various kinds of crises and identify whether their organization currently has access to it.
- "Do I routinely consider other team members' ideas or feedback when making decisions?": They sought out expertise to fill their blind spots and make informed decisions. Effective crisis leaders are those who know when—and how—to defer to others.
- "What systems or processes might I put into place to surface and capture others' perspectives?": They look at how communication is structured within their organization and whether there are barriers or silos that they need to proactively address.

## Resilience

During times of crisis, these thriving leaders remain calm and sustain their energy levels under pressure, to cope with and adapt to disruptive changes. They bounce back from setbacks. They also overcome major difficulties without engaging in dysfunctional behavior or harming others. Resilient leaders are genuinely, sincerely empathetic, walking compassionately in the shoes of employees, customers, and their broader ecosystems.

The well-being and resilience of self and others are more important now than ever before. Role modeling around well-being will be important for leadership success as well as the need for clear messaging on psychological first aid, well-being, and mental health from the business.

These leaders in the middle of a crisis are faced with a flurry of urgent issues across what seems like innumerable fronts. Resilient leaders zero in on the most pressing of these, establishing priority areas that can quickly cascade.

An essential focus in a crisis is to recognize the impact the uncertainty is having on the people that drive the organization. The priority should be safeguarding workers, ensuring their immediate health and safety, followed by their economic well-being. At such times, emotional intelligence is critical. In everything they do during a crisis, resilient leaders express empathy and compassion for the human side of the upheaval, for example, acknowledging how radically their employees' priorities have shifted away from work to be concerned about family health, accommodating extended school closures, and absorbing the human angst of life-threatening uncertainty. Resilient leaders also encourage their people to adopt a calm and methodical approach to whatever happens next.

Credibility is a valuable leadership commodity during a crisis. It's built on consistency, but consistency isn't just the ability to do the same thing over and over. It's also the ability to spring back from negative comments and adapt to rapid changes, to be resilient.

Mary Lynn Pulley and Michael Wakefield (2001) write in *Building Resiliency: How to Thrive in Times of Change* that resiliency is important because change is so pervasive. It's hard to imagine change as dramatic as that brought about by chaos, and resiliency creates a continuity of effective leadership around which people in an organization can rally.

Leadership consistency is like the smooth ride of a well-engineered car—the car's suspension system adapts to the bumps in the road to protect the passengers and provide stability. In the same way, a leader who can handle change and difficulty with flexibility, courage, and optimism protects others in the organization, provides stability in a tumultuous environment, and inspires trust.

Resiliency is a reflection of the mental toughness required to keep your leadership on the road and moving forward during the twists and turns of a crisis. During a crisis, leaders at all levels are faced with all kinds of extremely unpleasant possibilities, such as serious injury to themselves or others, the destruction of property and equipment, or worse. They must be resilient and mentally tough enough to handle the situation. There can be no indifference or resignation. When the leader hangs tough, it shows others in the organization that someone cares enough about them and their welfare to take the punishment and to keep springing back. To quit or resign is not an option because it would result in the loss of all influence and credibility.

## Agility

While much of the above is self-explanatory, the need for agility when facing future crises is especially important. One positive phenomenon of the crisis has been the speed at which the leaders of many of these organizations have accelerated their uptake of technology, built resilience into their supply chains, and created alternative revenue streams. Some of these changes, such as Unilever shifting from the production of skin care products to cleaning and hygiene products, were simply demand-driven. In other cases, these have been to develop or expand online distribution channels and/or move from B2B to B2C models. While many of these pivots are an extension of existing capacity and are aligned with the organization's strategy, some might be permanent. Importantly, the agile decision making that leads to these shifts needs to be embedded into the organizational DNA as organizations set the path to recovery.

Agility and resiliency are highly correlated concepts and both are essential for adapting to disruption and times of crisis. It is important to understand that they are not the same, yet they are often confused in management literature and also by business leaders and practitioners.

Several decades ago, businesses were built to last. The successful companies were the stable companies—those that consistently, dependably offered a product or service desired by the masses. The goal for those running these businesses was to eliminate uncertainty, complexity, and variability where possible.

Lengthy, tedious planning cycles and bureaucratic processes are hallmarks of this type of business. The uncertainty in complex projects is dealt with by planning experts who would attempt to predetermine every possible detail before implementation. Success is measured by the extent to which the plan is followed and predetermined milestones are achieved. While a traditional approach to business management persists in some types of organizations today, it is often being replaced by a more dynamic, agile approach.

Today, businesses are built to change. Rather than being viewed as problems to eliminate, complexity, uncertainty, and dynamism are seen as inevitable factors involved in meeting the ever-changing customer demands. The most successful organizations are those able to constantly evolve to continuously add value to their customers' lives.

Today's hyper-competitive world can be a tough place for many businesses. Large companies are always looking to produce better products while reducing costs, customers' needs evolve, and the world economy fluctuates at large. In a sentence, your business will face many threats. But how do you survive?

A successful business knows when to bend, pivot, and change to accommodate forces more powerful than itself, a process that requires *business agility*. Business agility can be used to adjust to market changes in addition to internal business changes.

Business agility refers to the company's ability to quickly adapt to changes and fluctuations in its business environment. The faster a company can adjust its business strategy, the higher its business agility. Business agility is an organizational method to help businesses adapt quickly to market changes that are either external or internal. If a business is set up to respond rapidly and with the flexibility to meet customer demands, they're more likely to thrive and keep those customers.

Resilient organizations are those that rebound and prosper after business disruption because they're adaptive, agile, and sustainable. Resilient organizations have resilient leaders who see change as opportunities for continued growth rather than a source of anxiety and fear. Response, recovery, and contingencies are the basis of resilience.

To achieve organizational high performance in an era of constant disruption and crisis, both *agility and resilience* are important. This author defines both terms as follows:

*Agility refers to the ability to make a rapid change and achieve flexibility in various aspects of the operations, in response to changes or disruptive events in the external environment that could be characterized as a volatile, uncertain, complex, ambiguous, and disruptive*

*(VUCAD) environment. It can also be viewed as the capacity for responding with speed and flexibly and decisively toward anticipating, initiating, and taking advantage of opportunities and avoiding any negative consequences of change.*

*Resilience refers to the ability to anticipate, prepare for, and recover from disasters, emergencies, and other disruptions, and protect and enhance workforce and customer engagement, supply network and financial performance, organizational productivity, and community well-being when disruption occurs. It can also be viewed as the capacity for resisting, absorbing, and responding, even reinventing, if necessary, in response to fast and/or disruptive change that cannot be avoided such as the "black swan" events.*

Leaders should also explore opportunities for developing collective agility where major challenges require entire systems to be agile and adaptable. Such challenges require whole-system collaboration and design rather than piecemeal solutions. The accelerated delivery of COVID vaccines in the United States is a recent illustration of whole-system design and collaboration across all stakeholders in the system. This ranges from manufacture, regulatory approval, vaccine distribution and tracking, supply chain coordination, and a range of healthcare systems and pharmacies. There are many advantages to encouraging a horizontal and vertical cross-section of the system to codesign the strategic outcomes as well as the business model and tactics. These include an outside-in perspective, facilitation of buy-in, identifying bottlenecks and problems early, and quicker decision making (Deloitte 2020a).

One major challenge may be the tension between traditional governance structures and processes that often focus on risk. Another may be fixed processes and the speed and agility required to take up opportunities in the new environment. Accordingly, governance structures and processes may need to adapt.

### Intelligence (Business Intelligence and Data Analytics)

We don't know when or where the next crisis will strike—or what form it will take. The only things we can control are how we prepare for crises and how we respond to them. In both instances, decision analytics plays a critical role.

When *Harvard Business Review* investigated why some companies had reached new levels of success in the years following the Great Recession of 2008–2010, the researchers concluded preparation was the differentiating factor (Gulati, Nohria, and Wohlgezogen 2010).

Crises change markets, industries, and economic processes. Hence the key to success is change management. One of the best ways to manage change is by making wise decisions about debt, workforce management, and new technologies. The best way to improve business decision making is by supporting those decisions with advanced data analytics.

In times of crisis, business intelligence (BI) is an area that leaders can leverage successfully when revenues are decreasing and budget problems come into play. By leveraging BI and big data analytics, leaders will be able to discover things that are not obvious or that they didn't know, such as the root cause of those revenue drops and how they affect specific levers within their organization.

## Data Analytics

Data analytics is an emerging field in the 21st century when using analytical tools has become a fundamental part of the business decision-making process, including operations on crisis management. The exponential growth of data, with technological advancement, inspires the creation of devices such as smartphones and the development of space technologies. As a result, the amount of information generated from these devices and technologies is surging, leading to the so-called big data, which has become a disruptive element in the workforce. Data analytics has been demonstrated to be an asset to identify patterns, predicting outcomes, and guiding corporate strategies (Ngai, Xiu, and Chau 2009).

Data analytics is a set of analytical and functional tools to gain insights into business processes and uncover hidden patterns from the BI view. It is the use of data, obtained from different sources, via statistical and quantitative analysis, explanatory and predictive models, and fact-based management to guide the decision making and activities of the stakeholders (Davenport and Harris 2007). It is a collection of theories and technologies that turn raw data into relevant and usable information for day-to-day operations, based on the analysis of datasets to deduce the information found within them. Some business questions can be answered to find potential prospects that will give a company a competitive edge in the market. These are "what happened?" in a descriptive sense, "why did it happen?" in a diagnostic sense, and "when might it happen?" in a predictive sense.

Data-driven decision making is observed as an essential part of business operations. It is achieved by extracting descriptive insights to observe current operations, predictive insights to forecast possible future events, and prescriptive insights to execute business strategies. Effective planning is a critical factor for allocating the necessary resources with minimal cost and time. The indicators that are gathered from the computational models are part of the crisis and risk management to be ready for any outcome. These insights can show an upcoming systemic risk, such that allocating resources will avoid these downturns or delay the losses.

Proper risk management is critical for each company during difficult times. Analytics can be used to manage business continuity and retention by monitoring, forecasting, and preparing for crisis management and incorporating them into the strategy. The decision-making process is an important aspect of business that affects economic development and the long-term viability of the business in the external environment it operates.

The use of business analytics in a data-driven setting shows that there is a way to enhance management capability by offering valuable insights. These observations will pave the way for a good business strategy that puts them ahead of the competition. Because of advancements in information technology, data analytics has enabled service technology systems to create innovative ways to respond to customer needs.

Business Intelligence

BI is a computer-supported system used for identification and to produce new insights and high-quality knowledge to support decision making (Božič and Dimovski 2019). BI is learning from the business experience, which explains the behavioral approach to using informatics and information technology to make decisions. It is an important part of organizational planning to gain intuitive sight and to execute the operations phase by phase based on these informal gatherings. Knowledge workers and data scientists are essential for each company to establish its corporate strategy and planning.

BI is a sequence of operational processes to provide the right information in the right format and to represent such information to the consumer in real time. Intelligent decision support systems and knowledge management databases are part of these advanced evolutionary stages. The multilayer framework is promoted by casual interdependencies and the holistic design of business analytics. BI systems' maturity is based on information content quality, information access quality, analytical corporate culture, and the use of information for decision making.

Data analytics can be used to evaluate these risks, known as black swan events, where the value creation would be preserved while focusing on evaluating contingencies that threaten the present business model.

Organizational ambidexterity is the ability to respond to changes in the business environment where each firm may encounter environmental ambiguity, which is defined as instances when business relationships are unclear because of a lack of information. A firm needs to achieve organizational ambidexterity when it faces a competitive environment. This requires companies to recognize new information to adjust dynamic capabilities while focusing on internal and external changes. Dynamic capabilities of the organizations evolve with sensing new opportunities that can influence organizational decision making. Competitive advantage is derived from a firm's ordinary capabilities that have been transformed through these decision capabilities.

During the DLI research, it was found that the organizations leveraged data analytics to enhance their dynamic strategic capability in corporate planning during these systemic risks and crises. It helps these organizations understand uncertain economic environments to stay competitive while the focus is on day-to-day operations. The business cycles are directly affected by value creation where the agile frameworks play a factor.

Most organizations have crisis management teams, protocols, and business continuity to guide current actions and forecast possible responses to future events including pandemics and unexpected downturn risks.

These policies need to reduce business-critical operations and travel, distribute all critical operations across the departments for effective decision making, diagnose employees at work, or ask them to stay at home if they are sick.

Although the main emphasis is containing and mitigating the risk from these unexpected events themselves, during the COVID-19 pandemic, these companies established a corporate plan for unanticipated business risks and downturns. These actions include updating BI daily, necessitating new strategies of mitigation rather than containment, using experts' knowledge and predictive forecasting understanding of what's happening and will happen including epidemic and public health intelligence, and establishing resilience principles in developing policies that also include consistent communication with the employees and evolvability for preparedness for the next possible crisis. These policies for dealing with and resolving the ability to forecast immediate results are get-ready scenarios for current and future situations. Dealing with and resolving the immediate problems that COVID-19 presents to each company's workforce as well as creating resilience protocols that can foresee similar cyclical events will enable businesses to continue operating throughout this pandemic crisis.

When dealing with black swan events like pandemics, data-driven decision making is a crucial tool, and predictive analytics can foresee similar catastrophes. Crisis management capacities of businesses will need to be more data-driven and based on forecasting technologies to prepare for probable pandemic-like situations.

Black swan is thought to be a systemic shock to financial markets and daily societal life that may change social standards. Data analytics are used in risk management as part of crisis management, where data-driven decision making is given top importance to control and prevent such disruptions.

### Shifting the Mental Model

In a crisis, leaders are compelled to try to implement measures that they have never attempted before. When a leader adopts a growth mindset in a crisis, the path to change tends to be less arduous, as individuals with a growth mindset believe their talents and abilities are developed through self-development and practice. They are open to new ideas and learning and see failures as opportunities.

Believing that your qualities are carved in stone—the *fixed mindset*—creates an urgency to prove yourself over and over. If you have only a certain amount of intelligence, a certain personality, and a certain moral character, then you'd better prove that you have a healthy dose of them. It simply wouldn't do to look or feel deficient in these most basic characteristics (Dweck 2006).

There's another mindset in which these traits are not simply a hand you're dealt and have to live with, always trying to convince yourself and others that you have a royal flush when you're secretly worried it's a pair of tens. In this mindset, the hand you're dealt is just the starting point for development. This *growth mindset* is based on the belief that your basic qualities are things you can cultivate through your efforts, your strategies, and help from others. Although people may differ in every way—in their initial talents and aptitudes, interests, or temperaments—everyone can change and grow through application and experience (Dweck 2006).

Those thriving leaders interviewed during the DLI research emphasized the importance of critical thinking, which helps them to establish situational awareness and impose effective strategy, direction, and action in situations that are exceptionally volatile and uncertain. In such circumstances, information available to decision makers is likely to be ambiguous. Also, there may be too much of it or too little, and what there is may appear to be unstructured, confusing, and possibly contradictory.

The situation is likely to be uncertain, and suitable courses of action may not be readily apparent or clear enough to support confident and effective decision making. However, this may be exactly when urgent choices and critical decisions have to be made. These leaders recognized these problems as characteristics of crises. They were able to leverage the business of managing information to establish situational awareness. This awareness, when shared with their crisis leadership team and key stakeholders, is the essential basis for effective choices of strategy, direction, and action. Shared situational awareness implies creating and maintaining a common understanding of what is going on, what that means (in terms of its implications), and what it might mean (in terms of reasonable deductions that can be made about future developments).

## What Is Critical Thinking?

Critical thinking is an active form of reflection which is deliberate, persistent, and careful. It challenges preconceptions, perceptions, and received wisdom. And it is, most important of all, focused on deciding what to believe and what to do. It is, therefore, inherently practical and generates a set of guidelines for the practitioner. It involves what some have called metacognition or the act of thinking about how we think.

Critical thinking aims to better understand the meaning and implications of information, conclusions, options, and decisions and to identify and evaluate the assumptions upon which thinking (our own and others') is based. It can bring a powerful rigor to crisis management if it is applied with perseverance, determination, and self-awareness.

Critical thinking in the business literature is often confused with skills like "problem solving." In reality, "problem solving" is quite different from "critical thinking."

Sometimes problem solving requires thinking skills, like how best to balance profit and loss statements, but not critical thinking skills—rational, reflective thinking. Some business-related problems, for example, require emotional intelligence, which is thinking that is neither rational nor reflective.

In other words, while critical thinking often refers to "problem solving," not all problem solving is an example of critical thinking. Critical thinking consists more of "habits of mind" providing a framework in which problem solving can occur. Often, these distinctions aren't clear in business education literature.

How and why is critical thinking applied in the workplace? Critical thinking in the workplace comes in many forms. We see critical thinking being used in teams to help effectively resolve problems. We even see critical thinking being used in the workplace to help teams figure out what issues exist, and then we see teams come up with possible answers for those issues.

Critical thinking is applied to leadership approaches because leaders need to have critical thinking skills, be able to understand logical relationships between ideas, recognize the importance and the relationship of an argument, as well as recognize mistakes in reasoning and then be able to make the right decisions.

The need for critical thinking in leadership has always been around. A model was developed in 1925, called the Watson–Glaser critical thinking model, which helps organizations identify factors in people that are important for critical thinking and judgment making, which explains why critical thinking needs to be a part of leadership approaches.

Pearson has developed the following RED model—Recognize assumptions, Evaluate arguments, and Draw conclusions (see Figure 4.2)—as a way to view and apply critical thinking principles when faced with a decision (Chartrand, Ishikawa, and Flander 2018).

*Recognize assumptions.* This is the ability to separate fact from opinion. It is deceptively easy to listen to a comment or presentation and assume the information presented is true even though no evidence was given to back it up. Perhaps the speaker is particularly credible or trustworthy or the information makes sense or matches our own view. We just don't question it. Noticing and questioning assumptions helps to reveal information gaps or unfounded logic. Taking it a step further, when we examine assumptions through the eyes of different people (e.g., the viewpoint of different stakeholders), the end result is a richer perspective on a topic.

*Why does it matter?* This is the ability to separate fact from opinion. It is deceptively easy to listen to a comment or presentation and assume

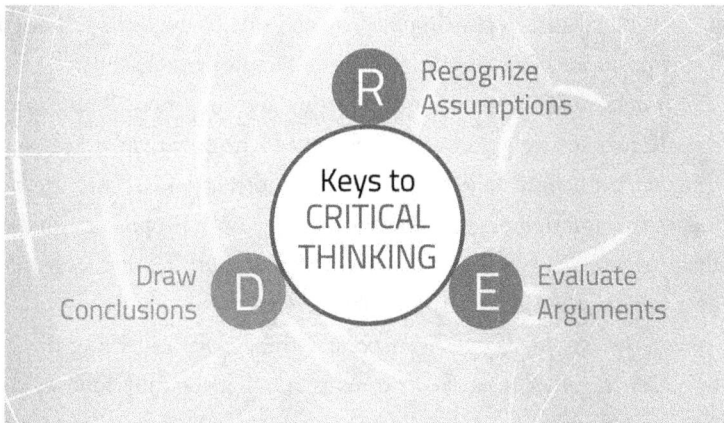

*Figure 4.2 The "RED" model of critical thinking*

the information presented is true even though no evidence was given to back it up. Noticing and questioning assumptions helps to reveal information gaps or unfounded logic. Taking it a step further, when we examine assumptions through the eyes of different people (e.g., the viewpoint of different stakeholders) the end result is a richer perspective on a topic.

*How/when to use it.* When you're gathering information, listening to what people say, or assessing a situation, think about what assumptions you have going in. Perhaps you assume that a trusted co-worker is providing reliable information, but is there really evidence to back it up? Learn to see gaps in logic and opinion disguised as fact.

*Evaluate arguments.* It is difficult to suspend judgment systematically and walk through various arguments and information with the impartiality of Sherlock Holmes. The art of evaluating arguments entails analyzing information objectively and accurately, questioning the quality of supporting evidence, and understanding how emotion influences the situation. Common barriers include confirmation bias, which is the tendency to seek out and agree with the information that is consistent with your own point of view or allow emotions—yours or others'—to get in the way of objective evaluation. People may quickly conclude simply to avoid conflict. Being able to remain objective and sort through the validity of different positions helps people draw more accurate conclusions.

*Why does it matter?* We often have problems sorting through conflicting information because we unknowingly let our emotions or pride get in the way or because we only hear what we want to hear (confirmation bias). Being able to remain objective and sort through the validity of different positions helps people draw more accurate conclusions.

*How/when to use it.* The art of evaluating arguments entails analyzing information objectively and accurately, questioning the quality of supporting evidence, and understanding how emotions—yours or others—influence the situation or get in the way of objectivity. People may quickly conclude simply to avoid conflict. Learn how to push all that aside, and analyze information accurately and objectively.

*Draw conclusions.* People who possess these skills can bring diverse information together to arrive at conclusions that logically follow from the available evidence, and they do not inappropriately generalize beyond the evidence. Furthermore, they will change their position when the evidence warrants doing so. They are often characterized as having "good judgment" because they typically arrive at a quality decision.

*Why does it matter?* People who possess this skill can bring diverse information together to arrive at conclusions that logically follow from the available evidence, and they do not inappropriately generalize beyond that evidence. Furthermore, they will change their position when the evidence warrants doing so. They are often characterized as having "good judgment" because of their quality decisions.

*How/when to use it.* This is the payoff. When you think critically, the true picture becomes clear, and you can make the tough decision or attack the difficult problem.

Each of these critical thinking skills fits together in a process that is both fluid and sequential.

When presented with information, people typically alternate between recognizing assumptions and evaluating arguments. Critical thinking is sequential in that recognizing faulty assumptions or weak arguments improves the likelihood of reaching an appropriate conclusion. It is helpful to focus on each of the RED skills individually when practicing skill development. With concentrated practice over time, typically several months, critical thinking skills can be significantly increased.

### Inspiring

During crises, leaders need to demonstrate inspirational and transformational leadership styles. Trust is more valuable than ever during times of crisis because it not only promotes resilience in the face of uncertainty but also provides solid ground for action and results in better financial performance. When leaders and organizations are centered on an authentic purpose, employees feel that their work has meaning.

Employees' trust in their organization is vital during crises and disruptions. It powerfully facilitates employees' ability to respond constructively to crises and change, and it underpins organizational agility and resilience. Yet it is during such episodes that trust is most threatened. During the COVID-19 pandemic, this conundrum has organizational leaders asking: How can we preserve employee trust in the face of the financial and other challenges posed by the outbreak?

Yet it is during crises and disruption—when trust is most required—that it is also more likely to be lost. The COVID-19 pandemic is posing just such a threat. It is requiring organizational leaders and policy makers to make rapid, large-scale changes to both sustain organizational viability and maintain the flexibility and ability to later scale up and rapidly return to their core business once the pandemic passes. To ensure organizational survival, they are having to make tough and unpopular decisions, such as cutting pay and work hours and laying off workers temporarily or permanently. The uncertainty and unpredictability of the pandemic have jolted employees out of their familiar ways, including their habitual trust in their employers, and has heightened their sense of vulnerability. In such a context, employees need and seek reassurance from their employer that their continued trust is deserved.

Leaders must take key practical actions to preserve trust. The DLI research shows that during crises, employee trust can not only be preserved but also be enhanced. These thriving leaders show that employees who feel a greater sense of connection are far more likely to ride out volatility and be available to help companies recover and grow when stability returns.

Central to reducing uncertainty is drawing on and reinforcing the familiar, established foundations of trust that already exist in the organization. These trust foundations are unique to each organization and include the values, purpose, relationships, practices, organizational structures, and processes that built and sustained employee trust before the crisis. For example, in one government agency we studied, trust was founded strongly on principles of fairness, integrity, and professional respect. In a manufacturing business, employee trust was based on a unionized culture and the strong relationships between line managers, workers, and trade unions at the local plant level. These trust foundations highlight what the organization needs to protect and continue to do to preserve employees' trust.

We believe that all leaders can be inspirational during times of crisis as all they need to do is unlock their inspirational potential and find an opportunity to demonstrate their capability. They need to develop the relevant skills which they can learn, grow, and develop to increase their impact and influence on their followers. It is important to understand from the start that becoming an inspirational leader requires focused effort, practice, and the ability to conduct self-reflection. Inspiration is personal; our source of inspiration is closely linked to our beliefs, values, and identity.

Inspirational leadership is both a mindset and a skill. It should be thought of as an action-orientated mindset where one individual can ignite a fire in another person's heart and/or mind and move a person or team of people to take action and achieve something greater than the current status quo. Inspirational leadership, at its core, is about finding ways to enhance the potential of those you lead in a way that works for them and inspiring others to push themselves, achieve more, and reach that potential. The methods by which this is done will vary from person to person, and business to business, but the outcome is always the same: People develop greater confidence in what they can do and apply this confidence in a way that benefits the organization they work for.

During times of crisis, when employees aren't just engaged, but inspired, that's when organizations see real breakthroughs. Inspired employees are themselves far more productive and, in turn, inspire those around them to strive for greater heights. The DLI research shows that while anyone can become an inspiring leader as it is believed that they're made, not born, in most companies, there are far too few of them. Those thriving leaders are inspiring as they leverage effectively their unique combination of strengths to motivate individuals and teams to take on bold missions—and hold them accountable for results. And they unlock higher performance through empowerment, not command and control.

While the research found that leaders who inspire are incredibly diverse, which underscores the need to find inspirational leaders that are right to motivate your organization, there is no universal archetype. A corollary of this finding is that anyone can become an inspirational leader by focusing on his or her strengths. Although DLI found that many different attributes help leaders inspire people, it also identified that there is one common trait that indicated matters more than any other: mindfulness. This enables the leaders to remain calm under stress, empathize, listen deeply, and remain present.

Often, leaders have been identified as possessing a remarkable quality that set them apart from others. It enabled them to have a powerful influence on others. It caused others to be attracted to them and enabled them to achieve remarkable outcomes. That quality has most frequently been labeled "charisma," a term coming from the Greek word meaning "gift." In ancient times, it was believed that this quality was indeed a divine gift that was bestowed upon some and not others. The practical consequence of this has been that unlike other leadership skills, such as being results focused, giving compelling oral presentations, or delegating, no one attempted to teach charisma.

Because the popular press often describes leaders as charismatic, this characteristic has then been used to explain this person's success. The probable reason is that many leaders fell into the seemingly logical trap of thinking that charisma, as the term was most often used, was simply a synonym for being inspiring. There were instances where countless leaders are identified by their colleagues as being highly inspiring and not charismatic. Conversely, some people are seen as quite charismatic and fail to meet the test of being inspiring and motivating—especially in the long run.

Some believe that inspiration is just something that leaders do on big occasions. They see it as that yearly speech where leaders get up in front of all the employees and get them all revved up and inspired. Inspiration is much more than this. The DLI research found that during the recent pandemic, everything a leader does every day has an impact on the employees. When a leader comes to work in the morning and is in a bad mood, that counts. When a leader comes in and is sharing with colleagues his or her optimism, excitement, and passion for the work, that counts. When a leader comes in, ducks into his or her office, and hides in his or her cave all day, that counts. But if a leader will just take a few minutes to go around and ask people how they're doing, thank them, and encourage them to do more, that counts. Everything leaders do counts. Everything every employee does on every level counts.

Inspirational leadership builds on inspirational appeals. It is probably the most powerful form of leadership and may well be the only soft approach that is scalable and that allows firms to thrive in situations characterized by ambiguity, complexity, and rapid change.

### Set the Recovery Path

A crisis may end, but it doesn't just fade away. Leaders can take several important and influential actions to ensure their organization and its employees not only recover but also prepare for a future crisis.

One of the biggest questions employees have asked their leaders during the COVID-19 pandemic is when this coronavirus madness will end so that they can get back to normal or business as usual. The reality is that it is going to be business as unusual. To prepare for the "new normal" or the "next normal," leaders need to answer the question "what can I do now to prepare for when things return to a new normal?" To achieve this, they need to reflect on what has happened and what lessons they have learned and then plan to start with a new vision.

They need to connect the conversation about why they and the leadership team are embarking on preparing the organization for the future, what the outcomes are likely to be, and how to go about it. Leaders need to stay firmly grounded in questions like "what's our goal here? What does success look like for us?" Leaders need to build a culture of accountability, foresight, a "people-first ahead of process and technology" mantra, and decisive adaptability. For many organizations, this means asking their workforce to work from home. If you are preparing for increased remote work, ensure that the organization has in place the right technology and the technical capacity to support it, including bandwidth, VPN infrastructure, authentication, access control mechanisms, and cybersecurity tools that can support peak traffic demands. Many leaders have confessed that their organizations were not ready for this!

### Reshaping the Organization for Recovery

Two important goals of leadership following a crisis are to rebuild and strengthen relationships (between the people in the organization and between the people and the organization) and to learn from the experience to prepare for the next crisis. In working toward those goals, one of the most effective things leaders can do after the crisis is to assure employees that the probability of the same crisis reoccurring is virtually nonexistent. Otherwise, anxiety levels will remain high in the organization and significantly impact morale and productivity. Leaders at all levels should talk to employees and personally share what preventive measures are being taken to avert another crisis. This allows the employees to ask questions, an act that can be therapeutic and calming.

Another more formal but particularly effective means of providing such reassurance is through updated and highly publicized company rules and regulations aimed at preventing a similar crisis. These revised rules can outline improved crisis assessment procedures, including early warning and detection, crisis indicators, and improved interpersonal communication methods among leaders and employees in general.

These assurances can be the first step in rebuilding and reviewing the organization's communication strategies. Clear and continuing communication is as essential after a crisis as it is before and during a crisis. Making sure those lines are open after a crisis helps leaders and the organization as a whole to learn from their experience and enhance their capability to deal with future crises. It also helps employees connect to the organization and connect and strengthen the bonds they developed during the crisis.

### Demonstrate Transformational and Authoritative (Visionary) Leadership Style

As signs of recovery tentatively creep back into the economy, forward-looking organizations are working to redefine their "business as usual" and arrive at a transformational strategy. Along the way, according to the DLI research, there are important aspects that these thriving leaders take into consideration in charting the way forward.

During the height of the pandemic, most organizations operated in crisis mode. As the world moves toward a postpandemic recovery, these thriving leaders guided their organizations out of emergency mode into something of a semblance of normality. Yet, they are mindful that the crisis remains in the background. Supply chains remain overstretched and working restrictions continue. So, it's still important to steer organizations on a transformational journey.

The concept of applying and adopting various leadership styles was popularized by psychologist Daniel Goleman through his evidence-based research on emotional intelligence. In his book *Primal Leadership: Realizing the Power of Emotional Intelligence*, Goleman describes six different

*Figure 4.3 Goleman's situational leadership styles framework*

styles of leadership (see Figure 4.3)—visionary, coaching, affiliative, democratic, pacesetting, and commanding (Goleman 2002)—and how the most effective leaders embrace all six styles, utilizing the appropriate style based on situational, organizational, or human cues (Goleman 2000).

Goleman describes the situation most appropriate for applying visionary leadership as one of directional change, where openness is critical for blazing new paths: "Visionary leaders articulate where a group is going, but not how it will get there—setting people free to innovate, experiment, take calculated risks."

However, when the visionary style is your only style, it can leave your team confused about their priorities, searching for vital details, dealing with "organizational whiplash" in the face of constant change, and unsure where the organization (and their career) is going.

Therefore, it can be critical for visionary leaders to balance their style and surround themselves with fellow C-levels, directors, managers, or team leads more adept at integrating the other leadership styles into the mix when being democratic, coaching, or a pacesetter isn't their strong suit.

## Importance of Authoritative Leadership During Crises

Authoritative leaders, also called visionary leaders, tend to approach leadership like a mentor guiding a mentee. Instead of telling their team to follow instructions and do as they say, authoritative leaders put themselves in the scenario and utilize a "come with me" approach. They have a firm understanding of the challenges to overcome and the goals to reach and have a clear vision for achieving success.

Authoritative leaders inspire motivation. They offer direction, guidance, and feedback to maintain enthusiasm and a sense of accomplishment throughout the crisis or business challenge.

At its heart, authoritative leadership depends on a thoroughly developed sense of emotional intelligence. To be effective, authoritative leaders must demonstrate certain emotional intelligence competencies, such as:

1. *Self-confidence*: to develop a vision and inspire others to follow it. Authoritative leaders provide direction and vision. They approach resolving challenges arising from the crisis from a position of confidence. They have a clear vision of what success looks like and give their team members clear direction and constructive feedback as they work toward achieving those organizational goals.

2. *Empathy and empathetic listening*: to understand and anticipate the emotions felt by team members at key junctures during the crisis. Authoritative leaders breed goodwill as for the authoritative leadership style to work, a person must approach his or her team from a position of empathy. By understanding the personal and professional emotions, desires, and worries of a team member, an authoritative leader is better able to identify potential roadblocks to performance and remove them, while simultaneously incentivizing success.

3. *Ability to adapt*: identify and remove barriers to change that may be required for success on the path of recovery from the crisis. Authoritative leaders bring clarity. They are effective because of their ability to inspire, motivate, and influence their team. Often, this motivation stems from their ability to understand a company's strategic goals and communicate them in a way that's easy for employees to follow. When everyone knows what the organization is striving toward, it's easy to ensure everyone is aligned.

### *Authoritative Versus Authoritarian Leadership*

While the terms "authoritative" and "authoritarian" leadership sound similar—and are often used interchangeably—they are very different.

Authoritative leaders guide their teams by example and inspire progression toward a common goal, whereas authoritarian leaders rely on commands and demand compliance without question. Authoritative leaders say, "Come with me"; authoritarian leaders say, "Do what I tell you." Authoritative leaders view success as something to be shared by the team; authoritarian leaders view success as stemming from themselves.

While authoritarian leadership, also called commanding leadership, is often viewed as a more negative approach, it can be highly effective in the right circumstances, particularly when a company or organization needs firm guidance through a crisis when compliance with the directives of the board or senior leadership team is crucial for the sustainability of the organization.

## Conclusion

Ideally, all of us would balance our intellectual, physical, spiritual, and emotional lives all of the time. But that's a difficult job, particularly when a crisis creates an imbalance and tips the scale toward the emotional end. This creates a special challenge for managers who must provide leadership to those who are in a state of emotional turmoil.

Occupying a designated leadership position isn't the same thing as being a leader, doesn't provide leadership on its own, and doesn't prove that the person in that position has the skills or knowledge to be an effective leader. There is a significant difference between being a successful leader because specific numbers were achieved and being an effective leader. After all, the numbers were achieved and the continuing support of direct reports is evident. Leaders who view themselves as successful because of position, salary, or longevity, but leave a high body count of former employees bobbing in their wake, are often surprised to find their careers derailed or sidelined. Nothing separates such leaders from their illusions as quickly and sharply as a crisis because it's then they realize they haven't built the skills necessary to lead effectively during such traumatic events.

An organization's senior leadership is key before, during, and after a crisis, and its quality can determine the length, severity, and ultimate consequences of the crisis. Leaders set the tone by their example and conduct during the crisis. By paying attention to the components of influence (especially communication, empathy, and caring), leaders can have a significant positive impact on the very human, emotionally charged climate that accompanies a crisis. That in turn can reduce the negative impact and duration of a crisis for the benefit of the organization.

Effective leaders often have a well-developed ability to influence others and can avoid using authoritarian or fear tactics to get results. This is an especially important capability in a crisis when strong leadership is essential, and getting results through others using threats, pressure, and coercion is generally unproductive and can even be harmful. Influencing techniques that are effective during normal times become even more critical during a crisis. Because influencing skills are applicable during normal business situations as well as in a crisis, leaders can develop these skills before the heat of a crisis is upon them.

If your day-to-day leadership doesn't bolster trust, garner respect, inspire confidence, and connect emotionally with your direct reports, it's highly improbable that your leadership will dramatically change just because a crisis is at hand.

Authoritative leadership can be particularly well suited for businesses undergoing a period of struggle or change. A department or team not meeting its goals in recent quarters; a shift in company ownership, leadership, or structure; a corporate turnaround after a decline; or a desire to innovate and change organizationally can all be appropriate situations for an authoritative approach.

It isn't, however, applicable to all business challenges. Skilled leaders can tailor their leadership style to whatever scenario they find themselves in.

# CHAPTER 5

# Crisis Management Strategy

## Introduction: Crisis Management

As the business community has learned through the COVID-19 pandemic, it's more important than ever for leaders to anticipate and plan for the possibility of an unplanned event. The more prepared you are to manage shocks, the less likely you'll fall victim to the serious harm a crisis has the potential to inflict.

Whereas risk management is traditionally a proactive discipline, crisis management (CM) is reactive. CM can be viewed as a specialized discipline within risk management, where specific practices are instituted in response to unexpected events that threaten a company's stability. Having an effective plan and resources in place mitigates the destructive nature of that reactivity.

To respond to ongoing uncertainty and change, businesses need to embrace a core set of capabilities and behaviors to embed agility and resilience. They need to go beyond their usual business analysis and think about a broader set of future scenarios; they need to plan not just for business as usual, but for any major disruptions that might affect them or a competitor, and they need to be able to act with agility to quickly counter existential threats and take advantage of new opportunities.

To succeed, CEOs need to have adaptability—the ability to change—and agility—the speed of response. This includes both plannings for whatever can go wrong and setting up a structure to respond quickly.

To do this, companies need to utilize a range of information and tools to gain insight into their current operations, performance, and market environment and plan for different future environments. These include external insights, such as third-party data and dynamic analytics that can quickly process real-time data and help shape insights into customer demands or concerns.

Scenario planning that utilizes data to help simulate how a company can be impacted by a host of situations, such as a market crash or a product recall, is another key activity. For example, many organizations have built cross-functional teams to look at potential scenarios and be ready to act once the way forward is clear.

To be adaptive and agile, people across different functions of a company need to be empowered to make the decisions to quickly execute change to meet any situation.

This starts with inclusive leadership from the top, which delegates rather than controls, and actively invites input from all levels and can be seen as taking appropriate action based on this input. The traditional top-down structure is likely to be too slow to respond to a threat in today's environment. A key step in change management is to ensure that people feel empowered, are more aware, and are likely to communicate early signs of disruption.

This is also a good time to make sure business units are sharing data, rather than keeping it in silos, to make sure all decision makers can act based on a full set of information.

Boards and leadership teams also need to make sure they have the right leaders in place, with the right skill sets for all situations. An organization may have the best leaders for a growth scenario, but these leaders might not be nimble enough in a turnaround situation.

CEOs, CFOs, and the board should regularly evaluate whether the leadership team has the essential skills for all situations. They can then identify which leaders should take point in different scenarios such as CM or operational restructuring.

Organizations face challenges that present varying levels of severity. But handled poorly, even a seemingly minor shock has the potential to escalate into a crisis that threatens the viability of a business. A crisis can disrupt operations, damage reputations, destroy shareholder value, and trigger other threats.

The media continues to be filled with stories about companies that fail to manage crises, costing them millions in damage, fines, reparations, lost revenue, and lost jobs.

Many of those failures can be tracked to a few common causes:

1. *Lack of attention to the identification and assessment of risks*
2. *Weak leadership commitment to effective risk mitigation and CM*

3. *No crisis communication plan*
4. *No process to assess, investigate, and mitigate a crisis*

As part of an effective enterprise risk management (ERM) program, leaders need to make the right moves when a crisis occurs to resolve the issue and protect the organization. The following *five steps,* when taken with care and commitment from the board of directors on down, can help ensure the enterprise is well prepared to protect itself when a crisis occurs.

### Step 1: Evaluate Corporate Governance, Risk Management, and Internal Controls

Organizations must commit to a regular evaluation of their corporate governance and risk management practices and internal controls. When addressed together, these three components provide the pillars for a strong CM program. Through a regular review of these pillars of effective governance, corporations can identify new and emerging risks, assess existing risks, and make the policy and process changes needed to address the behaviors that could lead to significant damage to the enterprise—before they evolve into a crisis.

### Step 2: Identify the Most Probable Crises and Assess Their Potential Impact

There are several kinds of crises that are possible in every organization, including natural disasters, unexpected injury or death of employee or customer, harassment or discrimination, workplace violence, employee malfeasance, cybercrime, white-collar crime, litigation or class action, fraud, mismanagement, and product defects/recalls. Other categories may be unique to the business. An enterprise-wide vulnerability assessment using clearly defined risk indicators will help to uncover the kinds of crises for which the organization needs to plan and prepare. Extra attention should be given to those crises that are deemed either highly likely to occur or to have the highest potential impact on the organization.

### Step 3: Create and Train a Crisis Management Team

Arguably the most important step in an effective ERM and crisis response program is having the crisis team in place. Internal and external experts should be identified and roles and responsibilities delineated. Regular training and crisis exercises are vital to assuring that the team is prepared to execute important response strategies and tasks. Internal expertise should include senior executive management, operations leaders from key areas, and leaders of compliance, internal audit, corporate communications/PR, human resources, legal, sales and marketing, among others.

External expertise may be needed to supplement the internal team and should include established relationships with outside providers of PR and communications, and legal and forensic counsel, among others. By having these key vendors in place well in advance, they can get to know the company and its leaders, facilitating better, faster responses when a crisis is declared.

### Step 4: Develop and Implement a Crisis Communication Plan

Effective communication response to a crisis has never been more important than in this highly charged age of instant communication. Organizations no longer have the luxury of waiting days to respond when an issue arises. Effective crisis communication plans include details on not only what to do but how to do it. Policies and processes, chains of command, roles, and responsibilities for communication should be detailed. Best-practice plans contain quick response guides for the most probable crises identified in the vulnerability assessment, including initial strategy and messaging that has been vetted and preapproved by management and legal.

Spokespersons should be identified and trained. Platforms to monitor media and social media should be implemented well in advance. Companies with operations in multiple countries should make sure that their communication plans address important cultural differences so that they can respond appropriately. Finally, the plan should be exercised and updated at least annually to assure that it is well integrated with an operational response and business continuity (BC) and recovery plans.

### Step 5: Develop a Crisis Response Plan

The CM team needs a written plan to effectively manage the crisis. The plan should address levels of crisis with thresholds for activating the team and implementing the plan. It should identify who will lead the response for each type of crisis. Procedures to assess, investigate, and mitigate the crisis are vital. Operational roles and responsibilities should be detailed and external support services identified and engaged.

As the business community has learned through the COVID-19 pandemic, it's more important than ever for leaders to anticipate and plan for the possibility of an unplanned event. The more prepared you are to manage shocks, the less likely you'll fall victim to the serious harm a crisis has the potential to inflict.

*Crisis management* (CM) is one of several interrelated core disciplines comprising ERM, along with emergency preparedness, disaster response, BC planning, supply chain risk mitigation, and cyber liability prevention. CM practices can help lessen the magnitude of emergencies and disasters while decreasing the uncertainty and anxiety associated with these events.

*Business continuity management* (BCM) is a holistic management process for identifying potential impacts from threats and for developing response plans. The objective is to increase an organization's resilience to business disruptions and to minimize the impact of such disruptions. Think of BCM as the strategic process for execution when a disaster occurs. The consequence of the activation of a BC plan is a result of a disaster. In its simplest form, your organization is denied access to either/ or its people, processes, or technological infrastructure.

The CM plan is often embedded into the BC plan or vice versa. This is not a problem unless the execution and responsibilities are delineated in both plans.

During a crisis, your organization is expected to execute the CM plan and during a disaster, the BC plan. The decision-making process for the handling of the crisis or disaster is shouldered by the senior management team. The execution of the necessary crisis response and should there be a denial of access to the "people, process, and technology infrastructure," the recovery activities under recovery strategies and BC plans will be executed.

What is confusing is the overlapping of activities for the crisis response and continuity of operations. It is good to start any discussion with the definition of a crisis and disaster. The question to ask when the incident occurs is, "Is this a crisis or a disaster?"

*Enterprise risk management* (ERM) is the process of identifying and addressing methodically the potential events that represent risks to the achievement of strategic objectives or to opportunities to gain a competitive advantage.

Whereas ERM is traditionally a proactive discipline, CM is reactive. CM can be viewed as a specialized discipline within risk management, where specific practices are instituted in response to unexpected events that threaten a company's stability. Having an effective plan and resources in place mitigates the destructive nature of that reactivity.

## The Board's Role in Overseeing Crisis Management

A corporate crisis can impact organizational culture, business operations, and reputation, all of which can have significant financial, legal, and regulatory ramifications. Therefore, a CM program should bring together a variety of stakeholders who can understand the potential implications and help plan for and recover from a crisis. The program should be managed by someone with in-depth legal and compliance experience who can manage day-to-day operational and tactical responses. It should also closely align the internal and external communications leaders to make sure the decisions and messaging are clearly and directly articulated to the key audiences.

The CM program should be a process within the company's broader resiliency toolkit and integrated into its ERM program. This integration helps safeguard that crisis response planning is aligned with and informed by the company's strategic plan and risk tolerances and that it is dynamic and evolves along with changes to risk assessments and prioritization. Most importantly, a robust ERM program is foundational for risk management, litigation prevention, and loss mitigation.

CEOs and the executive team are responsible for the organization and establishment of a CM capability; boards are responsible for safeguarding the governance and viability of the organization. So CM should be a central preoccupation for the board of every organization, small or large, local or global. Why, then, do we see so few boards actively participating in, overseeing, and assuring CM in the way they do other risks and contingency plans?

Outside of the board's responsibility for general risk oversight, the responsibility for the management of specific crises is often left unassigned. Boards should consider tasking a specific committee with the responsibility of developing a crisis response plan and running crisis response simulations from time to time. The executive or governance committees are well suited for this role and often have additional time, as compared to the audit committee, to take on this responsibility. Less frequent, but still used by 5 percent of the S&P 500, are special "risk committees" established by the board to specifically address the company's risk profile and develop crisis response plans. Whichever committee is selected, this group of directors should be tasked with developing and implementing each element of the crisis response plan, and most importantly that each individual involved in the crisis response plan is fully aware of the responsibility that comes with that role.

CM starts long before a crisis hits. It should be an integral part of the wider organization's resilience measures and not simply something to deploy when all other options have failed. The board should take a keen interest in the crisis capability of its executive teams. With its fiduciary duty and its responsibility to protect the interests of shareholders, this sits squarely within the board's mandate to oversee good governance and management of risk. It should be one part of the board's normal assessment of the ongoing viability and sustainability of its business (Deloitte Insights 2020).

Today's crisis response needs to be sure-footed and well practiced to win in this environment. The board needs to know its role in advance, not learn about it upon first contact.

Our interconnected world brings increasing complexity and dependency, with global supply chains vulnerable to disruption by international events—natural and man-made. Technology has altered the balance of risk between organizations and individuals. Lone individuals with the power of technology and social media, for example, can wreak havoc across an organization.

It is this complexity that makes it increasingly difficult to make sense of the core issues at play and the trade-offs that need to be made. Today's crisis response demands more frequent moves from business as usual to a CM mode of working. The board needs to understand why, when, and how the organization moves to crisis response and to be reassured that the response is effective.

## Conclusion

While prevention must always remain a priority, advanced crisis preparation is now imperative as avoiding crises entirely is nearly impossible. For example, the current cyber threat environment is such that it is likely only a matter of time before all businesses will suffer a cyber breach. Whether the cause of the crisis is a corporate malfeasance, a terrorist attack, or a natural disaster, a company's ability to manage a timely, well-coordinated crisis response and communicate with stakeholders is critical.

**Table 5.1 Questions for the board to consider in overseeing crisis management**

| |
|---|
| 1.  Has the company developed a crisis management "playbook" with decision process flows and escalation protocols? Do all the participants know their roles and the critical approval processes that are in place to be certain of quick and straightforward approvals? |
| 2.  Has the company considered and challenged itself as to the types of crises it may face, where and how likely such events might be? |
| 3.  Has the company identified the individuals who will lead communications during a crisis? |
| 4.  Has the company identified the external advisors in the various scenarios from whom the company plans on seeking counsel? If so, are agreements in place with the external advisors such that they can be mobilized quickly? Does the company have a place or virtual room secured to gather in the event of a crisis? |
| 5.  How often do senior leaders take part in tabletop exercises using realistic crisis scenarios? And what is the board's role in these? |
| 6.  Does the company's response planning prioritize communications with key stakeholders, including employees, customers, shareholders, and business partners? |
| 7.  If a crisis were to unfold today, how prepared is the company to react with precision, speed, and confidence? |

To help companies prepare for the challenge, boards should be asking a series of crucial questions (see Table 5.1) to determine that the management has a practical and relevant crisis response program and actively oversee and challenge all aspects of that program, including key considerations before, during, and after an event (Klemash et al. 2018). This includes determining that the management has the right framework in place and that it has sustainable capabilities to allow the company to react to and quickly recover from crisis events. In preparing for and especially when confronting a crisis, boards should also understand the roles and potential implications to key stakeholders. Boards should also participate in various simulations and tabletop exercises with management teams to enhance their effectiveness in responding to crises.

## The COBRA Model

When a board takes risk preparedness seriously, it lessens the likelihood that it will be summoned to manage a crisis. No preventative system, however, is perfect. Organizations may wish to adopt a variation of the crisis response system used in the United Kingdom at the board level.

The United Kingdom and other Commonwealth countries use a strategic, tactical, operational (STO) management structure to manage incidents. Each incident response is allocated one strategic commander on the team, one tactical commander, and as many operational commanders (geographic or thematic) as necessary to fulfill responsibilities. Thus, the strategic members function as the senior management of the response. On the political side are senior elected officials and policy makers, often referred to as the COBRA group because they meet in the Cabinet Officer Briefing Room A, located in Whitehall near 10 Downing Street, the rough equivalent of the Situation Room at the White House. A designated senior, the nonelected civil servant on each side in a formal liaison role, serves to foster an orderly flow of information between the two. This structure enables political leaders to have input into the handling of the operation while ensuring that they do not try to run it. Conversely, the strategic team members receive valuable information about the political ramifications of their decisions while remaining able to maintain an essential "battle rhythm" to keep pace with unfolding events (McNulty and Marcus 2019).

Now, translate this model to the corporate setting. Think of the corporate CM team as the equivalent of the U.K.-model strategic team and the board as the COBRA group.

Imagine a designated board liaison on the former and a counterpart member of the board on the latter (each with alternates). Assuming such roles in advance allows the CM team and the board to build familiarity, confidence, and trust. This is particularly important for the crisis manager who may have to convey hard truths to powerful board members in a vexing situation. Similarly, a board member who knows the crisis team members and how they work can provide valuable input while tempering the impulses of board members to intervene in operations.

In general, boards should not become directly involved in most crises. Responding to these is best left to senior managers who understand the details of the business. However, board members represent the shareholders and must be prepared to engage if needed. In our turbulent world, any board that is not paying attention to CM is courting disaster.

## Conclusion

It is not difficult to see how these cultural, structural, and personal fault lines can crack open in a crisis and combine to create a chasm. In essence, they all indicate insufficient trust between board members and senior managers. That may simply be frustrating in calm times but escalates rapidly once a crisis starts. It is striking how often these issues came up in our conversations with directors. The point they all made, in different ways, is that a lack of transparency and trust too often hampers the effectiveness of board–management dialogue even in normal times. In a crisis, poor relationship dynamics can prove fatal.

Healthy boardroom dynamics are crucial to help a company respond effectively in a crisis. As corporate crises are becoming more frequent and more intense, they are imposing unprecedented stresses on boards and senior management teams. In the worst cases, they can create a threat to a company's very existence.

Board members and senior management teams need to approach preparing for a crisis much more proactively. They should go beyond the conventional crisis playbook and simulation exercises by honestly assessing how well prepared they are to manage the turbulent dynamics of a crisis. That means candidly discussing roles and responsibilities while surfacing potential vulnerabilities in organizational dynamics well before a crisis hits and preemptively agreeing on the ground rules and remedies (McKinsey 2022b).

# CHAPTER 6

# Negotiating the New Balance

## Introduction

Climate change is a topic at the forefront of everyone's mind, with articles and images popping up regularly that showcase melting ice caps and animal deaths as a direct result of climate change. Everyone, from the smallest individual to the CEO of the largest corporation, has started taking steps to lessen their environmental impact.

With large companies though, it can be hard to find the balance between environmental mindedness and profit. What struggles do environmentally concerned business managers face daily? How do you balance being green and making a profit?

While there are plenty of companies with good intentions when it comes to improving the environmental impact of their businesses, there are not enough CEOs who think climate change is an actual threat to their businesses yet.

Research by the Centre for Executive Education (CEE), a global executive development and consulting firm based out of Singapore, uncovered that most CEOs and business owners are more concerned with overregulation, geopolitical uncertainty, and the possibility of cyber attacks than they are with climate change or the damage their business could be doing to the environment (Centre for Executive Education 2022).

The path to net-zero was always going to be fraught with complexities. Recently, several "weather fronts" have emerged, posing significant challenges to leaders across both the private and public sectors.

The Russian invasion of Ukraine and the resulting energy crisis in Europe are reminders that, fundamentally, disruption in energy markets can wreak havoc on the global economy. In response, countries are boosting the use of fossil fuels, including coal and gas, and extending the life of conventional energy infrastructure, which is under growing pressure.

Physical risks are proliferating. Europe saw a record-breaking heat in the summer of 2022. Floods devastated Pakistan in autumn of 2022, and tropical storms raged across Japan, Korea, and China. In the United States, Texas saw an unprecedented grid failure in 2021, with a near miss in California this year. There are important choices to be made, some of which entail trade-offs between climate mitigation and climate adaptation—for example, rebuilding versus relocating and investing in cooling versus keeping energy consumption down—all of which occur within a limited envelope of infrastructure funding.

Fossil fuels are used every single day in every corner of the globe. This unchecked consumption releases hundreds of thousands of tons of harmful pollutants into the air every single year. Where would we be, though, without the electricity produced by coal-burning power plants and the product transportation network of trucks, ships, and planes?

This is one of the biggest challenges that CEOs and business leaders face when trying to reduce their carbon footprint and make their company more environmental friendly. However, there are steps that companies can take to reduce their use of fossil fuels. Companies with large transport fleets can transition to biodiesel engines for large trucks and solar or electric vehicles for smaller individual cars. Solar- or wind-powered office buildings can help to reduce a company's use of coal-burning power plants (Centre for Executive Education 2022).

While these steps can help to reduce a company's carbon footprint, it doesn't make good business sense if it costs more to be environmentally friendly than the company is bringing in at the end of the year. That's where balance comes in.

## Balancing Corporate Sustainability and Financial Stability (Profitability)

Over the past few decades, most countries have experienced unprecedented levels of economic growth. Meanwhile, several macro trends are shifting the nature of the global economic activity, including growing urbanization, the shift of economic activity from agriculture and industrial production to services, and lower barriers to the mobility of labor, financial capital, and products. These trends have placed strong pressure on the environment and society. In particular, accelerating consumption of natural resources and carbon emissions threaten the capacity of the planet to sustain human activity. At the same time, unemployment, especially among young people, social inequality, and immobility threaten to erode the social fabric and stability of society. Finally, repeated corporate governance failures and a series of crises in the financial system have dramatically undermined trust in business on the part of civil society. These environmental, social, and governance (ESG) challenges are calling into question the legitimacy of capitalism, as it is largely being practiced today, as the preferred socioeconomic system.

Business leaders are grappling with these issues, unsure of their expectations or responsibilities if there is no direct and immediate impact on profits. Policy makers have long recognized their role in regulating externalities, but are often unable to move with the agility and dexterity needed to address these issues. Social expectations around the role of the corporation in society are changing, but the power of social movements and the lack of consensus add greater uncertainty to the already volatile business environments.

The challenge and the differentiating factor that is going to set companies apart moving forward is the ability to balance sustainability and profitability. Setting up a solar-powered factory is a great move toward sustainability, but it does you a little good if you leave yourself without the ability to buy the equipment or supplies needed to keep your company moving forward.

With that in mind, though, it is important not to discourage anyone from taking risks or trying something new as they embark on "experimentation," which is critical in the VUCAD (volatile, uncertain, complex, ambiguous, and disruptive)-driven business environment. You never know what amazing innovations will come from someone willing to take a risk and what that can do to help improve your industry as a whole.

There are many steps businesses can still take to improve their sustainability without negatively impacting their profitability. Finding the delicate balance between the two will depend on each business and the amazing and innovative minds behind them.

While the CEO or team of leaders may be accountable for sustainability, the responsibility should be shared by everyone in the company. Leaders must convey the importance of an organization-wide (and personal) commitment to sustainability and ensure that every employee understands what part they can play in their daily work.

Leaders who are tackling the cultural challenges may be pleasantly surprised that nearly everyone is likely to find part of the agenda that is important to them, whether it's addressing climate action or diversity, equity, and inclusion, which can create a more cohesive culture.

The leaders who are instrumental in building a culture of sustainability are typically those who display a genuine love for the work, the organization, and the planet. They tend to naturally gravitate toward an ESG agenda and they do it very passionately.

Every culture shift starts with an intention, then layering on tangible commitments over time. While these commitments must come from all levels of the organization, the executive leadership team and the board of directors must be ready to put in the work to model behavior, drive accountability to commitments, and be willing to act as both teachers and learners as the culture evolves.

Companies do not all define sustainability in the same terms, and they often use different frameworks and systems to measure progress. But even in companies that have embedded sustainability in their core, there is still the issue of tracking progress. Commitments to specific ESG targets are one way of measuring. Beyond the issue of defining sustainability, there are several obstacles leaders need to overcome to effectively implement and advance their sustainability work. While leaders have distinct priorities they want to address, there are common themes that CEOs, board chairs, CSOs, and CFOs all pointed out as challenges. One is the way their companies lay the foundation of sustainability work, which encompasses the development of a methodology, key performance indicators (KPIs), tools, and a data collection pipeline for more insights. This underscores the need for strategic leaders with the right skills who can align ESG with the existing business structure, which is already the case for some companies.

# The Board's Role in Corporate Sustainability

Corporate sustainability, which encompasses ESG concerns, is increasingly positioned at the top of board agendas around the world. It is essential for corporate competitiveness and a company's continued ability to successfully operationalize its business model. Encompassing topics ranging from environmental degradation and labor relations to safety incidents and scandals, sustainability affects all sectors and challenges even the most progressive companies and the most thoughtful directors. While investors have traditionally focused on the governance (G) element, they increasingly demand a holistic view from corporate boards on the interrelations between strategy, risk, and corporate sustainability that considers environmental (E) and social (S) factors.

While board members will not have all the answers, a significant part of their role can be to encourage constructive and ongoing conversations about integrating sustainability into the core of their companies.

The terms "sustainability" and "ESG" span environment, human capital, social capital, business models and innovation, and governance. Tackling these issues requires both short- and long-term vision, with the needs of both current and future generations given consideration. This means boards and their companies must factor in a wide range of possible outcomes and make bold decisions while remaining flexible to respond to shifting situations.

## Environmental (E) and Social (S)

Investors believe that well-managed companies will deal effectively with the E and S aspects of their businesses. Therefore they expect companies to identify and report on their material, business-specific E and S risks and opportunities and to explain how these are managed. This explanation should make clear how the approach taken by the company best serves the interests of shareholders and protects and enhances the long-term economic value of the company. The key performance indicators concerning E and S matters should also be disclosed and performance against them discussed, along with any peer group benchmarking and verification processes in place.

## Governance (G)

Investors typically focus on a company's board of directors. As the agent of shareholders, the board should set the company's strategic aims within a framework of prudent and effective controls, which enables risks to be assessed and managed. Corporate governance practices vary internationally, and expectations concerning individual companies are based on the legal and regulatory framework of each market. However, some overarching principles of corporate governance apply globally to promote and protect shareholder interests by:

1. Establishing an appropriate corporate governance structure
2. Supporting and overseeing management in setting strategy
3. Ensuring the integrity of financial statements
4. Making decisions regarding mergers, acquisitions, and disposals
5. Establishing appropriate executive compensation structures
6. Addressing business issues including environmental and social issues when they have the potential to materially affect the business

On the one hand, board members are keenly aware of the environmental and social requirements their companies must address—given emerging legislation and global reporting standards, sustainability-conscious investors and customers, and the increasingly clear link between long-term company performance and sustainability. Boards know that ESG goals can no longer be an afterthought, way down the agenda after financial governance and performance.

On the other hand, many board members tell us they feel ill-equipped to act on the ESG imperative in a structured and systematic way. Our research shows that many boards have not yet embedded the skills, mindset, and courage to pioneer a new way of doing business and change how long-term risks and opportunities are identified and assessed. This not only places their companies at risk—both reputationally and performance-wise among investors and customers—but also misses an opportunity to take the lead in finding ways to leave the planet in a better shape for future generations.

Sustainability is no longer a nice-to-have item on a board's agenda, appearing after financial governance and performance. Most farsighted boards know it is not a tick-box exercise either, included to merely meet legislative, procedural, or reporting requirements. Rather, sustainability—a term often used interchangeably with ESG—has moved to the core of a company's business. This awareness has been driven by the links between long-term company performance and ESG performance; investors with sustainability at the core of their decisions; and emerging legislation and global reporting standards.

This dichotomy suggests that board leaders and members need to challenge themselves on multiple fronts if they are to embed sustainability in the board's DNA. Questions to ask include:

1. *Do we have the deep commitment and courage required to act as stewards of sustainability?*
2. *Do we have the right mindset and mix of people on the board? Do we have enough knowledge about sustainability, and if not, how do we change this?*
3. *Do we have a clear understanding of the full scope of ESG as it relates to our company?*
4. *Do we put sustainability at the heart of our decision making?*

## Brief Case Studies of Organizations in Negotiating the New Balance Between Corporate Sustainability and Enterprise Risk Management

The application of the principle of sustainability in business and business management is an important key to the success of a company. A survey by McKinsey & Company (2011) shows that there has been an increase in the performance of companies that apply the principles of sustainability in the management of their companies.

Corporate sustainability is a relatively new concept as a business strategy by allocating resources from companies for ESG practices. A company that focuses on sustainability should maintain a balance among all stakeholders including owners while distributing resources. Nonetheless, many companies believe that the greener they are, the more effort will erode their competitiveness. They believe that efforts to achieve sustainability will add costs and will not provide direct financial benefits.

Enterprise risk management (ERM) has become a top priority for corporate boards and management over the past two decades. What many skeptics initially considered a fad has evolved into a global standard and regulatory requirement for managing risk.

Major multinationals, including General Electric (GE), Hitachi, and Procter & Gamble, realized early on that sustainability was neither a distraction nor a simple public image posturing. Properly executed, sustainability policies promote faster growth and reduce risk, which benefits the company and its stakeholders—including employees, shareholders, regulators, and the communities in which it operates. Sustainability touches every aspect of a company's ability to manage risk and grow its business.

Beyond regulatory compliance, ERM has produced business benefits—one of the first empirical studies showed firms that have implemented ERM enjoy an average 16.5 percent premium in market valuation (Hoyt and Liebenberg 2011).

The power of sustainability in driving growth transcends industries and geographic regions.

## Company Spotlight #1: General Electric (GE)

Throughout its 130-year history, GE has demonstrated a larger purpose of lifting the quality of life for people around the globe. GE's approximately 168,0001 employees work with customers, partners, communities, and governments in over 175 countries to deploy and innovate technology to solve the world's most pressing sustainability challenges across energy, health, and flight. Every day, the employees rise to the challenge of building a world that works, in service of a more connected, healthier, and more sustainable future (General Electric 2021).

In year 3 of the COVID-19 pandemic, it is clear that global recovery—both economic and societal—remains uneven. Supply chain constraints continue to challenge businesses; government budget shortfalls hinder efforts to provide essential services; and millions of people around the world have faced significant disruption to their education and employment. Throughout 2021, GE teams continued to assist healthcare providers, partners, communities, and patients around the world to address the ongoing health crisis, and they worked with local organizations in some of the hardest-hit communities to respond to humanitarian challenges.

The devastating war in Ukraine is no different, and the GE team stands proudly with the people of Ukraine. GE's number one priority has been the safety of its people in the region, and they have acted diligently both to relocate those in harm's way and to support its Ukrainian employees working elsewhere in Europe. GE has donated $4 million in medical equipment to those affected along with $500,000 for international aid groups to support refugees.

GE is taking steps today to further strengthen its ability to lead on some of the defining trends of our time—driving decarbonization through the energy transition, enabling precision health, and creating a smarter and more efficient future of flight. In November 2021, GE announced plans to form three independent, investment-grade companies that will be better positioned for long-term growth and improved service to customers, employees, and communities. They plan to spin off Healthcare first in early 2023, and combine Renewable Energy, Power, and Digital into one business to launch as an independent public company a year later, thus creating its third company focused on Aviation (General Electric 2021).

### Energy Transition

As a company whose equipment helps generate one-third of the world's electricity, GE has a responsibility to lead the industry's decarbonization efforts while solving the energy "trilemma" of affordable, reliable, and sustainable electricity, particularly for more than 750 million people without access. GE energy businesses provide powerful, integrated solutions with some of the most innovative onshore and offshore wind turbines, the most efficient gas turbines, as well as advanced technology to modernize and digitize electrical grids. For example, GE's powerful Haliade-X offshore wind turbine prototype in Rotterdam began operating at 14 MW. One Haliade-X 14 MW turbine can generate up to 74 GWh of gross annual energy production, saving up to 52,000 metric tons of $CO_2$, which is the equivalent of the emissions generated by 11,000 vehicles in one year. GE has over 7 GW of Haliade-X commitments worldwide (General Electric 2021).

### Future of Flight

Innovations that improve fuel efficiency are defining the future of flight, and Aviation is helping the industry make meaningful progress toward its goal of net-zero carbon emissions by 2050. GE Aviation is unique in the industry for the scale and ambition it is bringing to confront this problem, as it pursues solutions across sustainable aviation fuel (SAF) as well as hybrid electric and hydrogen-powered flight.

Today, all GE and partner engines can operate on approved SAF, which could lower life cycle carbon emissions by up to 80 percent compared to petroleum-based fuels. GE Aviation, together with GE Research, is advancing commercial hybrid electric propulsion systems through key partnerships with ARPA-E and NASA. Additionally, Airbus and CFM International are collaborating on tests of a modified GE Passport engine fueled by hydrogen. GE is also innovating the next generation of aircraft engines. CFM launched the Revolutionary Innovation for Sustainable Engines (RISE) program to demonstrate advanced technologies, with ground and flight tests expected in the middle of this decade. This program could ultimately lead to engines that would use 20 percent less fuel and reduce $CO_2$ emissions by 20 percent more than the most efficient jet engines built today (General Electric 2021).

### Conclusion

The UN Sustainable Development Goals (SDGs) represent a global agenda to address the most pressing challenges facing our world, including climate action, access to healthcare, and reducing inequities throughout the world. GE recognizes the importance and urgency of this global initiative and how GE plays a critical role in infrastructure, advancing the quality of life, and furthering global development sustainably. GE has been a signatory to the UN Global Compact since 2008 and the company sees a close alignment between the SDGs and its strategy and sustainability priorities (General Electric 2021).

## Company Spotlight #2: Hitachi Group

# HITACHI
## Inspire the Next

In the wake of the financial crisis following the collapse of Lehman Brothers in 2008, Hitachi made a major shift to the Social Innovation Business, which aims to solve social issues through cocreation with customers, leveraging on its core strengths in IT (information technology) × OT (operational technology) × products. For about 10 years until the last fiscal year in 2021, as one CEO passed the baton to another, Hitachi has been on a transformational journey to reform its business structure to further expand its Social Innovation Business (Hitachi 2021).

Hitachi believes a strong commitment to sustainability will be the growth driver. Sustainability is not a cost nor for compliance. It is value creation for the business first and a consequence for the society. The organization believes that sustainability is something nice to have, but it's a key driver for any business to survive in the mid- to long-term future. It has become increasingly accepted that the objective of maximizing shareholder value requires not only top competitive performance, but also attention to a variety of sustainability issues.

As indicated in its 2024 Mid-term Management Plan, Hitachi aims to enhance its corporate value through sustainability with a focus on planetary boundaries and well-being (Hitachi 2021).

## *Sustainability Initiatives Aligned to Business Strategies*

Speaking to the environment, to accelerate and promote the achievement of Hitachi's long-term environmental targets as measures, Hitachi developed two business strategies, GX for GROWTH (customer and society decarbonization) and GX for CORE (Hitachi decarbonization). Under GX for GROWTH, the organization will support customers in reducing $CO_2$ emissions by expanding Hitachi's greener and more efficient product portfolio and providing customers with end-to-end (E2E) solutions across sectors.

By fiscal 2024, Hitachi aims to contribute to reducing $CO_2$ emissions by approximately 100 million metric tons per year (Hitachi 2021). It will accelerate the development of various solutions realizing energy transition, the electrification of mobility, and energy saving. GX for CORE aims to decarbonize its operations. The organization aims to achieve reductions in Scope 1 and 2 (essentially, Scope 1 and 2 are those emissions that are owned or controlled by a company, whereas Scope 3 emissions are a consequence of the activities of the company but occur from sources not owned or controlled by it). Hitachi plans to achieve this goal by investing approximately 37 billion yen over the next three years to meet the carbon neutrality target in fiscal 2030 and 50 percent $CO_2$ emissions reduction throughout the value chain by the same fiscal year (Hitachi 2021).

In addition, Hitachi launched a framework for issuing green bonds to mobilize more funds to accelerate activities toward carbon neutrality. Based on these efforts, including the preparation of SBTi net-zero certification, it aims to improve ESG evaluation. At the same time, Hitachi is also looking to the future by investing in the R&D of green technologies, such as hydrogen, methanation, and direct air capture (DAC).

In terms of society, Hitachi believes that, through the inclusion of diverse talents, it will be able to collaborate and create innovation in data and technology in the digital age to realize a sustainable society and support people's well-being. In addition to strengthening the acquisition and development of digital talents, Hitachi aims to enhance employee engagement by creating a culture in which every employee can contribute to solving social issues and a work environment in which diversity, equity, and inclusion (DEI) are fostered on a global scale, thereby achieving both business growth and a sustainable society (Hitachi 2021).

*Conclusion*

All of the above are in line with Hitachi's mission to contribute to society but respecting human rights is essential. It is indispensable for the development and sustainability of the company. Under the Hitachi Group Human Rights Policy, the organization is promoting human rights due diligence (HRDD) and other efforts to embed human rights risk management into its operation and to see that people's rights and dignity are respected throughout the value chain.

## Company Spotlight #3: P&G

Environmental sustainability has been embedded into how P&G does business for decades. The organization continually works to improve its environmental impact and enable consumers and suppliers to do the same. In September 2021, P&G announced a comprehensive *Climate Transition Action Plan—Net Zero 2040* to accelerate action related to climate change. P&G set a new ambition to achieve net-zero greenhouse gas emissions across all of its operations and supply chain by 2040, with interim 2030 goals to ensure meaningful progress this decade (Procter & Gamble 2021).

P&G Community Impact work supports people and communities in difficult times. During the COVID-19 pandemic, P&G brought relief around the world through donations of products, cash, and personal protective equipment. At the same time, they were supporting those who have faced fires, floods, typhoons, hurricanes, and other emergencies. P&G Children's Safe Drinking Water Program, which is the organization's signature Community Impact initiative has provided more than 19 billion liters of clean water to people in need around the world.

P&G's Equality & Inclusion efforts are focused on helping create a world where equality and inclusion are achievable for all, inside and outside of P&G. The organization's diverse group of employees advance innovative ways to grow their business and support the communities they served. P&G uses its voice through films, advertising, and programs to advance equity in the industry and society at large. P&G believes when brands and businesses meaningfully engage in supporting equality, it leads to a better world for all.

### Ethical and Corporate Social Responsibility (CSR) as Cornerstone of P&G Strategy

Ethics & Corporate Responsibility is the foundation for everything that P&G does including its citizenship work. Building and sustaining a robust business for more than 180 years depends on maintaining strong ethical, compliance, and quality standards across everything P&G does. It is a critical reason consumers trust P&G, partners do business with them, and shareholders invest in them.

In 2021, P&G completed its third annual Global "It's Our Home" Ambition 2030 reward and recognition all-employee awards program (Procter & Gamble 2021). Importantly, that year the awards program was led in partnership with all of their businesses and regions around the world who owned the nomination and recognition process to continue to drive the integration into business strategies and action plans. P&G recognized hundreds of employees and teams from around the world.

P&G annual employee survey results in 2021 report that 72 percent agree that "my manager empowers me to contribute to my organization's sustainability efforts," which is a very strong baseline result.

### Conclusion

P&G is one of the most socially relevant companies on the planet. With that comes a responsibility, not only to consumers, employees, and shareowners, but also to their customers, communities, and the broader world alike.

Together, the people of P&G accept that responsibility—a responsibility none of the leadership team nor employees can deliver alone, but an objective that, together, working with each other and with valued partners, P&G can achieve and sustain so the organization continues to be a force for growth and a force for good.

## Company Spotlight #4: Standard Chartered Bank

Standard Chartered (SC), the London-based global bank, has embedded sustainability in its business strategy over the past 15 years.

At SC, the bank's purpose is to drive commerce and prosperity through their unique diversity. For over 150 years, SC has provided banking services that help people and companies to succeed, creating wealth, jobs, and growth across some of the world's most dynamic regions—Asia, Africa, and the Middle East (Standard Chartered 2022).

SC is committed to promoting economic and social development in the markets they serve, doing so sustainably and equitably in line with the bank's purpose and three-valued behaviors: *Never settle, Better together*, and *Do the right thing*. This Sustainability Philosophy sets out how SC integrates sustainability into its organizational decision making.

At SC, climate change is considered one of the greatest challenges facing the world today, given its widespread and proven impacts on the physical environment, and human health and its potential to adversely impact economic growth. SC believes it has a unique role to play in facilitating a just transition to net-zero carbon economies where it matters most—across Asia, Africa, and the Middle East (Standard Chartered 2022).

The bank's presence in 59 markets across the world—and spanning all stages of development—allow it to support the net-zero transition by engaging with a wide range of stakeholders including clients, governments, civil society, and academics on the impacts of climate change and ways these can be mitigated.

SC is committed to becoming net-zero in its own operations by 2025 and to purchasing carbon offsets for its residual Scope 1 and 2 carbon emissions annually to compensate for its residual emissions until this time.

According to SC's study, "Just in Time," emerging markets need U.S.$94.8 trillion to reach net-zero by 2050, underlining the importance of governments, and banks, in developed markets fulfilling the financing pledges made during COP26 (Standard Chartered 2022). The report shows that without help, emerging market populations could be U.S.$2 trillion poorer per year (U.S.$79.2 trillion poorer cumulatively between now and 2060, the date by which some key markets seek to achieve net-zero).

In a foreword to that "Just in Time" report, Bill Winters, SC Group chief executive, wrote:

> Our report shows that without help, emerging market populations could be USD2 trillion poorer per year (USD79.2 trillion poorer cumulatively between now and 2060—the date by which some key markets seek to achieve net zero).
>
> There is an opportunity for private investors to help drive a just transition, moving assets from developed to emerging markets with the help of the right policies and regulations.
>
> Private capital from developed markets could help boost household consumption in emerging markets by 4.5 percent on average each year between 2021 and 2060 and emerging market GDP would be 3.1 percent higher on average each year between 2021 and 2060.
>
> Reaching net zero is a vital landmark and hitting our goal by 2050 will help the world stave off the worst effects of climate change. However, it will not be easy—requiring great collaboration and even greater funding.

He further adds that:

> Banks and other financial institutions have a key role to play in developing and scaling the structures that will channel the trillions required for the net-zero transition in emerging markets.

To this end, Standard Chartered pledged to mobilize USD300 billion in green and transition financing, guided by our Transition Finance Framework. Our progress so far is encouraging, and the pace is picking up.

Overall, I remain confident in our collective ability to deliver a Just Transition to net zero.

I know that it will be difficult; we will all need to act with much greater urgency and relentlessly work through the difficult issues together. But then again, given the stakes involved, why wouldn't we?

### Conclusion

With less than 30 years to reach the goals laid out in the Paris Agreement, the pressure is on the world's largest multinational companies (MNCs) to start making headway on carbon net-zero and play their part in helping stave off the worst effects of global warming.

Suppliers cannot do it alone; MNCs, banks, and governments also have a role to play in aiding transition. Banks must provide the financing needed for companies in both emerging markets and carbon-intensive sectors to transition.

Governments, meanwhile, need to accelerate their net-zero plans, particularly switching away from electricity grids that are powered solely by fossil fuels to more renewable solutions, to help aid the transition.

We cannot combat the worst effects of climate change without policy makers, financial institutions, and companies working together. Decarbonization is vital for the survival of the planet and we must collaborate to ensure we reach our goals without leaving anyone behind.

## Lessons From Companies Who Failed in Their Corporate Sustainability

Companies such as GE, Hitachi, P&G, and SC are growing because they embrace sustainability and position themselves as good corporate citizens. Companies that downplay or ignore sustainability run a serious risk—sooner or later, they are likely to encounter avoidable problems with regulators, investors, or nongovernmental organizations, or inflict lasting damage to their reputation because of questionable operating practices.

A prime example of how dangerous it can be for organizations to ignore sustainability is the regulatory and public image backlash experienced by large banks after the financial crisis in 2008. While major financial institutions had enjoyed an image of security and reliability, the fallout from the financial crisis undermined decades of this positive reputation.

Even in light of this shifting public image, the industry has been slow to change. Some institutions have encountered problems since the crisis and admitted that individuals within their ranks were continuing to conduct risky and sometimes illegal practices that contributed to the crisis. All of this has left the reputation of an entire industry marred in a way that institutions are still working to overcome. Fair or not, the public perception was that banks had undermined consumer trust—an asset essential to their sustainability.

Manufacturers are at risk, too. A prime example is a well-documented circumstance of Hindustan Coca-Cola Beverages (HCCB), a subsidiary of The Coca-Cola Company. After the fallout around the water usage of several India-based bottling plants that impacted production, The Coca-Cola Company adjusted its thinking to acknowledge how critical a role sustainability plays in business strategy (Gangadhar 2017).

Similarly, when PepsiCo came under fire 15 years ago for excessive water usage in India, the company launched a program to achieve a "positive water balance"—saving more water than it uses through sustainable agriculture initiatives, recycling, and recovery. In its Corporate Citizenship Report 2010/11, PepsiCo India reported 10.143 million liters of water saved versus 5.826 million liters used in 2010. In effect, PepsiCo's production remained uninterrupted as the company silenced critics and mitigated a business risk through its sustainability initiatives (Sattarkhanova 2021).

High CSR and ESG scores are also strongly correlated to a superior corporate financial performance by both accounting and market measures. Companies that integrate sustainability into their ERM program will likely outperform their peers by every measure and enhance their stature as model corporate citizens.

To enjoy these advantages, however, companies must do more than make empty gestures. When sustainability first emerged as a management concern in the early 1990s—about the same time as ERM—it was a far cry from what was to come. Early policy statements did well to address environmental stewardship but fell short of establishing numerical targets and metrics for success. A modern sustainability policy is both broader in scope and more focused—incorporating quantifiable objectives and target dates for employee health and safety, environment, corporate governance, shareholder relations, and community outreach.

Although many companies now recognize how important sustainability is, few have yet to incorporate it into their ERM frameworks. However, as illustrated above, sustainability does involve significant strategic, business, and operational risks.

The following are the critical issues and questions for ensuring the balance between corporate sustainability, governance, and ERM:

1. *Governance and policy*: How should the board and management be organized to provide effective risk governance and oversight? What policies should be established to communicate expectations and risk tolerance levels?
2. *Risk assessment and quantification*: How should the company make more informed, risk-based business decisions?
3. *Risk management*: What strategies should the company implement to optimize its risk/return profile?
4. *Reporting, monitoring, and feedback*: How should board and management reports be structured to provide effective monitoring of risk, including objective feedback loops?

### Governance and Policy

A good governance structure conveys the message that sustainability matters to senior management and the board of directors. Excellence starts at the board level, with a committee to set policy and monitor progress toward tangible sustainability goals—a structure used in major companies across multiple industries.

A 2014 study by the Sustainability Investment Institute found 277 companies in the Standard & Poor's 500 Index that monitors sustainability at the board level (DeSimone 2014). Of these, 32 percent charge the public affairs committee with responsibility, and 34 percent rely on the governance and nominating committee. Only 11 percent designate the audit or risk committees, a choice that implies a significant opportunity to integrate sustainability and ERM. Policy implementation is delegated to an operating council of senior managers who handle day-to-day sustainability efforts—the council may also establish smaller working groups to tackle specific topics.

A good governance structure conveys the message that sustainability matters to senior management and the board of directors.

A key component of ERM is a risk appetite statement that clearly defines specific metrics and risks tolerance levels for the core risks faced by the organization. In this regard, an effective sustainability policy sets numerical goals with target dates where appropriate—for example, a commitment to reduce total carbon dioxide emissions from the 2025 level by 30 percent no later than 2030. This example highlights the details critical to a successful policy:

- How will the company achieve the savings (e.g., changing its fuel mix, emissions scrubbing, switching to a hybrid vehicle fleet)?
- How much will the initiative cost?
- How will the company monitor progress?
- Who will review progress internally?
- Which outside entity will conduct independent monitoring and to whom will that entity report?

The policy should establish a purpose related to the business, too. A water reduction target may be a top priority for The Coca-Cola Company or PepsiCo, but not for a bank such as SC.

Once a goal is set, the company must pursue the implications through its entire business operations, including third-party entities. To illustrate, a carbon dioxide emissions reduction target affects logistics, the supply chain, transport policy, manufacturing policy, air travel, premises management (e.g., HVAC, lighting, furniture, carpet purchases), and so on.

Data collection alone poses a challenge—companies must adopt technologies to capture data across risk and sustainability domains, and throughout their supply chain. Companies cannot cheat their way to targets through outsourcing, either. They must engage third-party vendors in the process and be willing to change vendors if the current ones refuse to cooperate.

Goals should be tailored to each company's specific business even though this makes it difficult to compare results at different companies. Consider that L'Oreal is aiming to cut water consumption by 60 percent whereas The Coca-Cola Company aims to cut water consumption by 20 percent by 2020—these goals reveal how common sustainability issues must be viewed relative to every company. L'Oreal does not count the relatively modest amount of water used as a raw material in its water footprint—only water used in washing vessels and other manufacturing processes. The Coca-Cola Company does count water used as a raw material—its goal would be meaningless if it did not. If both companies achieve their objectives, which has delivered better performance?

Sustainability committees looking for best practices or examples among peer companies must take such nuances into account.

### Risk Assessment

Whenever possible, companies should assess and measure risks to facilitate the monitoring of progress. Suppose a company set a target for the year 2020 in 2012—what percentage of that target has it achieved in 2014? If the answer is less than 25 percent, why, and how does it affect the probability of meeting the target on time?

Negative goals—zero hazardous waste spills, for example—cannot be measured this way. The company must rely on incident reporting, but it should also establish a mechanism to escalate problems up the risk hierarchy to trigger remedial action.

A significant obstacle to effective ERM derives from different perceptions of risk within the company. The CFO may focus on risks that affect financial performance and future growth, and the head of operations would focus on health, safety, environmental, and manufacturing risks. Meanwhile, the head of procurement would focus on supply chain risks, including child labor and conflict minerals. Finally, the head of human resources would focus on risks relating to diversity, resource management, and training.

Companies must break down these silos to establish an enterprise-wide risk assessment. Only then can they establish appropriate priorities for risk management and avoid potential duplication of risk mitigation strategies. A holistic view enables risk managers to identify offsetting risks that reduce net exposure and may obviate the need for hedging or insurance in whole or in part.

To facilitate ERM, the key players should meet at least quarterly to share their concerns and discuss enterprise-wide cross-discipline solutions. Each unit should prepare a risk control self-assessment (RCSA), setting out the probability and severity of key risks, what risk controls exist, and how effective they are. Risk managers use RCSAs to develop risk mitigation strategies appropriate for the company as a whole. By adding new pieces, sustainability simply completes the risk management puzzle—it does not require separate or special treatment.

### Risk Management

Assessment is only the first step—a company cannot manage a risk until it has determined how much of that risk it is willing to bear. It needs to make business decisions within the context of a risk appetite statement, prepared by risk professionals but reviewed and approved by the board. The statement spells out quantitative limits applicable across the entire company. For example, a financial institution may commit to make socially beneficial impact investments, like microfinance or community development loans of a minimum fixed dollar amount or a target percentage of its portfolio.

Assessment is only the first step—a company cannot manage a risk until it has determined how much of that risk it is willing to bear.

Once the risk appetite is defined, risk managers can prioritize the risks they need to mitigate and how best to achieve the desired result. Community outreach is often the starting point in risk mitigation because many jurisdictions require a renewable license to operate. The decision to renew rests with local politicians, who must answer to the populations they govern. Licensing may represent a barrier to entry, as western retailers have discovered during their ongoing negotiations with local authorities to obtain operating permits for potentially lucrative markets in emerging nations.

Companies must factor the cost of maintaining licenses, including overcoming barriers to entry and license-related community outreach, into pricing decisions to ensure they receive adequate compensation for the risks they assume. For risks transferred to third parties through insurance, hedging, or alternative risk transfer mechanisms, pricing must reflect the associated costs. Companies typically transfer risk if the amount would otherwise exceed their appetite for that risk or if a third party is willing to assume the risk at a cost lower than the company's own cost of capital.

In the sustainability context, risk transfer demands an intense focus on the supply chain, including indirect sources. For example, a consumer products company is at risk not only for the ingredients it purchases but also for the supply chain behind those ingredients. If child labor is used to gather saffron for a chemical company that makes a yellow pigment sold to a branded food manufacturer, the media would pounce on the consumer products company. No matter how infinitesimal the quantity of pigment in the end product, reporters would target a household name rather than an anonymous ingredient manufacturer the public has never heard of. Justified or not, these types of stories rarely provide credit for postexposure remedies.

### Data Management, Reporting, Monitoring, and Feedback

Risk and sustainability data are complex and distributed throughout an organization. To report effectively regularly, companies must invest in technology that aids in the collection, analysis, and management of risk, financial performance, and sustainability data. Furthermore, technology must allow for easy linkage of data across these disciplines in real time.

The ideal format for reporting is a dashboard report. It summarizes KPIs and key risk indicators (KRIs) on the first page and allows users to drill down into greater detail about each item. Sustainability fits neatly into this structure once risk managers identify appropriate KPIs and KRIs for the associated risks.

Ideally, management would review the ERM dashboard report, including the sustainability component, at monthly meetings and present the results to the board regularly—no less than once a quarter, more often if significant problems arise. The purpose of reporting is not only to keep senior management informed. If corporate culture treats risk dashboard reports as a compliance function, the company will never realize the full benefit of ERM.

Companies need to embrace sustainability with the same cultural commitment required for successful ERM. The emphasis must come from the top, infuse the business model, and work its way into everything the company does.

In a successful ERM program, dashboard reports become a critical management tool that triggers remedial action whenever needed. The company has a feedback loop—risk information flows up to senior management and the board, who study the implications, decide what to do in areas of concern, and pass appropriate instructions back down to business units. Senior management not only is well informed but often has an opportunity to take corrective action before problems escalate into serious threats to business strategy.

## Conclusion

The intent to create a better world is there, and targets are only the first step. Leaders must dedicate resources and people to carry out their ESG intentions over the long term. What will set companies apart is the willingness to lead—rather than simply trying not to lose. This is a space where leaders cannot have all the answers and must be willing to take some leaps of faith to enact real change.

As companies gear up to incorporate sustainability more holistically, current operating approaches are no longer enough to support this new vision and meet new demands related to ESG. For some, change will mean more upfront investment in talent, such as the appointment of a sustainability officer; for other companies, progress will come from an internal cultural shift. The nuance here is to strike the right balance between vision, action, and outcome in the long run.

Sustainability has become an important business objective for leading companies because it supports their ability to grow and prosper over the long run. The modern corporation owes a fiduciary duty to its shareholders but cannot succeed without taking into account the interests of other key stakeholders.

Companies must back up principles with action. If a supplier cannot assure a retailer that conflict minerals were not used in the manufacturing or packaging of a product, a retailer can threaten to drop the product or the supplier. A mining company may lose its license to operate unless it fosters good relations with local communities affected by its operations.

Even regulators have begun to embrace sustainability. In the United States, the Office of the Comptroller of the Currency and the Federal Reserve Board now requires bank examiners to look for appropriate and sustainable remediation to risk management deficiencies. A quick fix or one-time improvement will no longer suffice.

Sustainability leaders recognize a symbiotic relationship between the market for their products and their roles in society at large. A company today ignores societal relations at its peril. The nonrenewal of a single license to operate could have devastating consequences. Integrating sustainability into ERM puts companies in control of their destinies, enabling them to be proactive and forestall stakeholder pressures that might otherwise pose a threat to existing operations or future growth.

# CHAPTER 7

# Transforming a Digital-Driven Culture

## Introduction

A digital revolution is currently underway. Technology has disrupted every aspect of our life and society: info-communication, education, health care, transportation and logistics, farming, and manufacturing. Blockchain and cryptocurrencies are disrupting banking systems. Metaverse, Web 3.0 (focused on the use of technologies like machine learning and AI to provide relevant content for each user instead of just the content other end users have provided), hyperconnectivity, through communication systems, sensors, wearables, and smart devices, have blurred the boundary between the physical and digital worlds.

Leaders need to understand the implications of megatrends of disruption, innovative disruptive technologies, big data, and, more importantly, how to leverage them to help their companies connect to customers and stakeholders with efficiency and precision, creating new opportunities and staying ahead of the competition. Digital platforms offer fundamental improvements to traditional business models, can transform entire industries, and are critical drivers of growth. Web-based enterprises that leverage digital infrastructure can enter markets quickly and move with agility in the current era of the Fourth Industrial Revolution (Bawany 2020).

Digitization has an impact on companies in various sectors. In each case, the impact is a different one, which makes it essential for companies to have a good understanding and view of what they face and how digitization will affect their businesses: which opportunities can be seized and which threats must be faced.

The business world is rapidly digitizing, breaking down industry barriers, and creating new opportunities while destroying long-successful business models, which could be viewed as digital disruption. Although sweeping technology-enabled change often takes longer than we expect, history shows that the impact of such change can be more significant than we ever imagined. Think steam engines, cars, airplanes, TVs, telephones, and, most recently, mobile phones and e-books. With e-books, the market has been slow to develop. Traditionalists said you wouldn't be able to replace the experience of a paper book. But e-books are gaining traction—they are cheaper than paper books, faster to acquire, and more searchable. Although the margins on them are thinner than that of traditional books, the market is growing.

Given the amount of turmoil digital disruption is causing, it's time for companies to evaluate these threats and opportunities and start creating new business and operating models for the future—the more-connected future of digital ecosystems.

Over the past 10 years, we have seen that business is no longer as usual due to the impact of digital transformation at the workplace with the increasing utilization of digital technology to reengineer business processes, organizational structures, and customer experiences to meet the demands of today's VUCA-driven and hypercompetitive business environment.

Many leaders today find it challenging to cope with the increasing pace and unpredictability of change. For many companies, the root cause of this change is disruption fueled by the digitization of products, processes, and business models. Organizations need to ensure that they equip their leaders with the right mindset along with the relevant skills, competencies, and behaviors that are required to succeed in environments characterized by such disruption.

One of the critical challenges is that many leaders are not ready for the digital transformation of their organizations. This is reflected in the research on "Transforming Your Company Into a Digital-Driven Business," which was conducted with 1,874 leaders across the Asia Pacific, North America, and Europe seeking their views on digital transformation and their readiness to implement it. One of the profound findings is that almost half of the companies and leaders were not prepared for a digital-driven world in 2019 (Blain and Speculand 2019).

Not only do disruptive brands deliver what the customer needs from them, but they take this one step further by creating a unique customer experience, as we have seen in Chapter 1 on how disruptors such as Uber and Netflix accomplish this. These disruptors are continually evolving to improve their products and services, responding to their customers' existing behavior, and then finding ways to influence how they will behave next. Interestingly, Netflix now faces competition of its own such as Apple, Disney, NBCUniversal, Paramount, Sony, 21st Century Fox, and Warner Bros (Marvin 2019). Disruption never stops.

## The Digital Revolution and Industry 4.0

The digital revolution is turning the traditional rules of the game upside down, as we have seen in 2014, when the mobile car-booking company Uber Technologies Inc. garnered $1.2 billion in equity funding to boost its international expansion and which was valued at $40 billion bolstering its rank as the most highly valued U.S. technology start-up (Saitto 2014).

Many venture capitalists believe the future of the blockchain and cryptocurrency to be extremely bright. Bitcoin empowers users by eliminating or minimizing many financial intermediaries. This has the potential to be a massive disruption for the global financial system and, at the same time, presents enormous opportunities (Desjardins 2014).

Today's society, including businesses, government, and individuals are responding to shifts that would have seemed unimaginable even a few years ago. Artificial intelligence (AI), robotics, Internet of Things (IoT), blockchain technology, and cloud computing are reinventing the workforce and will continue to impact the workplace for many years to come (Bawany 2018a). Drones and driverless cars are transforming supply chains and logistics, resulting in enhancing the quality of life.

The preferences and expectations of the "millennial" generation (better known as Gen Y), as well as that of "digital natives" also known as Gen Z (those born from 1995 to 2010) who have grown up in a wholly digital world, are changing consumer behavior. They have altered the consumption patterns and demand for everything from transportation, travel, accommodation, education, and lifestyle pursuits (Bawany 2015c).

The way we live and work is about to go through a profound change. For some countries, this has already been happening for quite some time now. The rapid advances in many technologies are expected to continue disrupting many of the industries in the various economies, and the impact will be felt across the globe. Yet from the research by the Centre for Executive Education (CEE) and Executive Development Associates (EDA) validated by other research (Blain and Speculand 2019), we have found that most businesses and their leaders aren't prepared for the coming age of disruption—and sadly we believe many of the unprepared won't survive in the highly disruptive, intensely volatile, uncertain, complex, and ambiguous (VUCA) world.

## The Fourth Industrial Revolution (Industry 4.0)

Digitization has an impact on all organizations across various sectors or industries. In each case, the impact is a different one, which makes it essential for companies to have a good understanding and view of what they face and how digitization will affect their company: which opportunities can be seized and which threats must be faced (Bawany 2018a).

The impact of digital disruption must be managed alongside the more general VUCA operating conditions of recent years (Bawany 2016a). An ability to calculate and manage/mitigate risk will, therefore, be another essential requirement of leaders seeking to propel their organizations into the digital age. Navigating a course through these challenging conditions may also force leaders to look at their leadership style and decide whether it needs to be adjusted.

Professor Klaus Schwab, the founder and executive chairman of the World Economic Forum (WEF), has published a book entitled *The Fourth Industrial Revolution* in which he describes how this fourth revolution is fundamentally different from the previous three, which were characterized mainly by advances in technology (Schwab 2017).

Schwab defines the first three industrial revolutions as the steam-enabled transport and mechanical production revolution of the late 18th century; the electricity-enabled mass production revolution of the late 19th century; and the computer-enabled technology revolution of the 1960s.

The Fourth Industrial Revolution (or Industry 4.0 as it is more commonly known) represents the combination of AI, robotics, cyber-physical systems, the IoT, and the Internet of Systems (IoS). In short, it is the idea of smart factories in which machines are augmented with web connectivity and connected to a system that can visualize the entire production chain and make decisions on its own. In this fourth revolution, a range of new technologies will evolve that combine the physical, digital, and biological worlds (see Figure 7.1). These new technologies will impact all disciplines, economies, and industries, and even challenge our ideas about what it means to be human.

Technological innovation is on the brink of fuelling momentous change throughout the global economy, generating great benefits and challenges in equal measure. To thrive in this environment, Schwab argues, public–private research collaborations should increase and should be structured toward building knowledge and human capital to the benefit of all.

There will be enormous managerial leadership challenges as the impact of technology and the disruption will result in an exogenous force over which leaders would have little or no control at times. However, it is the role of leaders to guide their teams and to be mindful of these forces when making business decisions that would impact the sustainability of their organizations. They should thus grasp the opportunity and power to shape the Fourth Industrial Revolution and direct it toward a future that reflects the organization's values and success.

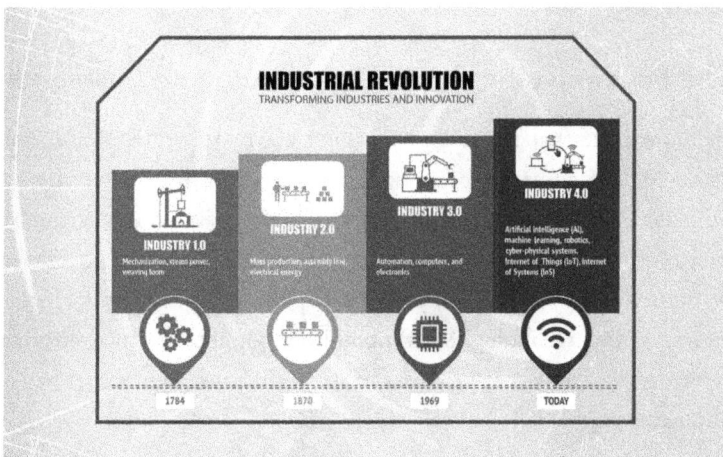

*Figure 7.1  The evolution of the Industrial Revolution*

To do this, however, leaders must develop a comprehensive and collective shared view of how technology is affecting the lives of their employees and, at a macro level, how it is reshaping the economic, social, cultural, and human environments. There has never been a time of more exceptional promise or one of greater potential peril. Today's leaders and decision makers, however, are too often trapped in traditional, linear thinking, or too absorbed by the multiple crises demanding their attention, to think strategically about the forces of disruption and innovation shaping their organization's future.

In the end, it all comes down to people and values. Leaders need to shape a future that works for all stakeholders by putting people first and empowering them. In its most pessimistic, dehumanized form, the Fourth Industrial Revolution may indeed have the potential to "robotize" humanity and thus deprive us of our hearts and soul. But as a complement to the best parts of human nature, creativity, empathy, and stewardship, it can also lift humanity into a new collective and moral consciousness based on a shared sense of destiny. It is incumbent upon all of us to make sure the latter prevails.

Leading in Industry 4.0 would require the next-generation leaders to be "disruptive leaders" who can adapt to these new technologies, and to be able to do so effectively means that the relevant leadership skills and competencies would need to be developed and demonstrated proficiently.

## The Disruptive Impact of Digitalization on Businesses

It is undeniable that technology has long been a 'disruptive force, radically changing the nature of work and society. In the 19th century, the Industrial Revolution altered our world profoundly and permanently. Electrification, the automobile, and mass production, just to name a few massive technological changes, reshaped the 20th century. Today, powerful digital technologies and ubiquitous connectivity have created a knowledge economy that promises to spark the most significant changes in human history.

A vast range of ever-improving advanced technologies is driving the disruptive innovation that has changed our world and defines the century to come. Advanced technologies are defined as emerging technologies that may enable new ways of doing business that result in more economical consumer trade-offs. *Disruptive innovation*, a term coined by Harvard professor Clayton Christensen, describes "a process by which a product or service takes root initially in simple applications at the bottom of a market and then relentlessly moves upmarket, eventually displacing established competitors" (Christensen 1997).

The coming age of disruption will forever change the nature of business, work, and society in all countries. We already see the first signs of the change to come. Technology is lowering barriers to entry, increasing efficiency and cost savings, and even launching new industries. It has given rise to a "freelance" or "gig economy" of independent workers, collaboration without boundaries, and technological unemployment (Clark 2013).

Disruptive innovation has the potential to impact every business, no matter its size, sector, or location. No business is immune. The development and application of advanced technology are accelerating at such an exponential rate that people have difficulty coming to grips with the pace of change. Among the key factors propelling these advanced technologies is the exponential growth in computer processing power—and the staggering drop in the price of computer chips.

Each period of technology-driven disruption has seen business models go extinct and be replaced by ones never considered. Some companies couldn't evolve and went out of business. In contrast, others adapted, seized opportunities, and continued to thrive by taking advantage of the new environment. What's different today is that technology is advancing at a pace we have never experienced before in human history—and the pace of change will only increase.

Advanced technologies are driving disruptive innovations that will bring significant and permanent change to the business landscape. These advanced technologies have considerable disruptive potential, including but not limited to advanced robotics and AI. Whether profound change comes from these technologies, others, or some combination that has yet to be conceived, the incredibly disruptive potential of these advanced technologies will illustrate the importance of preparedness by all organizations.

## Deployment of Robotics in Manufacturing

Robots have transformed how businesses manufacture goods large and small and replaced the need for human labor in a vast range of applications, from the manufacturing floor to fulfilling warehouse orders to maintaining nuclear reactors. As robots become more useful and less expensive, these numbers will increase, and robots will permeate more and more aspects of business and life.

The convergence of robotics with AI, connected devices, cloud computing, biometrics, and other technologies is creating the potential for large-scale, exponential disruption. Today, robots perform many increasingly complex tasks 24/7 without the need for breaks, holidays, insurance, or contract negotiations.

Robots enable companies to lower labor costs, achieve better productivity, and deliver consistent, superior quality (Mudhar 2015). We have seen them being deployed in automobile manufacturing plants and others. As robots evolve from executors of repetitive tasks to adaptable AI systems, we will see them take on many roles and duties once believed to be beyond them.

The use of robots can already open up new opportunities to improve efficiency and achieve cost savings. As robots become more commonplace, it's clear that businesses and governments will need to reconsider their traditional thinking about their labor force and the skills it will require in the future.

## Leveraging Artificial Intelligence

AI is broadly defined as the simulation of human intelligence by machines, mainly as constructed by complex computer systems. Many processes of human cognition and reasoning can be simulated by computer coding and by the development of logarithms that carry out tasks independently of their base programming. These include essential learning (acquiring information and the rules for using it), self-correction (recognizing mistakes and rectifying them), and reasoning. Reasoning simply means applying specific rules to conclude (rightly or wrongly). AI, therefore, represents a new form of intelligence, some may say a higher form, but one that can perform much faster and more efficiently.

As we have explored earlier, Industry 4.0 denotes the Fourth Industrial Revolution, which is the latest step in human progress where artificially intelligent systems coordinate automated production industries. Today, a web of connected applications are all talking to each other, to streamline everything from timescales to labor costs. This doesn't mean that the human workforce will be entirely replaced with robots, but is a more complicated evolution of the way we apply the processing capacity of machines.

One of the significant changes will involve factory automation. While programmable logic controllers and distributed control systems have already begun to impact manufacturing, most machinery and processes still run on a rules-based approach. Robots are used successfully for a range of warehouse tasks that include picking, packing, and palletizing. Still, these kinds of bots are programmed to address only a fixed range of activities. Artificially intelligent systems will be able to make their own decisions in response to unexpected or unfamiliar situations, making technical systems more flexible.

Industry 4.0 is a wake-up call for manufacturers who are suddenly faced with a paradigm shift in the design and operation of their production processes. This poses several significant challenges, not least of which is the financing of plant conversion and finding people with the right IT skills to manage the new systems. Mechanical engineering will move over as software engineering becomes more important, introducing smart systems that can analyze and assess big data sets. Much of these data can be optimized by the machines themselves, as they learn progressively how to identify faults and correct them, or to evaluate optimal design options. In automated processes, AI can streamline systems, by using visual recognition to identify the underlying causes of quality issues and predictive reasoning to identify potential machine failures.

As the world becomes increasingly automated, the IoT is already transforming our domestic and business lives. Nowhere is this more apparent than in the use of AI and robotics in the manufacturing industry, with all the benefits offered by Industry 4.0.

Automated systems governing smart manufacturing, enabled by IoT devices, give us the IIoT (Industrial Internet of Things), which allows for the expansion and streamlining of all aspects of the business. Besides, the deployment of AI and robots is particularly useful in industry as they increase product quality, production efficiency, and overall speed.

The introduction of collaborative robots (or "cobots") is becoming increasingly common in the industry as well as in laboratory work and commerce. The industrial robots that might come to mind when you think of physical bots operating in 4Ds-type environments need separation from humans to operate safely. However, cobots are meant to operate in conjunction with and in proximity to humans to perform their tasks.

Indeed, unlike their more isolated counterparts, cobots are intentionally built to interact with humans in a shared workspace physically. Humans would provide the power to make the machines move. In contrast, the cobots would provide control and steering to place objects with precision. In this way, humans are safe because they controlled the power of the robot while gaining all the advantages in assistive capabilities that the machine would provide (Walch 2019).

Cobots can take instructions from humans to work more productively with them, including instructions that were not initially anticipated in the initial programming. Robots do not get bored, hungry, or tired. The capabilities of AI are far beyond human capacity when it comes to such things as miniaturization and precision measurements, and they deliver vastly superior quality assurance.

## The Future of Work

Historically, technological improvements that develop the production process have been one of the most determinants of industrial revolutions. The usage in the industry of advanced technologies such as metaverse, extended reality, virtual reality, augmented reality, AI, machine learning nanotechnology, quantum computing, synthetic biology, and robotics is regarded as the beginning of Industry 4.0.

It is expected that Industry 4.0 creates better prospects in the production process while bringing some changes in social, economic, environmental, and political systems. Undoubtedly, among those changes, employment issues and the future of work take part at the top. With the transition to Industry 4.0, some reports have suggested that automation and robots are more likely to replace many jobs performed by labor and lead to massive job losses; others claim that Industry 4.0 will provide net employment increase by creating new jobs and employment fields. Nevertheless, the effect of Industry 4.0 on employment and the future of work is still mostly ambiguous.

Increased digitalization and automation are expected to affect jobs significantly. New types of jobs and employment are changing the nature and conditions of work by altering skills requirements and replacing traditional patterns of work. They offer opportunities, especially for developing countries, to enter new, fast-growing sectors and catch up with more advanced economies. At the same time, new technologies are affecting the functioning of labor markets and challenging the effectiveness of existing labor market institutions, with far-reaching consequences for the number of jobs in the workplace.

The development of automation enabled by technologies, including robotics, AI, and cobots, brings the promise of higher productivity, increased efficiencies, safety, and convenience. Still, these technologies also raise difficult questions about the broader impact of automation on jobs, skills, wages, and the nature of work itself. Many activities that workers carry out today have the potential to be automated.

Technological change has reshaped the workplace continually over the past two centuries since the industrial revolution. Still, the speed with which automation technologies are developing today and the scale at which they could disrupt the world of work are massive without precedent.

Research by McKinsey Global Institute published in *Harvard Business Review* revealed that, on a global scale, the adaptation of currently demonstrated automation technologies could affect 50 percent of the world economy, or 1.2 billion employees and $14.6 trillion in wages. Only four countries—China, India, Japan, and the United States—account for just over half of these totals. There are sizable differences in automation potential between countries, based mainly on the structure of their economies, the relative level of wages, and the size and dynamics of the workforce (Chui, Manyika, and Miremadi 2017).

As machines evolve and acquire more advanced performance capabilities that match or exceed human capabilities, the adoption of automation will pick up. However, the technical feasibility to automate does not necessarily translate into the deployment of automation in the workplace and the automation of jobs. The technical potential is only the first of several elements that must be considered. A second element is a cost of developing and deploying both the hardware and the software for automation. The supply-and-demand dynamics of labor are the third factor. If workers with sufficient skills for the given occupation are in abundant supply and significantly less expensive than automation, this could slow the rate of adoption. A fourth to be considered are the benefits of automation beyond labor substitution—including higher levels of output, better quality and fewer errors, and capabilities that surpass human ability.

## Introduction to Digital Transformation (DT/DX)

Digitalization is rapidly changing the way companies operate and create value in the era of the Fourth Industrial Revolution. The emergence of technology-centered business models is also challenging established organizations to reimagine and reinvent themselves to remain relevant to the marketplace. Digital readiness is important as it seems that while many organizations are either experiencing or expect to experience some form of significant digital disruption, few appear genuinely prepared.

Digital transformation (DT/DX) is the process of integrating and leveraging digital technologies (including but not limited to AI, robotics, the IoT, the IoS, big data, cloud computing, and blockchain technologies) into all aspects of an organization. It transcends traditional roles like sales, marketing, operations, finance, strategy, IT, and customer services to create new or enhance existing business processes, culture, and customer experience (CX) to meet changing market requirements.

DT/DX is not just about disruption or technology. It's about creating and delivering a compelling value proposition that focuses on the integration of the three pillars of strategy: people, process, and technology (PPT). It is the reimagining of the business in the digital era with an obsession with the customers and with everyone adopting a customer-centric mindset (which begins and ends with how the organization thinks about and engages with its customers). DT/DX also focuses on delivering value for various stakeholders (particularly its customers) and continuously innovating and acquiring relevant digital capabilities in response to the rapidly changing highly disruptive and digital-driven marketplace. DT/DX is a strategic imperative for all organizations (private, public/government, and nonprofit) to remain relevant in the highly disruptive, digital, and VUCA-driven era of Industry 4.0 (Bawany 2020).

Most businesses are experiencing the "knowing-doing gap," where they are failing to transcend the gap between knowing what is needed and doing what is required to combine emerging technology with new processes and skills to remain competitive. This presents a significant risk to the organization, its operating model, and the talent it acquires and retains. Although the presence of a contingent workforce and access to technology, such as AI, machine learning, cloud computing, data analytics, and robots, opens doors to opportunities for the organization, it also stokes fears of redundancy among existing employees, which need to be addressed promptly and effectively; otherwise, this would impact on the organizational climate, employee morale, productivity, and performance.

When reviewing organizations that have undergone or are going through DT/DX, far less attention is observed to have been dedicated to addressing the people and cultural aspects of change management and change leadership than the processes and technology behind the transformation. Businesses must adopt the "PPT" mantra, which is putting people ahead of process and technology. That said, conversations about managing employee experience as a core component of DT/DX have risen in recent years.

Advanced technologies are creating innovations at a speed and on a scale that has never been seen before. AI has the potential to diversify human thinking rather than replace it. It has a multiplier effort, where groups of machines and humans collaborate to innovate and solve problems that will contribute to a more productive and inclusive world.

However, it would be wise to remember that technology is an enabler, a force for positive change. The only way we can experience the best of these types of technological advancements is never to forget that it's all about people; in other words, unlocking the positive potential that technology brings requires fundamental shifts in the collective mindset of the employees. Organizations need to develop a culture that fosters change and a learning organization that cultivates a spirit of continuous learning, unlearning, and relearning (Bawany 2020).

The growing awareness and recognition of the impact of transformation on people and culture underscore the urgency to place cultural change at the center of any DT/DX agenda. Cultural transformation in a highly digitalized world includes best practices approaches that will help organizations understand how they can embed successful digital cultural transformation initiatives within their organization.

Corporate culture could be simply defined as how things are done around here or how a company works and operates. Culture can also be viewed as being comprised of the values and a particular set of behaviors that define how things get done in an organization. A healthy culture provides the guidelines, the tacit code of conduct, that steer individuals to act appropriately and make choices that advance the organization's goals and strategy. Leadership, purpose, and how work can implement a vision also play a role in describing a corporate culture.

DT/DX is the key to business competitiveness in a changing and increasingly demanding market. However, for this transformation to be successful, the right corporate culture is needed to promote innovation and creativity within companies.

## The Digital-Driven Organization Culture

As organizations embark on DT/DX at the workplace, it's critical to create a culture in which everyone is digitally savvy and demonstrates a "disruptive mentality," where they continuously seek to redefine how they create and deliver value for customers by leveraging digital technologies. But DT/DX calls for more than just updating technology or redesigning products. Failure to align the effort with employee values and behaviors can create additional risks to an organization's culture if not managed properly, whereas a comprehensive and collaborative effort can help shift the culture to understand, embrace, and advance DT/DX.

DT/DX demands vision, leadership, and process change alongside powering core operations with technology. Therefore, DT/DX requires introducing change at the most fundamental level, addressing how things get done everywhere in the organization. DT/DX affects the company culture itself. Without addressing culture change, DT/DX is bound to be a superficial attempt. When organizations undertake DT/DX and focus only on technology at the expense of culture, that can hinder progress in many areas. Leaders must remember that technology is only an embalmer of DT/DX, but unless leaders can impact and influence their teams throughout the process, efforts can stall or be less successful than they could be, and they may also lose the highly valued talent that is critical to driving the successful implementation of the DT/DX initiatives at the workplace (Bawany 2020).

Furthermore, failing to align the goals of a DT/DX with employee values and behavior can present additional risks to an organization's culture, such as low morale and an inability to attract talent with the right digital skill set. Ensuring the transformation aligns with the culture reduces challenges and helps avoid potential hurdles toward achieving the organization's DT/DX objectives.

The elements of a digital-driven culture such as customer-centricity, disruptive mentality, innovation, data-driven decision making, collaboration, open and trust-based partnership, as well as agility and flexibility, can be found in Figure 7.2.

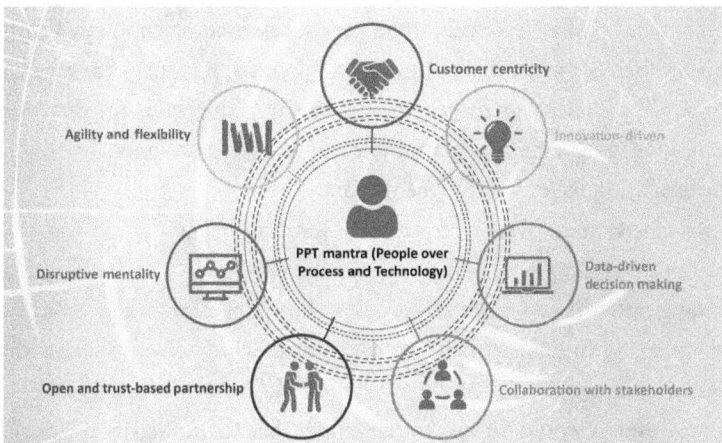

*Figure 7.2  The elements of digital-driven organizational culture*

# The Importance of Culture for Successful Digital Transformation

Digitalization is rapidly changing the way companies operate and create value in the era of the Fourth Industrial Revolution. The emergence of technology-centered business models is also challenging established organizations to reimagine and reinvent themselves to remain relevant to the marketplace. Digital readiness is important as it seems that while many organizations are either experiencing or expect to experience some form of significant digital disruption, few appear genuinely prepared.

Most businesses are experiencing the "knowing-doing gap" where they are failing to transcend the gap between knowing what is needed and doing what is required to combine emerging technology with new processes and skills to remain competitive. This presents a significant risk to the organization, its operating model, and the talent it acquires and retains. While the presence of a contingent workforce and access to technology, such as AI, machine learning, cloud computing, data analytics, and robots, opens doors to opportunities for the organization, it also stokes fears of redundancy among existing employees, which need to be addressed promptly and effectively as this would impact on the organizational climate, employee morale, productivity, and performance.

When reviewing organizations that have undergone or are going through digital transformation, it has been shown that far less attention is dedicated to addressing the people and cultural aspects of change management and change leadership than the processes and technology behind the transformation. Businesses must adopt the "PPT" mantra, which is putting *People* ahead of *Process* and *Technology*. That said, conversations about managing employee experience as a core component of digital transformation have risen in recent years.

Advanced technologies are creating innovations at a speed and scale that has never been seen before. AI has the potential to diversify human thinking rather than replace it. AI has a multiplier effort where groups of machines and humans collaborate to innovate and solve problems that will contribute to a more productive and inclusive world.

However, it would be wise to remember that technology is an enabler, a force for positive change. The only way we can experience the best of these types of technological advancements is never to forget that it's all about people. In other words, unlocking the positive potential that technology brings requires fundamental shifts in the collective mindset of the employees. Organizations need to develop a culture that fosters change and that of a learning organization that cultivates a spirit of continuous learning, unlearning, and relearning.

The growing awareness and recognition of the impact of transformation on people and culture underscore the urgency to place cultural change at the center of any digital transformation agenda. Cultural transformation in a highly digitalized world includes best practices approaches that will help organizations understand how they can embed successful digital cultural transformation initiatives within their organization.

Corporate culture could be simply defined as *how things are done around here* or how a company works and operates. Culture can also be viewed as comprising the values and a particular set of behaviors that define how things get done in an organization. Leadership, purpose, and how work can implement a vision also play a role in describing a corporate culture.

Digital transformation is the key to business competitiveness in a changing and increasingly demanding market. However, for this transformation to be successful, the right corporate culture is needed to promote innovation and creativity within companies.

## Benefits of a Digital-Driven Culture

1. **Better Customer Experience**

   It's all about intelligently connecting things, people, and businesses—with speed as the key to digital business success. If it is done right, more can be known about the customer, and then the organization can do more and care for its customers leading to customer retention and profits in the long run (Bawany 2015a). The world's obsession with the latest technology, social media, and apps revolves around a desire for an easier life. People want valuable solutions to their problems. More importantly, they want it fast. The customer experience is at the heart of the digital-driven strategy. As a result, the primary focus of digital transformation is to use cutting-edge technology to improve the customer experience. Those companies at the forefront of the digital revolution will earn much more authority, trust, and respect from customers. But how is this achieved?

New digital technologies empower today's customers significantly by offering them the opportunity to research, compare, and rate products and services more efficiently. Digital innovations of products and services in one industry strongly influence customer preferences, which then are projected as expectations on products and services of other industries as well. An in-depth understanding of the behavior or impact of the newly connected customer is the main initiative for digital transformation. Organizations will be able to uncover unmet customer needs by leveraging the design thinking approach toward developing innovative products and solutions. This customer-centricity will require a whole new mindset in the leaders at all levels, as well as the employees.

2. **Enhanced Collaboration and Decision-Making**
   Many people fear change. The thought of the entire organization making a massive digital transformation can be a daunting prospect for a workforce from leadership to entry-level employees. All processes and strategies, down to the core structure and company culture, need to be addressed. However, in that, there is an opportunity for unity throughout the workforce. Highly effective communication is critical to ensure a smooth transition to digital culture.

   Digital organizations move faster than traditional ones, and their flatter hierarchy helps speed decision making. A digital culture serves as a code of conduct that gives employees the latitude to make judgment calls and on-the-spot decisions.

   Leaders need to leverage managerial coaching, support, and encouragement; employees can break down multigenerational gaps and social divides to engage in conversation and learn together. Effective leadership is required to improve the digital intelligence of the workforce. The foundation for a smooth digital transformation is built upon digital congruence (Kane et al. 2016), which essentially is a concept where the culture, people, structure, and tasks of an organization are aligned with each other and with the organization's strategy and challenges of the digital environment. When all departments are aligned, a robust company culture forms, resulting in a successful digital transformation.

3. **Achieving Cost Efficiency and Revenue Optimization**

The other benefit of a digital-driven organization is the ability to leverage "big data" and track metrics and analyze the data gained during digital marketing efforts. Using these insights would allow businesses to optimize their strategies and processes for even better results. At the same time, it will allow the achievement of cost efficiency and revenue optimization.

It's possible to make massive changes to both by integrating data-based insights into the company culture. Using data-driven insights to understand customers and feeds into business strategy enables hyperpersonalization or mass customization, relevancy, real-time feedback, and agility. This involves businesses making use of both structured (personal customer information) and unstructured data (social media metrics), pulling together data from many sides of the business to help drive the transformation journey. The importance of data in decision making should not be underestimated. With the right leadership sponsorship to encourage this attitude throughout an organization, the road to a higher ROI will be achieved.

4. **Attracting and Retaining Right Talent**

Having a digital culture is particularly important in attracting digital talent, the demand for which is rapidly outpacing the supply. Large, established companies must often employ new methods for attracting, developing, and retaining the talent needed to support their digital transformation. Millennials (Gen Yers) and digital natives (Gen Zers) are generally drawn to digital companies, with their promise of a collaborative, creative environment and greater autonomy.

These new generations of employees no longer want to work in an environment that is a 9-to-5 routine. Establishing a digital culture allows them to become a part of the collaborative, creative, and autonomous workplace that they desire. With the competition to attract and retain the best talent, it becomes more and more critical to ensure that the employee value proposition, as well as the employer branding, is compelling to attract the right talent. Digital culture also increases employee engagement as it has a model that permits them to bring their best self to work, voice their opinions, and create an impact. They would feel empowered, engaged, innovative, and more productive.

5. **Foster Innovation and Creativity**

A digital culture will enable organizations to foster a workplace that motivates employees to try new things. It is essential to ensure that the workforce has the right skills and mindset to leverage the data and insights offered for this to work. Innovation doesn't necessarily mean coming up with new or breakthrough ideas but also reinventing old models or finding a new application for existing products or solutions. Using digital technologies and insights considerably enhances the learning agility of the workforce, helping them optimize mundane tasks effectively and efficiently. Leaders need to establish an organizational climate of an open and trust-based partnership with their teams to enable them to share these new ideas (Bawany 2014c).

Companies with a strong focus on innovation and learning will result in further growth with their employees being a critical factor for success. As a result, an organizational climate that promotes creativity is created, and experimentation and openness to new ideas are encouraged. To achieve this transformation and adapt to rapidly changing conditions, current practices and processes need to be critically scrutinized.

Employees are encouraged and empowered to take risks and forge ahead with their ideas. They, therefore, play an active role in shaping the company. The company's business model is continually analyzed and adapted to suit changing market conditions and new technological trends. The company strives to bring about changes in the market, even if this bears risks. An intrapreneurial instead of risk-averse culture is crucial where failures are accepted as part of the development process and coming unstuck is seen as an essential learning process. As a result, there will be a willingness and desire for the employees to rise to new challenges.

# Barriers to the Development of a Digital Transformation Culture

In today's highly disruptive digital-driven landscape of Industry 4.0, every organization needs to adapt to succeed. Businesses that are unable to keep up with the ever-advancing digital capabilities risk getting outmaneuvered by their competitors, as innovations in mobile, and social media platforms, data science, cloud computing, AI, and machine learning continually change how customers expect to engage with a company. Digital transformation is now an ever-important business imperative that is being felt in every industry, at every level (Bawany 2020).

In an extensive survey by SAP, in collaboration with Oxford Economics in 2017, of over 3,000 business leaders, 96 percent maintained that digital transformation was a priority for them, and only a paltry 3 percent had completed their initiatives (SAP Center for Business Insight and Oxford Economics 2017). It is relatively easy for the boardroom to move digital transformation up its agenda, but delivering it is another matter. The impetus for a digital revolution is there, so what is going on? What are the barriers to the success of digital transformation projects?

From the Centre of Executive Education (CEE) extensive global consulting engagements in partnering with clients on digital transformation and drawing on CEE executive coaches' discussions with C-suite clients, various reasons, explored below, are key factors that have been consistently cited, validated by other research, as the barriers toward a successful digital transformation within their organizations.

1. Lack of the CEO's and senior leadership's involvement
   The lack of buy-in and involvement of the CEO and senior leadership team may reflect on their underestimating or misunderstanding of the strategic importance of culture in the digital transformation journey of their organization. As with any transformation, leaders who guide a digital transformation are often preoccupied with structural and process changes and overlook the people's side, only to wonder why the effort faltered. It's well established that cultural change is a crucial determinant of a successful transformation, especially so for digital transformations. The behaviors that embody a digital culture represent a significant shift from long-standing norms and particularly challenge traditional power structures, decision-making authority, and fundamental views of competition and cooperation among employees. It is imperative to put *People ahead of Process and Technology*, which the author named the "PPT" mantra (Bawany 2020).

As mentioned earlier, Laurent-Pierre Baculard, in his *Harvard Business Review* in 2017, emphasized the importance of the CEO's role in leading digital transformation. While CEOs are under pressure to launch transformation initiatives, including the deployment of new and sophisticated technologies under severe cost constraints, they recognize that while leading digital transformation, they would need to look well beyond achieving technological excellence to building a highly agile culture and organization (Baculard 2017).

Another research that supports the lack of senior leadership support is found in the findings of the survey commissioned by Wipro Digital in 2019. When asked about their most significant barriers to a transformation's success, 59 percent of respondents cited inconsistent sponsorship from senior leadership as one of their top five concerns; 56 percent selected not being able to train their existing teams to change or use new technology, methods, or processes; and 54 percent indicated needing better alignment with business stakeholders (Wipro Digital 2019).

2. A prevailing culture that is not conducive to digital transformation

Digital technologies can make organizations faster, smarter, and better at what they do. Many leaders widely acknowledge the promise of digital. Yet, the majority of digital transformations fail not just because of challenges with adopting new technologies or finding the right know-how. The prevailing culture of how people work together to transform the organization is critical. Digital innovation can be successful only in a culture of collaboration. People have to be able to work across boundaries and explore new ideas. In reality, most organizations are stuck in their prevailing culture of change-resistant silos and hierarchies with clear boundaries between areas of responsibility.

Digital innovation requires the opposite: collaborative cross-functional and self-directed teams that are not afraid of uncertain outcomes. The lack of willingness to share and collaborate is a challenge not only at the ecosystem level but also inside the organization. Issues of ownership and control of processes, information, and systems make people reluctant to share their knowledge. Digital innovation with its collaborative cross-functional teams is often very different from what employees are used to with regard to functions and hierarchies—resistance is inevitable.

These behaviors can impede change in any situation. More importantly, they are especially harmful to digital transformation initiatives, given the pace of technological advances. Therefore, unlocking an organization's full potential requires a shift in both the leaders' and employees' mindsets and mental models to embrace the speed and agility made possible by digital technologies. Organizations succeed best with digital transformations when they match any investments in technology with the leadership commitment at all levels to reshape the culture with the support of the employees.

3. **The lack of relevant digital skill sets**

A digital organization is also a learning organization, as continuous learning is of considerable significance during digital transformation. The landscape of today's workplace isn't what it was 20 years ago. Today's environment is both fast-paced and competitive, which makes it all the more important that employers find a way to keep employees energized, often with an employee development plan.

A gap exists between the role employees are prepared for and the reality they are encountering on the job. This mismatch of abilities and expectations is jeopardizing transformational efforts. Customer-centric organizations understand that creating a competitive user and customer experience demands specialized skills. These range across many areas, among them: cybersecurity, development of new technologies, UX (user experience), and human-centered design.

Even companies that employ individuals with relevant skills often find it challenging to maximize their potential. In the 2020 PwC's "Digital IQ" survey, one-quarter (25 percent) of 2,380 respondents said they use external resources even when they have skilled workers in-house. The reason for this is that it is often too challenging to upskill or reskill rapidly or too slow to work with internal teams (PwC 2020).

Leaders who have established themselves as digital leaders are those who have adopted a learning mindset. Within the landscape of digital transformation, changes occur too fast for any employee to get comfortable with their skill set. Businesses must step up their educational game and equip their staff with the tools to succeed. This changing nature of work requires additional training strategies focused on enhancing learning agility, transferability of skills, and opportunities to explore adjacent, in-demand skills.

Digital transformation is an area of skills development that demands attention. Companies need to improve the effectiveness of their online communications now that digital channels are one of the main techniques customers use for selecting and buying products and services. Business and HR leaders need to ensure that their employees acquire a new relevant suite of digital skills and knowledge and embedding learning into the overall transformation strategy. This would demonstrate the organization's commitment to the professional and career development needs of the employees, which could be potentially achieved by developing a corporate culture that leverages the managerial coaching approach (Bawany 2015d).

## Development of a New "Digital DNA"

CEOs and senior leadership teams would need to review their "Corporate DNA" statement, which may include a commitment to passion, quality, integrity, engagement, people development, and innovation, to ensure that the principles and the company's systems support the new digital culture (Bawany 2020).

To reinforce passion and people development, leaders would need to create a job rotation program and allow employees to work on a digital project of their choosing. Leaders could also promote quality and integrity through a digital expert network and digital modules in the company's onboarding and training programs. To bolster engagement, leaders could organize an annual digital summit and introduce a collaboration award for teams that devised bold new ideas. The company could promote innovation by upgrading equipment and redecorating the work environment to make it more futuristic and inspiring.

Organizations are beginning to come of age digitally, transforming how work gets done to thrive in the digital era. This transformation is unprecedently complex, making it more critical than ever to get the vision right and approach change iteratively. Deloitte and Sloan Management

Review (SMR), in 2017, collaborated on a global survey of more than 3,500 managers and executives and conducted 15 interviews with executives and thought leaders, which highlighted some unique characteristics of companies that are growing into mature digital organizations. Notable among these is a sharp focus on cultivating a "digitally minded culture" scaling smaller, iterative digital experiments into more significant, enterprise-wide initiatives, and finding creative ways of resourcing these initiatives in the face of other competing and more immediate investment priorities (Kane et al. 2017).

The research has also identified 23 traits that comprise an organization's *Digital DNA*, the qualities that digitally mature organizations share, which enable them to be more agile and adaptive at their core. These digital DNA traits include an organization's ability to be intentionally collaborative, continuously innovate, customer-centricity, dynamic skills building, shifting decision rights and power, "democratizing" information, failing forward and learning faster, and operating with morphing team structures—to name a few. Understanding an organization's digital DNA is essential to digital enablement and becoming a truly digital organization—and it's just one of several drivers that can help accelerate the organization's drive toward a digital-driven culture (Bawany 2020).

To accelerate the digital transformation within their organizations, CEOs and business leaders would need to identify critical Digital DNA traits that are needed and weave them into how the organization organizes, operates, and behaves through small, tactical actions designed to create a scalable impact.

## Challenges in the Implementation of DT/DX at the Workplace

People are one of the pillars of your organization, along with the relevant process and the right technology that would be required to drive the successful implementation of DT/DX at the workplace. The overriding concern for most companies considering a digital push is employee adoption and its potential impact on the company's culture and organizational structure. Many of the employees may feel that their jobs are threatened by these disruptive changes at the workplace, with a consequential impact on their morale or productivity. They may not have the required digital skill sets to thrive in this new normal (Bawany 2020).

To be able to develop a digital-driven corporate culture that minimizes employee pushback or resistance, there is a need to focus on being agile and build a customer-centric culture. A great example would be Zappos, the popular shoe company. When they first started, they knew they were entering a saturated industry. There are hundreds of businesses that sell shoes, so how could they do it better? They decided to differentiate themselves by developing a "Branded Customer Experience" by focusing on three primary areas: excellent customer service, employee training and development, and customer-centric culture. As a result, over the years they have been highly successful owing to customer loyalty, and this resulted in their being acquired by Amazon.

The key to change is to work on building a CX from the bottom up. It is important to focus on customer journeys. If the organization can optimize the touchpoints along this journey instead of merely trying to win sales, then the organization stands a better chance at keeping customers around longer, just as Zappos did. This provides the opportunity to improve sales and retention, which means stable growth in the years to come.

Putting the customer first has been the mantra of many companies. However correct the mantra may be, perhaps it's time to question its wisdom. Some companies already have, putting the customer second, after their employees. The results are surprising and enlightening—engaged and contented employees and companies cited for their best practices. Moreover, customers are satisfied. This *results-based leadership (RBL) framework* presents an operating model and a proven approach for putting employees first (Bawany 2014a).

Steady, long-term competitiveness requires an organization to be committed to putting employees first and developing quality training programs that are linked to its strategic objectives. Without a true commitment to the employees at all levels throughout an organization, the journey to enhance organizational performance will be an elusive adventure. Quality employees equate to organizational success; unqualified and poorly trained employees equate to organizational failure. An organization's employees have always made the difference between a truly successful organization and a mediocre entity, but it's amazing how often managers overlook or discount this fundamental recipe for economic survival. Organizations with cultures that focus on their people and that invest in their future will, in the long run, be more competitive than those whose cultures view employees as mere costs to be reduced in times of trouble (Bawany 2014a).

One of the most significant obstacles to achieving DT/DX goals is cultural and behavioral challenges. DT/DX requires significant structural and process changes. However, traditional incumbents have a strong organizational culture and can face resistance to implementing new workflows. From long-term employees to risk-averse managers to corporate politics, several cultural factors can hinder a digital initiative.

The other challenge arises when the prevailing or legacy organizational culture and structure are not designed to fit into the required highly collaborative structure that is critical in a digital-driven workplace. Even if there is a robust DT/DX strategy, governing organization-wide change can be a huge challenge. Failing to communicate the importance of DT/DX across the enterprise might lead to resistance among the employees to change. Employees usually resist any change until they are made aware of the real impact the change will bring in their work life. Organizations can confront these cultural barriers by creating a workforce transition plan as part of their DT/DX initiative. This plan should include communicating to employees the DT/DX strategy, objectives, and timing. It should also consist of identified skill gaps. Once identified, organizations can create opportunities to upskill existing employees to meet future needs. Workforce transition plans acknowledge that DT/DXs are a marathon and not a sprint and manage cultural change throughout the process.

Another challenge is the lack of clarity on the DT/DX budget. A prudent financial investment for DT/DX initiatives is one of the biggest hurdles that could hamper the entire project. Setting up a limited budget for building digital solutions and transformation processes can be bewildering for most business heads, who are under considerable market pressure to deliver software applications faster to their customers. As a result, they tend to focus more on the tools and operational end states that promise performance benefits instead of the value those performance improvements will provide to their customers and the company. This tendency can create additional DT/DX challenges through abrupt shifts in organizational structures and business workflows without the internal alignment and readiness to operate within them. Many companies also often continue to rely on previous success metrics that do not apply to the new processes. These missteps can doom a DT/DX.

When creating a DT/DX initiative, it is imperative to begin by defining what success means. A well-defined strategy requires a vision for what the digitally transformed company will be as well as new metrics that will capture progress toward that vision. The DT/DX vision should incorporate the company's existing core competencies and strengths and the means of augmenting them through conversion.

## Key Success Factors for the Implementation of Digital Transformation

First and foremost is to build a culture of innovation in all business areas because DT/DX affects all functions of the company, including strategy, finance, operations, marketing, production, HR, and IT. Successful digital-driven organizations have developed the right structures to support change with new forms of collaboration and cross-functional teamwork. This can be realized by a digital innovation culture that promotes disruptive innovation and the establishment of digital business models, which is characterized by a digital vision that is understood by every employee of the organization and other stakeholders. Effective communication is crucial during a DT/DX, more specifically, to convey a story of change that helps employees understand where the organization is heading, why it is changing, and why the changes are significant.

The other key to successful DX is to empower the team to new ways of working by ensuring that they have the relevant tools to do their job. The employees also need to demonstrate a "disruptive mentality" with behavioral changes such as calculated risk taking, increased collaboration, and customer-centricity. Organizations may be able to achieve this by reinforcing new behaviors and ways of operating through structured processes, long known to be a technique that promotes organizational change. One related key to effective transformation is the development of new forms of working practices. Organizations that have established at least one new way of working, such as continuous learning or open work environments, are more likely to experience successful transformations as part of their change efforts than others. Another approach to empowering workers is to ensure that individuals in critical positions play their parts in facilitating progress. Success depends on both senior leaders and those involved during the transformation.

It is also crucial for the organization to have "disruptive digital leaders" who are committed to the transformation agenda. When people in key positions (both the organization's senior leaders and those in transformation-specific roles) are more engaged in a DT/DX than they were in previous attempts to achieve transformation, the success of a transformation is higher. Hence, the advancement of talent and expertise around the organization's DT/DX initiative may lead to successful implementation outcomes. Technology doesn't solve business problems—people do. Having the right leadership for DT/DX efforts is critical to achieving the organization's goals. Regardless of whether your DT/DX initiatives are headed by your CxOs, business unit heads, or IT department, having clear priorities, responsibilities, and metrics for accountability is crucial to the smooth and efficient running of your implementation plans. Organizations should consider creating a digital transformation office (DTO), which is responsible for ensuring that individual initiatives are executed against the company's long-term vision. The DTO should be supported, or even led by, an executive sponsor.

The clearest indicator of commitment to transformation is the allocation of budget and definition of a strategic plan for change within every part of the business. As executives develop strategies and set investment priorities, it is critical to communicate that change is coming and that everyone is obligated to make it happen. Process optimization and modernization that have occurred at the tactical level are valuable, but the culture will not change until visible efforts are underway to achieve foundational change. Every employee, regardless of level or function, must be brought along the DT/DX journey. Communicating the intent, the plan, successes, failures, and progress is critical to changing the culture. Training that reinforces key strategies and intent is important as is "practicing what you preach." Any product or service innovation that is offered to customers should be deployed internally. Partnerships will be critical to the integration of "ready-to-wear" digital services, and partners must be provided guidelines that make inclusion easy and secure. Multitenant operations and support systems must be efficiently deployed and available via secure cloud-based platforms.

When a company begins its DT/DX journey, it must first define the business case supporting its DX initiatives. In other words, what is the business goal that it wishes to achieve? This process should be driven from the outside in. Companies need to start from a customer-driven perspective to best align their transformation efforts with their customers' current and continually evolving needs. The reason the "why" is important is that it allows the DX and the company to visualize future success and enables them to concentrate their efforts and resources in a single cohesive direction. Measures of success aligned to the "business why" must also be defined. This positions the team to start selling the DX concept within the organization with the intent of removing roadblocks and gaining support. This internal selling plan has three steps (Centre for Executive Education 2020).

The board and senior leadership team, led by the CEO, must understand and be supportive of the DX activities and must be willing to drive this support, through communication, training, hiring, reorganization adjustments, compensation incentives, cultural adjustment, and other needed factors down through their organizations. Without it, your DX initiative will likely fail. Furthermore, the DX initiative should have dedicated strategic funding, not simply be carved out of your existing operational budget. This is required because DX is a long-term investment, not a short-term operational expense. Additionally, having separate funding illustrates to those working on DX, and the company at large, the value and importance of DX to senior management.

Research by the CEE along with the consulting engagements of the Disruptive Leadership Institute (DLI) has identified several best practices (Centre for Executive Education 2020), all of which make a digital transformation more likely to succeed as seen in Figure 7.3. These characteristics fall into six categories:

1. Have a clear digital vision and transformation agenda.
2. Create a culture of obsession with the customer (customer-centricity).

*Figure 7.3  Key success factors for DT/DX implementation*

3. Develop a digital-driven organizational culture that is fit for the purpose.
4. Ensure a clear communication strategy for the digital-driven culture.
5. Adopt a data-driven approach to problem solving and decision making.
6. Deploy the right talent (leader and team members) with the digital skill set.

## Case Study of Successful Digital Transformation @ DBS Bank

The urgency for organizations to transform themselves in the face of technology-fueled disruption has been a critical challenge in many industries. In the banking sector, incumbent players are dealing with the emergence of financial technology, or fintech, firms that threaten them in a range of business segments.

One bank that has taken this challenge head-on is Singapore-based DBS Group, which embarked on an organization-wide transformation in 2009.

### Background of DBS Bank

DBS is a leading financial services group in Asia with a presence in 18 markets. Headquartered and listed in Singapore, DBS is in the three key Asian axes of growth: Greater China, Southeast Asia (SEA), and South Asia. The bank's "AA-" and "Aa1" credit ratings are among the highest in the world (DBS 2022).

DBS is also the largest among the three local banks in Singapore and had a humble start in 1968 as a government-linked bank. Over the years, with the gradual opening up of the banking industry in Singapore in the 1990s, DBS merged with another local bank, Post Office Savings Bank (POSB), in 1998 to retain competitiveness over foreign-based banks coming into Singapore. Over time, DBS grew to be the largest bank in Singapore and the largest bank by assets in SEA. It further expanded overseas with operations and branches in China, Malaysia, Hong Kong, Indonesia, Thailand, Philippines, Vietnam, Dubai, Japan, South Korea, Myanmar, and Taiwan. The bank acknowledges the passion, commitment, and can-do spirit in all its 28,000 staff, representing over 40 nationalities (DBS 2022).

From 2016 to 2018, DBS was most favored by investors. The share price of SEA's largest bank by assets roughly doubled during that period, with gains outstripping those of its main local rivals (Economist 2018). The market's optimism about DBS was partially attributed to the bank's digital prowess.

DBS was first named "Best Bank in the World" by Global Finance in 2018, marking its inaugural win of a global Best Bank accolade (Platt 2018). The magazine profiled DBS as a financial institution that was "pointing the way to the future for the entire industry with its digital transformation, strong financials, and good corporate citizenship" (DBS 2022).

The bank would go on to receive equivalent accolades from U.K.-based Euromoney (World's Best Bank—2019, 2021) and Financial Times publication The Banker (Global Bank of the Year—2018, 2021), and would take Global Finance's top award twice more, in 2020 and 2022, bringing its total haul of global Best Bank awards to seven in five consecutive years (2018–2022)—a feat unmatched by any other bank globally.

DBS was this year also recognized by U.S.-based Fast Company in its Top 100 Best Workplaces for Innovators list, ranking 29th globally, and is the only Singapore-headquartered company to feature on the list.

### Lessons From DBS Digital Transformation Journey

The bank initiated its digital strategy in 2009 under the relentless push of its new CEO Piyush Gupta. Between 2009 and 2014, DBS invested heavily in technology and undertook radical changes to "rewire" the entire enterprise for digital innovation. Key thrusts of its digital transformation involved revamping its technology and operations organization, developing scalable digital platforms, leveraging technology to redesign its customer experience, and fostering internal incubation as well as external partnerships for digital innovation (Sia, Soh, and Chong 2015).

David Gledhill, the then chief information officer (CIO) of DBS Bank, who has since retired, noted that those were foundational years that set the stage for its next phase of growth. In the first phase of its transformation, DBS achieved a 9 percent compound annual growth rate (CAGR) in income and a 13 percent CAGR in net profit (Bawany 2020).

When DBS embarked on its digital transformation journey, a new organizational unit called Digibank was created to spearhead the bank's expansion into new markets; the bank launched the Digital Mindset program to help change the company from within (Kaganer, Gregory, and Codrean 2015).

Key moments of the transformational journey include the strategy taken by Gupta to improve the bank's customer satisfaction ratings while also revolutionizing the way banking services were seen internally. Externally, the bank was using digital technology opportunities to expand into new countries where partnerships and acquisitions were not an option. Internally, top management was using the Digital Mindset program extensively to revolutionize business processes and ideation. The challenge facing the DBS senior leadership team was how to make this type of thinking sustainable, how to reach everyone in the bank, and what to do next to keep the momentum going (Bawany 2020).

The threats posed by financial technology ("fintech") disruption were relentless, with many fintech startups emerging and offering a wide range of innovative financial products and services. One such case was the Chinese e-commerce giant Alibaba. It had been expanding in the region with a controlling stake in Singapore-based Lazada, the top e-commerce player in SEA. Alibaba affiliate Ant Financial merged Lazada's HelloPay with its flagship Alipay payment platform. Alibaba also led a U.S.$1.1 billion investment round in Tokopedia, a major e-commerce platform in Indonesia (Sun 2018).

Similarly, Grab, SEA's leading ride-hailing company, also began promoting GrabPay. This mobile e-wallet could be linked to customers' credit and debit cards. Moreover, the competition was even coming from nontech incumbents that had a large consumer base and strong branding, such as budget airline AirAsia.

At the same time, DBS also faced growing institutional constraints for organic expansion and acquisition-led growth in the region, specifically in the emerging SEA and South Asia markets. The advent of fintech, however, opened up new possibilities. Instead of building banks the traditional way, DBS saw opportunities in driving technology-led growth in these emerging markets (Bawany 2020).

In 2015, DBS embarked on the second phase of its digital transformation, with a renewed mission to leverage technology to "Make Banking Joyful." DBS developed the new brand promise, "Live More, Bank Less," which captured this new vision of simple, effortless banking for its customers. Support from the bank's board was strong, with an annual technology budget commitment of U.S.$600 million (Bawany 2020).

The bank's ambitious digital transformation was grounded on three fundamental "philosophical shifts" to reinvent DBS by becoming *digital to the core, embedding DBS in the customer journey, and creating a 26,000-person start-up.*

## DBS DT/DX Key Success Factors

### 1. CEO-Driven Digital Transformation

Piyush Gupta is an Indian-born banker who spent 27 years at Citibank in Asia before becoming CEO of DBS in 2009 (DBS 2022).

In an interview with McKinsey in 2017, he clearly states the *raison d'etre* for the bank's digital transformation journey:

That said, with so much money going into fintech, we have reached a tipping point in the last couple of years. Incumbent players are wrestling with the challenges of how to transform themselves. In Asia, and notably in China, the actions of new players, such as Alibaba and Tencent, and of established banks, like Minsheng, Ping An, and ICBC, have made this all the more visible. In 2013, the DBS board, therefore, took the view that the future for us and our industry would have to be digital. We felt that if we didn't lead the charge, frankly, we might die. (McKinsey 2017)

Indeed, with the development of technologies in recent years, a scenario of banking where customers did not require banks but simply transferred money directly from payer to payee had become more practically feasible. The idea of a peer-to-peer payment scheme was not new. But its feasibility as a wide-scale implementation had grown with the availability of advanced technologies, like secured payments, encrypted network transmissions, digital identity certificates, and affordable mobile smartphones. Customers' need for an intermediary agent such as a bank to effect their payments diminished as payment alternatives grew.

During an interview with Forbes Asia in June 2014, as if sounding an alarm bell in the financial industry, Gupta publicly highlighted the need to move swiftly into digital banking fundamentally (Tan 2014). Whether people or businesses, customers required banking services, not banks, to get things done. This was true in the past. People initially queued up at bank branches to physically perform all kinds of services, including updating bank books and withdrawing cash. When ATMs and postal mail of bank statements came about, visits to bank branches were made less necessary. When the Web and Internet banking offered various safe, convenient remote banking services, there was even lesser reason to visit banks. People did not want to go to banks for banks' sake; they just needed banking services (Bawany 2020).

As the digital transformation architect, Gupta and his senior leadership team set out to take on these disruptive challenges by way of setting a new aspiration: to make banking joyful—by making it invisible, like stepping out of an Uber having already paid. This perspective led to the setting of three pillars, as mentioned earlier: becoming digital to the core, embedding into the customer journey, and changing the culture to act like "a 27,000-person start-up."

To change behaviors, the transformation team settled on five key traits or DNA for the digital culture: agility, being a learning organization, being customer-obsessed, being data driven, as well as experimenting and taking risks. The team targeted inefficient meetings as a blocker to change and a hindrance to innovation. Meetings often started and ran late without leading to decisions. Worse, meetings often lacked purpose and were dominated by a few voices, while others sat in defensive silence (Bawany 2020).

In 2019, DBS was ranked by *Harvard Business Review* as among the top 10 companies in the world to have made successful strategic transformations in the last decade. The study, conducted by strategy consulting firm Innosight, involved the screening of all companies in the S&P 500 and Global 2000 using three lenses: new growth, repositioning the core, and financials (Anthony, Trotter, and Schwartz 2019).

With this, DBS joins the likes of Netflix, Amazon, Microsoft, Tencent, and Alibaba, which were similarly recognized. The Innosight study found that the top 20 most transformative companies had certain ingrained behaviors.

"These included creating a higher-purpose mission, seizing the digital opportunity via new platforms and business models, and ensuring that innovation was not isolated to a department but was a strategic capability," said DBS. In the press statement, Gupta said a "startup culture" has infused the entire organization. "Conventional wisdom is that it is difficult for a legacy company to transform at scale. Our journey has shown otherwise, and what has worked for us is attacking the core, making transformation mainstream by changing culture company-wide," he said (DBS 2019).

2. **Becoming Digital to the Core: DBS' "GANDALF" Digital Transformation Philosophy**
When Gupta joined the bank in 2009, he was tasked with turning around a conservative, bureaucratic institution full of outdated

technology. He divided DBS's digital transformation into two phases. First, the bank revamped its back-end technology, building in-house expertise. Then he was ready to build the digital bank. He once declared, "Our aim was to be the 'D' in GANDALF—a term we coined to refer to Google, Amazon, Netflix, Apple, LinkedIn, and Facebook. We wanted to operate more like a tech company." To do that, he had to change the mindset of 26,000 employees. Training programs were revamped, experimentation encouraged across every department, and partnerships forged with startups and universities. "It was the mandate of the entire organization," Gupta says (Scott and Cobban 2019).

In their quest to "become the D in GANDALF," the bank realized that merely setting up a digital disruption team would not be enough. Instead, they fundamentally reorganized the organization to bring the customer and technology teams together and empower them to think holistically about the digital customer experience. This process helped employees see their role in the transformation and allow change agents to help others along on the journey naturally. Leaders gave their teams the space to take risks, emphasizing a "we're all in this together" approach and building a culture that endorses experimentation and understands failure, but has circuit breakers in place to protect the business from too much risk. The DBS success story is a people story, proving that employees are capable of fundamental change—as long as they receive positive and integrated messaging, support for execution, and a soft landing for inevitable missteps along the way.

3. **Focus on Talent and Creating the Digital Workplace**
   In addition to transforming customer-facing applications, DBS also uses digital to empower their employees, helping them to work smarter and driving gains in efficiency and productivity. Moreover, employee-focused aspects of digital complement efforts to improve the banking experience for consumers. By providing more and better digital services, DBS can capture data and generate a refined, high-resolution profile of their customer's preferences and behaviors. Still, those data are meaningless unless employees can readily access them and use them to improve the bank's offerings (Bawany 2020).

Strategies for creating the digital workplace include driving engagement and enablement to improve productivity and employee experiences, as well as expanding the use of analytics across the bank. The right solution includes social, mobile, cloud, and analytics, and it is tailored to a bank's unique situation to redesign the way its employees work. Through this approach, work becomes more mobile and collaborative, and processes become more flexible. Employees can access information and documents whenever, wherever, and however they want, across platforms and systems. Employees can assemble a 360-degree view of the customer and easily incorporate data from each interaction so that the profile becomes more refined over time. Communication increases across business units and functions. Customer service becomes more responsive (DBS 2022).

At DBS, people are the key differentiator and form the cornerstone of the bank transformation strategy, and the bank aspired to cultivate its people to embrace startup qualities of being customer obsessed, data driven, risk taking, agile, and continually learning.

The bank is passionate about being a learning organization and has created a culture that allows the people a myriad of opportunities to learn, reskill, and upskill to equip them with digital capabilities, especially it' legacy workforce, some of whom had been with the bank for over 30 years. DBS also revamped the way the people were trained through various programs and initiatives such as hackathons and gamification, among others. There is an encouragement to adopt the practice of lifelong and continuous learning. Young talents in the management associate program were also tapped into a reversed mentoring program where C-suite leaders were taught social media and its business potential.

DBS supported flexible staff participation in internal crowdsourcing, customer journeys, and pilot projects on emerging technologies. Projects in one department could be made open to volunteers from other departments. The HR department also sorted out a flexible working scheme to allow bank staff to leave their day role and join a new team (either on a part-time or full-time basis) to work on innovative ideas (DBS 2022).

DBS's culture is generally collaborative and harmonious, less political, and more family-like. It is, however, hierarchical; and decisions were generally made from the top, which resulted in less empowered employees. They were not very comfortable with making decisions. This is not ideal as the bank competes in a world that has high levels of volatility, uncertainty, complexity, and ambiguity (VUCA). The challenge is to shift not only the mindset of the people that the bank competitors are not limited to banks, but also the fintech companies and platform players. The people are empowered and encouraged to experiment, celebrate failures, and become teachers by sharing their lessons with other colleagues.

As part of the digital transformation strategy, the bank focused on changing its culture to a startup culture by being "Agile," focusing relentlessly on the customer, using data to help the employees to make better decisions, being digital to the core, and continuously experimenting to improve. One of the initiatives that the bank implemented was to experiment with agile workspaces by creating what is known as JoySpace, enabling the employees to work in squads for better collaboration and ideation, breaking down silos, and focusing relentlessly on the customer (DBS 2022).

## Conclusion

MIT SMR released a profound leadership resource that illuminates what it takes to lead in 2020. "The New Leadership Playbook for the Digital Age" report summarizes findings from the comprehensive SMR—Cognizant's "2020 Future of Leadership Global Executive Study and Research Project," making the case that organizations must empower leaders to change their ways of working to succeed in a new digital economy of the Fourth Industrial Revolution (Bawany 2020).

The objective of the research is straightforward: to explore how the changing nature of competition, work, and society is influencing the future of leadership. The authors surveyed 4,394 global leaders from more than 120 countries, conducted 27 executive interviews, and facilitated focus-group exchanges with next-gen leaders worldwide. The findings are as sobering as they are inspiring. They serve as a warning for today's leaders, as well as an invitation to reimagine leadership for the new economy. Reliance on antiquated and ineffective leadership approaches by the current generation of leaders is undermining organizational performance. Today's trailblazing leaders increasingly recognize that to transform their organizations credibly, they must credibly transform themselves first and their teams (Ready et al. 2020).

# CHAPTER 8

# Coaching and Development of "Disruptive Leaders"

## Introduction: Who Are the "Disruptive Leaders"?

What does it mean to be a "disruptive leader," also known at times as a "disruptive digital leader"? Is it a title reserved only for leaders of technology giants or businesses with seemingly bottomless budgets? The truth is that any business can excel in digital leadership, regardless of its size or budget. But doing so requires more than just savvy IT leaders. It requires leaders across the business who understand why digital technology is essential and how to use it.

Disruptive leaders demonstrate innovative thinking and experimentation to keep the business agile. Their ability to disrupt the status quo or challenge conventional wisdom and discover creative possibilities is one of the driving factors behind an organization's ability to transform by changing its business model and generating new opportunities for growth in the VUCA and digital-driven business environment (Gibson, West, and Pastrovich 2020).

Disruptive leaders don't change for the sake of change. It's about incorporating change into the modus operandi of the organization, which, of course, is easier said than done. The ideal disruptive leader doesn't need to talk about disruption because it's practically how they get things done. Disruptive leaders engage and empower their high-performance team, coach, and guide them along the way, and at the same time stay focused on the mission of the transformation agenda. It is the quickest and most effective way to jump-start ideas and behaviors that drive innovation at the workplace, which gives a much-needed sustainable competitive advantage to the organization.

The founder and CEO of Virgin Group, Sir Richard Branson, is an excellent example of a disruptive leader. He disrupts every market he enters. Simultaneously, he works toward building trust with both his customers and employees by adopting the "Employee First Philosophy" (Bawany 2015a), where he put staff first, customer second, and shareholders third, effectively; in the end, the shareholders do well, and the customers do better. As a result, the staff is rewarded and happy (Mistry 2017). Branson inspires inventive and unconventional action, and his excitement is contagious. Above all else, the Virgin Group founder thinks that leaders need to know how to listen. "Listening is one of the most important skills that anyone can have," he says.

> That's a very Virgin trait. Listening enables us to learn from each other, from the marketplace, and from the mistake that must be made to get anywhere that is original and disruptive. I learn so much from guests and employees that way. (Clarkson 2017)

Disruptive leaders empower their team members in the processes, maintaining transparency and allowing for timelier decision making. Such leaders demonstrate a leadership style where they expect the unexpected and thrive with the highest levels of uncertainty, being ideal for guiding the team and transmitting calm and trust. One such prominent disruptive leader, known for his creative vision and entrepreneurial skills, was the late Steve Jobs. He was responsible for the success of the company he cofounded, Apple Inc. Jobs was known for being the first one to voice harsh criticism and practice that he defended based on his drive for the results of his team. Jobs could be incredibly demanding of those who worked for him. Yet there are many unpleasant bosses in the world. Jobs was different because he was compelling, charismatic, and inspired people to achieve great things. While Jobs was tough on people, he was fun to work with, engaging, and engendered tremendous loyalty among those who worked for him (Isaacson 2012).

According to research by global organizational consulting firm Korn Ferry, corporate leadership is ill-prepared to meet the challenges of tomorrow in the digital workplace; 67 percent of the investors included in its study on "self-disruptive leaders" "believe that traditional leadership is not fit for the future." The study captured the sentiment of nearly 800 investors and included a detailed analysis of more than 150,000 leaders (Korn Ferry 2019).

The disruptive leader is continually looking for better solutions and innovative or new ways to establish new systems and processes with the view of making an impact on the business, without worrying about shaking up things or experimenting with obtaining the necessary results. They demonstrate learning agility where they continuously learn about and stay abreast of digital trends, the implications of those trends for their business, and how to leverage the new technologies. That doesn't mean they have to know the technical details of how the technology works, but rather why it's important and how to use it.

Disruptive leaders are facing an almost overwhelming task of restoring confidence and respect in leadership and business during times of continuous disruption and chaos at the workplace. They are being called upon to guide organizations through times of turbulence and uncertainty, to show the way forward, and to set an example during the implementation of their organization's transformation agenda in the face of an increasingly disruptive digital-driven global economy in the era of the Fourth Industrial Revolution (Industry 4.0).

They achieve results by aligning their teams to the organization's business strategy and goals. They are aware of the differences between each of their team members, in the way they prefer to work and communicate across the diverse, multigenerational workforce. They make decisions by managing effective stakeholder relationships with empathy and social skills as well as creating a common understanding, a shared sense of purpose, and a relentless commitment to action (Bawany 2019).

Disruptive leaders can envision the future, motivate, inspire, and engage their employees as well as be able to adapt to the changing needs of both internal and external stakeholders (Bawany 2020).

Disruptive leaders who want to make a significant difference for themselves and their organizations need to embrace new skills in today's increasingly disruptive competitive environment. While new behaviors are essential, so are new mindsets. Leading disruptive innovation requires a new set of assumptions, many of which are based on a personal sense of humility—the recognition that they don't have all the answers and that disruptive innovation is all about finding clarity through embracing uncertainty (Wade, Tarling, and Neubauer 2017).

Leading transformation is a challenge, and even the most effective change agents have moments of struggle. When leading through times of disruption, these leaders develop collaborative skills with different stakeholders. Disruptive leaders need to consider what their stakeholders are thinking and always feeling. Especially when the disruption is severe or new, their team members will likely experience fear, anger, resentment, and pessimism. These leaders can demonstrate empathy and active listening at the same time—a desire for genuine curiosity to understand and have a trust-based open dialogue with these stakeholders, including their team members, to address any issues they have and bring them along on the digital transformation journey (Freakley 2019). It has often been said that there is no leadership without followership. The best disruptive leaders rely on their humility, authenticity, as well as emotional and social–emotional intelligence to help motivate and inspire those around them.

In essence, the heart of the leadership challenge that confronts today's disruptive leaders is learning how to lead in situations of ever-greater volatility and uncertainty in a globalized business environment. On top of this, they need to deal with scale, complexity, and new organizational forms that often break away from the traditional organizational models and structures within which many have learned their "leadership trade" (Bawany 2019).

## Disruptive Leadership Competencies

A survey of the current research and perspectives on high potentials who could be disruptive leaders (e.g., Bawany 2015b, 2019, 2020; Bolt and Hagemann 2009; Campbell and Smith 2010; Chamorro-Premuzic, Adler, and Kaiser 2017; Charan, Drotter, and Noel 2001; Corporate Leadership Council 2005; Gallup 2018; Hagemann and Bawany 2016b; Ready, Conger, and Hill 2010; Silzer and Church 2009), as well as similar research on disruptive and digital leadership (e.g., Freakley 2019; Gibson, West, and Pastrovich 2020; Harvard Business Review 2015; Korn Ferry 2019; Mortlock et al. 2019; Wade, Tarling, and Neubauer 2017), indicates specific disruptive leadership qualities.

Leading in an era of constant disruption and times of crises would require a distinct set of competencies and these include, but are not

1  Disruptive Mentality (innovative-driven)

2  Visionary and Entrepreneurial Skills (creativity)

3  Cognitive Readiness and Critical Thinking (mental agility)

4  Resilience and Adaptability (change agility)

5  Empathy and Social Skills (people agility)

6  Driving for Success (results agility)

*Figure 8.1  Competencies of the "disruptive digital leader"*

limited to, a combination of variables such as visionary and entrepreneurial skills, innovation-driven mindset, and experimentation (disruptive mentality), cognitive readiness and critical thinking (mental agility), emotional resilience, empathy, and social skills (people agility), driving for success (results agility), and resilience and adaptability (change agility) (Bawany 2020) (see Figure 8.1).

## Disruptive Mentality (Innovation Driven)

Disruptive leaders empower their employees to innovate and cocreate by developing and providing the pathways for these employees to quickly move concepts into experiments and learning or impact across the organization. Such leaders make innovation a priority and give employees and teams the time and space to collaborate, experiment, and learn with new digital tools like virtual reality, machine learning, and automation.

It also means allowing them to find creative ways to innovate and provide support amid the COVID-19 crisis, as we have seen with several distilleries and cosmetic companies worldwide that are innovating and pivoting to produce hand sanitizers for their communities.

In a disruptive business environment, organizations must be able to innovate faster than their competitors. Disruptive leaders would encourage innovation at the needed velocity by establishing a culture of innovation and creativity. They visibly champion this belief at every level of the organization, actively role-modeling a culture that encourages risk-taking and discovery. They encourage speed and embrace learning from inevitable failures along the way, equipping themselves much better to succeed in the digital world.

These leaders are open to new ideas with cognitive readiness and critical thinking skills and find ways to test theories, develop relationships with others who are known for their innovation, and challenge themselves to view every problem from diverse perspectives. They are plugged into emerging technologies, bravely experimenting and rapidly learning through what works and, just as importantly, what doesn't. Their innovative mindset is infectious, and they promote it throughout the organization's culture.

Disruptive leaders are not afraid to take risks or fail; without such an attitude, innovation and progress are not possible. They create an environment in which employees are allowed to fail and make mistakes without repercussions. This encourages employees to experiment and innovate and helps the company grow.

These leaders don't just experiment with technology but are also willing to try new management and leadership techniques. They realize that part of a digital strategy is to change management methods. The traditional hierarchical organizational structure, with the strict division between boss and employee, is often obstructive to digital transformation. Digital teams should have the freedom to make decisions and to organize themselves and their work independently. They are curious and creative and operate well in ambiguous situations. They engage in continuous experimentation and learn by listening to many and varied voices, including those from the younger workforce by adopting *reverse mentoring*.

### Visionary and Entrepreneurial Skills

Vision is even more vital in turbulent times of digital transformation at the workplace. When building a digital transformation strategy, disruptive leaders sell the idea of the long-term benefits the new technologies will bring. These leaders can envision where they want their organizations to be so that they can better weather disruptive environmental changes such as economic downturns or new competition. They can make business decisions to counter the turbulence while keeping the organization's vision in mind.

Vision is ultimately an action-oriented responsibility of a leader that transcends articulating the desired outcome and communicating it to others. It also includes translating that plan into action to accomplish the desired result. They are also able to identify strategic issues, opportunities, and risks successfully. They communicate the links between the organization's strategy and the business unit's goals. They generate and communicate broad and compelling organizational direction, inspiring others to pursue that same direction while also conveying a sense of optimism (while grounded in reality) and enthusiasm about future possibilities.

These disruptive leaders can not only create a compelling and inspired vision or sense of core purpose and communicate it to the organization but also generate a sense of expectancy and optimism in others, vibrantly recruiting support for the vision. When their team members are provided with a compelling vision, they will have a clear sense of direction and be empowered by the vision to make decisions. At the same time, they are inspired to give their best in cooperation with their colleagues entirely.

### Cognitive Readiness and Critical Thinking (Mental Agility)

Mental agility—they are excellent critical thinkers who are comfortable with complexity, scrutinize problems, and make new connections.

The suite of cognitive readiness skills can be viewed as part of the advanced thinking skills that make leaders ready to confront whatever new and complex problems they might face. Cognitive readiness is the mental preparation that leaders develop so that they, and their teams, are prepared to face the ongoing dynamic, ill-defined, and unpredictable challenges in the highly disruptive and VUCA-driven business environment. The cognitive readiness skills will develop, enhance, or sustain a leader's ability to navigate successfully in this new normal.

The EDA has identified the following seven key cognitive readiness skills, collectively known as Paragon[7] (Figure 8.2), which will develop,

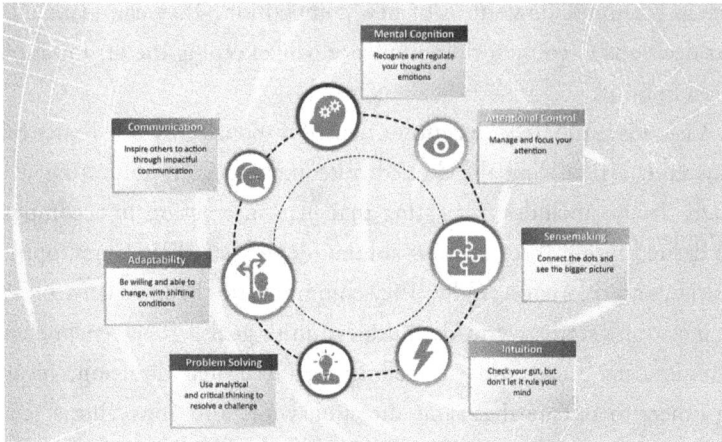

*Figure 8.2 Paragon[7] cognitive readiness competencies*

enhance, or sustain a leader's ability to navigate successfully in this new normal (Hagemann and Bawany 2016b):

1. Mental cognition: Recognize and regulate your thoughts and emotions.
2. Attentional control: Manage and focus your attention.
3. Sensemaking: Connect the dots and see the bigger picture.
4. Intuition: Check your gut, but don't let it rule your mind.
5. Problem solving: Use analytical and creative methods to resolve a challenge.
6. Adaptability: Be willing and able to change, with shifting conditions.
7. Communication: Inspire others to action; create fluid communication pathways.

The detailed descriptors of each of these seven cognitive readiness competencies can be found in Table 8.1.

Overall, heightened cognitive readiness allows leaders to maintain a better sense of self-control in stressful situations, which is crucial when resolving complex problems and decision making.

### Resilience and Adaptability (Change Agility)

To achieve achieving organizational high performance in an era of constant disruption and crisis, both agility and resilience are important.

**Table 8.1** *Descriptors of Paragon[7] cognitive readiness competencies*

| Metacognition | Attentional Control | Sensemaking |
|---|---|---|
| *Metacognition is monitoring and managing your emotional and mental processes*<br><br>Metacognition comes from the words "meta" meaning beyond and "cognition" meaning thinking. It describes the ability to control your mental and emotional processes and, in turn, manage behaviors and maximize performance. Metacognition involves self-awareness and the use of intentional strategies to self-regulate your cognition, emotions, and actions. Metacognitive individuals and organizations engage in reflective practice. They take time to plan before, during, and after situations | *Attentional control ("mindfulness") is the skill of actively managing your attention as a finite resource*<br><br>Attentional control, or mindfulness, is the conscious control of your own attention. People or organizations with high levels of attentional control pick up on weak signals. They can direct and sustain their attention deliberately, without being diverted by distractions, and they can stay focused, even if that sustained attention becomes unpleasant. You can help develop your attentional control "muscles" by practicing attentional shifting and focusing exercises | *Sensemaking is the ability to quickly connect the dots to gain understanding*<br><br>Sensemaking is pattern-based reasoning; in other words, it's the process of developing an understanding of an event or situation, particularly when it's complex and you lack clear, complete, and orderly data. Good sensemakers "put the pieces together" quickly and overcome information gaps. They discern meaning from patterns and recognize how parts of a system fit into the bigger picture, how individual elements interact, and how short-term goals impact long-term strategies |

| Intuition | Problem Solving | Adaptability | Communication |
|---|---|---|---|
| *Intuition comes from your "fast thinking" (elephant) cognitive system*<br><br>Intuition is fast; our minds quickly generate intuitive judgments without active deliberation. We all use intuition—especially under VUCA conditions—but our intuition isn't always reliable. It's important to know when it can be trusted and how to best use it | *Problem solving is an analytical approach to resolving difficult issues*<br><br>Problem solving relies upon three factors: subject-matter knowledge, motivation, and problem-solving "meta-skill," which is a mental list of problem-solving techniques and decision strategies typically associated with critical thinking and decision analysis tools | *Adaptability is the ability and willingness to change with shifting conditions*<br><br>Adaptability is the consistent willingness and ability to alter attitudes, thoughts, and behaviors to appropriately respond to the actual or anticipated change in the environment. This includes flexibility, resilience, responsiveness, and agility | *Communication is about conveying deeper intent and understanding*<br><br>Communication is the conveyance of information and sentiments. Clear, honest, and frequent communication facilitates team performance. Beyond that, you can use linguistic tools to help increase saliency, clarity, relevance, and persuasive value |

*Agility* refers to the ability to make a rapid change and achieve flexibility in various aspects of the operations, in response to changes or disruptive events in the external environment. It can also be viewed as the capacity for responding with speed and flexibly and decisively toward anticipating, initiating, and taking advantage of opportunities and avoiding any negative consequences of change.

*Resilience* refers to the ability to anticipate, prepare for, and recover from disasters, emergencies, and other disruptions and protect and enhance workforce and customer engagement, supply network and financial performance, organizational productivity, and community well-being when disruption occurs. It can also be viewed as the capacity for resisting, absorbing, and responding, even reinventing, if necessary, in response to fast and/or disruptive change that cannot be avoided such as "black swan" events (Taleb 2007).

Change agility—they are curious, like to experiment, and can effectively deal with the discomfort of change.

While resilience is the ability to quickly recover from any difficulties, adaptability is taking those same difficult situations and adjusting to them, accordingly, creating a positive outcome. Being adaptable means the leader is able or willing to change to suit different conditions. If the leader is resilient, then he or she will be able to withstand or recover quickly from unexpected or difficult conditions, adapting to (and often enjoying) change regularly.

The inability to develop or adapt was the most frequently cited reason for career derailment among leaders. That's because inflexible leaders limit the adaptability of others. New initiatives may be halted or stifled. Resistance to change may undermine critical projects or system-wide implementation. Employee enthusiasm, cooperation, morale, and creativity are jeopardized, making it more difficult to run a business or organization. Agile leaders are, first and foremost, good learners; hence, they have learning agility and are hyperaware. They scan internal and external environments constantly to anticipate and navigate opportunities and threats in a disruptive, digital environment. They take evidence-based decisions, make use of data and information, and execute fast, often valuing speed over perfection. Agile leaders engage with others, motivate, and inspire them to achieve the desired results (Bawany 2020).

In the VUCA-driven digital era, disruptive leaders can adapt to the business and respond effectively to the ambiguity that is present in the business environment. They can communicate across the organization and move quickly to apply appropriate solutions to the pressing challenges at hand. They can manage the pressure and adapt to constant changes and make decisions with agility.

Disruptive leaders can lead an agile transformation successfully by adapting their leadership style and approach to managing their teams and projects. The mindsets and skills they have carefully honed over years of experience may not necessarily be relevant or sufficient to lead digitally focused organizations. Hence, by evolving their ability to adapt, these disruptive leaders can transform their organizations into agile enterprises engineered for the digital economy.

Learning agility is the ability to incorporate new material quickly. It also involves consistently upskilling self and team and leveraging digital learning experiences and platforms. It has been found that the ability to learn quickly and use that information in business is the strongest predictor of success. Those with agility show strong leadership qualities.

Those with various abilities learn quickly from information and experience, take risks, strive for growth, and exhibit resiliency. These disruptive leaders absorb information through books and classes, peer learning, action learning-based workplace projects, direct experience, and reflections on past performances. Even failure can prove valuable to those with agility because they grow and adapt quickly from their unsuccessful experiences.

When examining organizations, such as DBS Bank, that have been successful in their digital transformation, as we have seen in the earlier chapter, these disruptive leaders can adapt successfully and transform themselves by adopting new personal mindsets and behaviors. Although it is not an easy task, they can change their mindset or adjust it to the new context, which is an attribute of disruptive leaders.

Disruptive leaders who demonstrate resilience can withstand shocks, manage complexity, are quick to learn, and are agile enough to recover from tough times or times of crisis. Resilience can be viewed as the speed and strength of one's response to tragedy and adversity. These leaders demonstrate the ability to lead when considerable ambiguity exists about the best way forward. They listen carefully to voices inside and outside the company for new information that might require a change of direction, and they think creatively about new ways of doing things.

They thrive in crises as they can balance their focus between the immediate challenges of a dynamic situation and the need to anticipate midterm disruptions. They are curious about issues that are emerging, in addition to those that have emerged. This might involve running simulations to identify how their business can anticipate potential challenges ahead.

Disruptive leaders act decisively and rapidly to institute revised arrangements to prevent business disruption and potential business failure. They don't dwell on failure but rather acknowledge the situation, learn from their mistakes, and move forward.

They can stay focused, productive, and energetic, despite the inevitable chaos and change swirling around them. They are skilled in helping their team to do the same for everyone, as well as the organization, to succeed and thrive.

They have a habit of looking at stress as a challenge to overcome, and this motivates them to address the causes of their stress in positive ways. This active approach can be contrasted with a more common approach, where stress is viewed as an unfortunate or even paralyzing force that overwhelms rather than motivates.

These leaders accept challenges and work to overcome and even master them. Even in intractable situations, they would work toward exploring possibilities that do exist and pursue them. They are committed to an active, engaged outlook toward challenges, which motivates them to actively attempt to influence their surroundings and to persevere even when their attempts don't seem to be working out. Resilient people are dedicated to finding that meaning—toward taking an active, problem-solving approach to situations.

### Empathy and Social Skills (People Agility)

People agility—they know themselves very well and can readily deal with a wide variety of people and tough situations.

Teamwork and collaboration are significant for organizations to embark on digital transformation. At a basic level, all employees, including leaders, must be able to develop a productive relationship to get along and earn the support of supervisors and co-workers.

Emotional resilience allows an individual to remain comfortable with the anxiety that often accompanies uncertainty and to think "out of the box," displaying on-the-job creativity and applying new ideas to achieve results. Conversely, people who are uncomfortable with risk and change may impact the organizational climate and undermine innovative ideas or be slow to respond to a shift in the marketplace.

Emotional intelligence (EI) is the ability to manage ourselves and our relationships effectively. It consists of four fundamental capabilities: self-awareness, self-management, social awareness, and social skill. Each capability, in turn, is composed of specific sets of competencies (Goleman 2000).

According to Goleman, social skill or relationship management is the fourth EI component, which poses a more complex picture. In a fundamental sense, the effectiveness of our relationship skills hinges on our ability to attune ourselves to or influence the emotions of another person. That ability, in turn, builds on other domains of EI, particularly self-management and social awareness. If we cannot control our emotional outbursts or impulses and if we lack empathy, then it is less likely that we will be effective in our relationships (Goleman 2000).

Disruptive leaders are those who are successful in assuming more significant, more complex jobs as they are first able to manage themselves—to handle increased pressure, deal constructively with adversity, and act with dignity and integrity. Second, they can establish and maintain cooperative working relationships, build a broad network of contacts and form alliances, and be influential and persuasive with a range of different stakeholders involved in the implementation of digital transformation projects as well as the management of crises at the workplace.

These skills can be improved further with proper executive development support, including training and coaching (Bawany 2015b).

The next crucial disruptive digital leadership competency is that of emotional and social intelligence (ESI). EI has become a major topic of interest in organizations since the publication of a bestseller by the same name in 1995 by Daniel Goleman (Goleman 1995). The early definitions of social intelligence influenced the way EI was later conceptualized.

Contemporary theorists like Peter Salovey and John Mayer originally viewed EI as part of social intelligence (Salovey and Mayer 1990), which suggests that both concepts are related and may, in all likelihood, represent interrelated components of the same construct.

Because individuals in organizations can rarely be successful alone, they must influence, lead, and coordinate their efforts with others to achieve their goals—to translate vision into action. A leader's success rests in large part upon the ability to influence and relate to the different groups in the organization: the superiors, peers, and direct reports.

In 1998, in *Working with Emotional Intelligence*, author Daniel Goleman set out a framework of EI that reflects how an individual's potential for mastering the skills of self-awareness, self-management, social awareness, and relationship management translates into on-the-job success for a leader. This model is based on EI competencies that have been identified in extensive published research on hundreds of corporations and organizations as distinguishing outstanding performers (Goleman 1998).

Emotional competence is defined as "a learned capability based on emotional intelligence that results in an outstanding performance at work" (Goleman 1988). To be adept at an emotional competence like customer service or conflict management requires an underlying ability in EI fundamentals, specifically social awareness and relationship management. However, emotional competencies are learned abilities: Having social awareness or skill at managing relationships does not guarantee we have mastered the additional learning required to handle a customer adeptly or to resolve a conflict—just that a leader has the potential to become skilled at these competencies.

## The Emotional and Social Intelligence Leadership Competency Framework

EI is the capacity for recognizing our own feelings and those of others, for motivating ourselves, and for managing emotions effectively in ourselves and others. Emotional and social competency is a learned capacity, based on EI, which contributes to effective performance at work.

ESI competencies are job skills that can, and indeed must, be learned. An underlying EI ability is necessary, though not sufficient, to manifest competence in any one of the four EI domains or clusters (Goleman 2000). The competencies are classified into four clusters of distinct areas of ability:

1. *Self-awareness*
2. *Self-management*
3. *Social awareness*
4. *Relationship management*

Nested within each of those four areas are specific, learned competencies that set the best leaders and performers apart from the average (see Figure 8.3).

The framework illustrates, for example, that we cannot demonstrate the competencies of trustworthiness and conscientiousness without mastery of the fundamental ability of self-management, or the competencies of influence, communication, and conflict management, without a handle on managing relationships.

*Self-awareness* concerns knowing one's internal states, preferences, resources, and intuitions. The self-awareness cluster contains *three competencies*:

1. Emotional self-awareness: recognizing one's emotions and their effects
2. Accurate self-assessment: knowing one's strengths and limits
3. Self-confidence: a strong sense of one's self-worth and capabilities

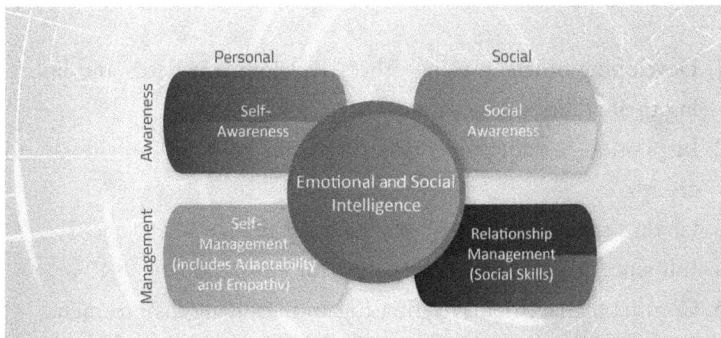

*Figure 8.3  The Goleman emotional and social intelligence (ESI) leadership competency framework*

*Self-management* refers to managing one's internal states, impulses, and resources. The self-management cluster contains *six competencies*:

1. Emotional self-control: keeping disruptive emotions and impulses in check
2. Transparency: maintaining integrity and acting congruently with one's values
3. Adaptability: flexibility in handling change
4. Achievement: striving to improve or meet a standard of excellence
5. Initiative: readiness to act on opportunities
6. Optimism: persistence in pursuing goals despite obstacles and setbacks

*Social awareness* refers to how people handle relationships and awareness of others' feelings, needs, and concerns. The social awareness cluster contains *three competencies*:

1. Empathy: Sensing others' feelings and perspectives and taking an active interest in their concerns
2. Organizational awareness: reading a group's emotional currents and power relationships
3. Service orientation: anticipating, recognizing, and meeting customers' needs

*Relationship management* concerns the skill or adeptness at inducing desirable responses in others. The relationship management cluster contains *six competencies*:

1. Developing others: sensing others' development needs and bolstering their abilities
2. Inspirational leadership: inspiring and guiding individuals and groups
3. Change catalyst: initiating or managing change
4. Influence: wielding effective tactics for persuasion
5. Conflict management: negotiating and resolving disagreements
6. Teamwork and collaboration: working with others toward shared goals; creating group synergy in pursuing collective goals.

## Importance of Emotional Intelligence Skills in the Digital-Driven Workplace

In a digital-driven workplace, artificial intelligence (AI), robots, and other cognitive systems are being deployed across every industry, revolutionizing the world in which we work. The challenge is in how well humans are being understood by these advanced technological systems and how well they can be empathetic to individual customer journeys.

In today's technologically driven world, "empathy" has become crucial for disruptive leaders and employees alike, the primary reason being that as technology takes an increasingly central place in all our lives, we've become more aware of the importance of human touchpoints in delivering robust and meaningful customer experience.

For a company to provide exceptional customer service, employees must first understand customers, their needs, and the context in which they operate. If there is no empathy or understanding of a customer's needs, and no evidence that they are valued, they will never feel fully engaged, regardless of the technology used to deliver and enable the customer experience.

Disruptive leaders are those who successfully understand the importance of empathy and bring it directly to bear on the customer experience journey. With so much competition and customer expectations at an all-time high, these leaders can offer a tangible, emotional connection that truly sets companies apart.

These leaders have been able to act with empathy and involve relevant human touchpoints in the customer journey. They also leverage big data analytics (a form of advanced analytics involving complex applications with elements such as predictive models, statistical algorithms, and what-if analysis powered by high-performance analytics systems).

This would enable them to examine the information they have available to develop a more holistic understanding of their clients and prospects, as well as the pain points they can help alleviate. Such a level of empathy and understanding cannot currently be reached without human involvement.

However, technology can help in creating a holistic view of the customer, servicing most customer requests automatically. One of the real benefits is that this frees employees to add higher value in addressing complex customer requests and providing empathy when it is genuinely required.

### Driving for Success (Results Agility)

Results agility—they deliver results in first-time situations by inspiring teams; they exhibit the sort of presence that builds confidence in themselves and others.

Although organizations are grappling with the market disruptions arising from digital transformation, results-driven disruptive leaders can not only keep pace with the ever-changing business environment but also ensure the successful adoption of digital solutions, achieving desired outcomes, and aligning all employees to the established digital transformation imperatives with the set performance standards or KPIs.

Digital transformation is challenging how these disruptive leaders interact, communicate, develop, and oversee the performances of their people. It creates an environment of teamwork where people can continuously learn, adopt, and adapt to digital systems. However, in the digital era, the physical presence of leaders has been mostly substituted with a virtual form of leadership owing to the networked organizational structures, thus further adding to the challenge of connecting emotionally and establishing the much-desired interpersonal connection with the team (Bawany 2020).

During the massive disruption caused by the COVID-19 pandemic in early 2020, these disruptive leaders can change the hearts and minds of the organization and help all employees see themselves in the new digital version of the company in the aftermath of the COVID-19 crisis. As a result, they can drive lasting change and develop the desired transformation culture despite the unprecedented crisis.

Results-driven disruptive leaders can seize the opportunity to set an example by embracing the current situation as an opportunity to reinvent themselves as digitally aware leaders and help their teams see the opportunity amid the chaos (Bawany 2019). Amid the crisis, disruptive leaders, when presented with unique challenges, will seize the opportunities—to leverage technology to unlock new opportunities around customer experiences, products, and operations.

From a talent management perspective, the organization must identify potential leaders who are future leaders. They are likely to stay in the long term and add value as well as make a significant contribution to the organization. Thus, another attribute of disruptive leaders is that they should feel a sense of engagement toward the organization and remain committed to its mission and values. This is particularly important in this digital age when marketable employees typically have much better career opportunities and are thus less likely to stay with a single organization throughout their working life.

Employee engagement and retention are a constant struggle for businesses all over the world. In fact, according to data from Gallup, "87% of employees worldwide are not engaged." An engaged employee is more likely to stay with an organization, produce a strong performance as a leader, and inspire others to action than a disengaged one (Gallup 2018).

Some of the hallmarks of engaged disruptive leaders to look for when assessing potential leadership candidates include how enthusiastic they are about the industry their company serves, as leaders set the tone for their teams. Their enthusiasm or reticence will thus spread to others quickly, affecting performance. The other attribute includes how often they go above and beyond the minimum requirements of their job because engaged employees will volunteer to be part of task forces and projects and work harder and take ownership of their work to make sure it is completed in the right way the first time and has achieved the desired results and met or exceeded the set performance standards or KPI. Highly engaged, disruptive leaders aren't just productive—they show everyone around them the best traits of themselves, inspiring others to be more productive as well.

## The Results-Based Leadership Framework

There is currently extensive published research on the direct link between leadership effectiveness and sustained organizational performance. Hence, the development of the disruptive leader's capability should be of primary concern for all organizations operating in Industry 4.0, since the contribution and motivation of the employees are key to achieving the organizational goals and objectives. While all organization needs financial resource, technical and professional knowledge and expertise, relevant systems, and processes, success cannot be assured and sustained unless the leaders can utilize these resources creatively and effectively. Arguably, the organizations that are best placed to survive and thrive in the disruptive business environment of Industry 4.0 are those which have a strong focus on leadership development practices and a good understanding of what effective leadership means to them (Bawany 2020).

Disruptive leaders must focus on effectively engaging all stakeholders, in particular, the employees, in delivering sustainable results for their organization. In the era of the Industry 4.0 workplace and at a time of continued significant transition and challenge, leaders at all levels will have a responsibility to ensure that the organization's mission and purpose are at the heart of what they do.

The concept of "engagement" can be defined in many ways. Essentially, engagement is a measure of how an organization values its employees and how employees value their organization and recognize that every individual is at liberty to decide whether to do the minimum required of them or to do more. Engagement can also be taken to represent the degree of empowerment to which staff are involved in decision making and/or the openness and perceived effectiveness of communication. Hence, leaders at all levels have a key role in cultivating a strong culture of engagement. This, in essence, is the foundation of the "results-based leadership" (RBL) framework for a digital-driven organization (see Figure 8.4).

*Step 1*: The basic premise of the RBL framework is that a highly effective transformational disruptive digital leader would start with a strong sense of self-leadership, in particular, developing a high level of self-awareness of his or her strengths and area of development in the crucial competencies for a disruptive digital leader as discussed in the preceding chapter. These include but are not necessarily limited to agility, adaptability, emotional resilience and social skills, empathy, cognitive readiness, critical thinking, driving for results, innovativeness, and resilience. Next, he or she needs to lead and engage the team by coaching them to success by adopting the proven SCORE™ High-Performance Team Framework, which could be found in Chapter 9.

*Step 2*: Organizational climate (sometimes known as corporate climate) simply refers to how employees feel about working in the

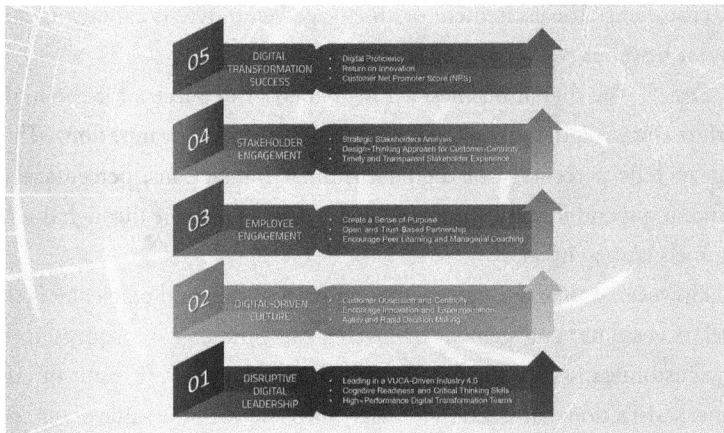

*Figure 8.4  The results-based leadership (RBL) framework*

organization. Organizational climate is the process of quantifying the culture of an organization. It is a set of properties of the work environment, perceived directly or indirectly by the employees, that is assumed to be a major force in influencing employee behavior and engagement. By implementing step 1 effectively along with the relevant contemporary human resource practices such as flexible work arrangements like "work from anywhere" (WFA) including workplace flexibility, flexible work hours, telecommuting, and "work from home," the leader will create an organizational climate of an open trust-based partnership between themselves and the employees who will be highly engaged and would want to remain in the organization, especially those who have highly marketable talent.

*Step 3*: The level of employee engagement is dependent on the organizational climate. Employees who are engaged and motivated are instrumental in delivering the required customer service experience for the client, which will result in customer engagement and retention. Consequently, engaged employees will result in employee loyalty, which will reduce the attrition rate and the operating costs of hiring new staff.

*Step 4*: Employees who feel fully committed to the organization for which they work take great pride in doing their job. They do more than is expected of them and go that extra mile. In so doing, engaged employees, in particular, the frontline service staff or customer-interfacing employees, will have an impact and inevitably influence the buying behaviors of the customers. The excitement of an engaged employee is contagious and cannot help but rub off on the customer.

*Step 5*: The digital business KPIs or metrics of success for the high-performance digital organization differ for each organization. They may include percentage of digital customer interactions, percentage of marketing spend that is digital, and percentage of revenue through digital channels among others.

However, one of the factors driving profitability and efficiency is the level of customer engagement or loyalty, since the cost of acquisition of new customers is reduced significantly. Loyalty is a direct result of customer satisfaction. Satisfaction is largely influenced by the value of services provided to customers. Value is created by satisfied, loyal, and productive employees, especially customer-interfacing service employees. Employee satisfaction, in turn, results primarily from the internal high-quality support services and organizational policies that enable the frontline team to deliver excellent service to customers.

Managers often fail to appreciate how profoundly the organizational climate can influence financial results. It can account for nearly a third of financial performance (Goleman 2000). Organizational climate, in turn, is influenced by leadership style and by the way or manner in which the leader motivates direct reports, gathers and uses information, makes decisions, manages change initiatives, and handles crises.

The fundamentals remain that all organizations, including those digitally driven, need to continuously deliver service value and build good customer relationships to generate sustainable results through their satisfied and loyal customers. Employees being at the forefront of the service delivery chain hold the key to building this satisfied and loyal customer base.

## Importance of Communication Skills for Disruptive Leaders

Developing excellent communication skills is essential to effective disruptive leadership. The leader must be able to share knowledge and ideas to transmit a sense of urgency and enthusiasm to others during the implementation of digital transformation initiatives. If a leader can't get a message across clearly and motivate others to act on it, then having a message doesn't even matter. Disruptive leadership also means communicating with others, so they are influenced and motivated to perform actions that further common goals and lead toward desired outcomes.

Communication is the key to driving successful digital transformation in the workplace. It helps disruptive leaders connect with employees, keep the workforce abreast of changes so they can move with them, and empowers staff to adapt and learn to stay current and focused. A successful disruptive leader must also bear in mind that while technology is important, the people part of the transformation is just as crucial. They can better impact and influence their team members if they possess excellent communication skills and avoid possible conflicts. Communication is the key to generating workforce willingness. It is the lever that helps leaders change beliefs, cultivate understanding, and create buy-in. In successful transformations, leaders connect with and gain the full support of the workforce with authentic, compelling, and consistent communication.

To achieve extraordinary success in leadership, the digital leader not only needs a clear vision of the digital transformational goals and objectives but also to know how to communicate these objectives to team members and other stakeholders. Hence, effective communication is an essential element of leadership. Disruptive leaders are communication champions who inspire and unite people around a common sense of purpose and identity. They lead strategic conversations that get people talking across boundaries about the vision, key strategic themes, and the values that can help the group or organization achieve desired outcomes (Bawany 2014e).

The strategic conversation is communication that takes place across boundaries and hierarchical levels about the group or organization's vision, critical strategic themes, and values that can help achieve desired outcomes. This is achieved by actively listening to others to understand their attitudes and values, needs, personal goals, and desires, as well as selecting the right communication channels and facilitating dialogue. Inspiring someone without effective communication is almost impossible.

Leaders must keep in mind that all good organizations achieve their goals through effective communication at all levels of the organization. To achieve this, they have an organized system of communicating at different levels of the organization.

As technology continues to disrupt the workplace, one of the key factors that would impact the success of the digital transformation is the talented employees, including the leaders, who can use existing digital technologies and adapt to evolving methods and new approaches. Without them, organizations will struggle to benefit as they should from the latest advances in Industry 4.0—everything from robots to AI, data science, virtual reality, blockchain technologies, cloud computing, the Internet of Things, and new digital business models.

Even if the technologies themselves are evolving and relatively easily acquired and deployed, having the right team of disruptive leaders who can lead the digital transformation implementation successfully will be scarce. Digitally talented people are already so highly in demand that many large, traditional companies must reinvent themselves to attract them.

Organizations should respond to this challenge by building new pools of skilled digital talent. To do so, they must identify the skills and attributes of these high-potential employees and assess and develop them into disruptive leaders who will lead successful digital transformation initiatives (Bawany 2020).

## Importance of Empathy as Competency for Disruptive Leaders

In Industry 4.0, advanced technologies such as AI, robotics, *cobots*, and robotic process automation (RPA) have gained a rapidly expanding foothold in the workplace, faster than many organizations ever expected. Leading companies are recognizing that these technologies are most effective when they complement humans, not replace them.

As these technologies permeate the workplace, cognitive readiness competencies such as critical thinking, creativity, problem solving, and emotional and social intelligence gain in importance. One of the critical ESI skills that a leader needs to demonstrate in the digital-driven workplace is empathy (Bawany 2019).

Empathy is a competence that gives people an astute awareness of others' emotions, concerns, and needs. The empathic individual can read emotional currents, picking up on nonverbal cues such as tone of voice or facial expression (Goleman 2000).

As companies increasingly embark on digital transformation at the workplace with the deployment of technology solutions to drive innovation, customer satisfaction, productivity, and revenue as well as profitability, the potential risk of losing touch with the employees grows hence this will impact the open and trust-based partnership between them and the leaders. Trust is most fragile during times of organizational change and transformation. Empathy builds trust and respect, which is crucial for digital transformation initiatives.

In crafting the organization's digital transformation strategy, leaders need to be able to identify and communicate the pain points that organizations are struggling with the various stakeholders including customers and internal employees and define actionable solutions. Disruptive leaders need to understand developing technologies, and their impact on the business, as well as gaps that exist in the organization to achieve its digital transformation objectives. Once again, the leaders must demonstrate at all times empathy, honesty, and open communication during the entire transformation journey, especially when facing challenging situations such as managing layoffs, resulting from transformation efforts, with both "organizational justice" (refers to employee perceptions of fairness in the workplace) and "procedural justice" (refers to employee perceptions of fairness of processes used to reach specific outcomes or decisions and how the decision is being communicated including transparency and mutual respect).

Empathy could also be viewed as demonstrating the ability to sense others' feelings and how they see things as well as taking an active interest in their concerns. A leader picks up cues to what's being felt and thought by listening attentively to understand the other person's point of view, the terms in which they think about what's going on (Bawany 2019).

For example, in the healthcare industry, empathy and the jobs connected with it will be valued more and more in the future. It makes complete sense. Automation, robots, and AI will perform certain cognitive tasks brilliantly to the extent that humans will not be able to compete. Where could humans have a chance? Although AI will perform diagnostic tasks or robots might be able to do surgeries, could they talk to a patient with empathy about the risks and consequences of an operation?

Moreover, as digital health simplifies administration and cuts down on monotonous tasks, the workload of doctors and nurses will be reduced, so they will be able to concentrate on what matters: healing the patient and guiding him through the entire process with care. It is believed that, eventually, AI would be able to mimic even such soft skills but as we are social beings, we will always need the human touch.

Many leaders and managers vaguely understand the impact empathy has on leadership effectiveness. One of the reasons, we have found, is that very few of them have been trained or taught how to cultivate empathy in their lives and work as a daily practice (Bawany 2017).

Empathetic leaders put themselves in their followers' shoes and attempt to see things from their perspective. Empathy doesn't mean agreeing with someone. Empathy is not sympathy. Empathy doesn't mean telling them that they are right or even addressing their concern. Demonstrating empathy shows that you care enough to give someone else's issue the same level of respect and attention they do.

Empathy can also be seen as demonstrating active concern for people and their needs by forming close and supportive relationships with others. Leaders who lack empathy may be perceived by others as cold, uncaring, and having little interest in them as people. Leaders who score high on this competency work to develop close bonds with others. They spend time getting to know people and can give their colleagues the feeling that they are personally involved with them. They tend to emphasize the importance of being generous and kind and displaying a sincere interest in the well-being of others. If carried to extremes, however, this closeness may cloud a leader's objectivity and result in decisions that do not properly consider the organization's best interests. Hence it would be crucial for the leader to bear in mind the saying "familiarity breeds contempt" (Bawany 2019).

Organizations would need to incorporate a different form of development activities for their disruptive digital leaders, which are likely to include executive coaching, mentoring and action learning workplace projects, stretch assignments, and executive education. Other development activities include psychometric assessments and managerial coaching and performance feedback, and customized leadership master-class training programs. All these activities have strong developmental value as components of an overall executive leadership development strategy. Additionally, the organization needs to ensure that these leaders are also equipped with cognitive readiness skills and ESI competencies needed for sustained success and effectiveness in a disruptive and digital-driven environment and workplace (Bawany 2019).

## Case Study of the Importance of Empathy in Disruptive Leadership: Satya Nadella, CEO of Microsoft Corporation

In today's hypercompetitive, disruptive VUCA-driven business environment, we need a new breed of CEOs and business leaders who are defined less by commanding and controlling or autocratic/coercive and pacesetting leadership styles, rather more by inspiring and empowering, or authoritative/visionary and coaching leadership styles (Bawany 2017).

A good example of a leader that demonstrates this approach effectively and successfully is Satya Nadella. He became CEO of Microsoft in February 2014 and in less than four years he transformed the company's culture into a more empathic one that opened new possibilities not only for learning and cooperation, but also for innovation and understanding customers' needs (Bawany 2020).

This cultural shift concerned both employees' inclusion, by hiring a diverse workforce, and customers' inclusion, by providing products and services and by developing inspiring technologies allowing disabled customers to have accessible experiences.

Unlike his predecessor, the notoriously combative Steve Ballmer, Nadella has dramatically revived Microsoft's reputation and its relevance by emphasizing collaboration and what he calls a "learn-it-all" culture versus the company's historical know-it-all one. As Fast Company's senior editor Harry McCracken explains in "Microsoft Rewrites the Code," the results have been eye-popping: more than $250 billion in market value gains in less than four years—a feat that, quantitatively, puts Nadella in the league of Jeff Bezos of Amazon, Tim Cook of Apple, Larry Page of Google, and Mark Zuckerberg of Facebook (McCracken 2017).

Nadella demonstrates ontological humility: When a few months into his tenure, he made a major faux pas at a conference for women engineers that spawned a wave of criticism. He owned the mistake and admitted to biases that he hadn't realized. The episode ended up building his credibility in the long run (Bawany 2019).

Nadella's leadership style is to emphasize what's been done right. He starts each senior leadership meeting with a segment called "Researcher of the Amazing," showcasing something inspiring at the company, and by doing so he created an organizational climate of trust-based partnership with his team of co-leaders.

Nadella is a strong believer in talent management and has been personally involved in the recruitment of new talent into the company. He has emphasized the importance of an outsider's perspective in steering the organization to greater heights. He has put even more focus on unleashing the potential within the leadership team, including high-potential leaders. He has created a high-performance-driven culture with his empowering and coaching style of leadership, which relies on managerial coaching as an organizational development tool. He also believes that resistance to change is a behavior, rather than a fixed personality trait, and that can be addressed with coaching (Bawany 2019).

The skills and behaviors mentioned above clearly contributed to the foundations of Nadella's inclusive leadership style.

In his memoir, *Hit Refresh: The Quest to Rediscover Microsoft's Soul and Imagine a Better Future for Everyone* published in 2017, Nadella says his highest priority is renewing the company culture with "a growing sense of empathy."

In addition to confidence, a CEO must have empathy, Nadella said. This is a quality one doesn't typically see on a list of top CEO character traits. But in Nadella's view, empathy is, among other things, a key source of business innovation. He said that although many regard it as a "soft skill," not especially relevant to the "hard work of business," it is a wellspring for innovation since innovation comes from one's ability to grasp customers' unmet, unarticulated needs (Nadella, Shaw, and Nichols 2017).

He demonstrates empathy as he recognizes that his co-leaders' and employees' perspectives are real and important to them. It may not be real, or important, to him, but it is very real and important to them. He gives it the same level of respect and attention they do. A leader's empathy for employees' needs to become more creative; there is also a need for them to have an in-depth understanding of customers' requirements; collaboration with former competitors, the value of which may have been underestimated previously; humility, by accepting errors, his and his employees; and learning from them (Bawany 2020).

Nadella's empathy was honed over years of experience as a father, both to his first child, Zain, who was born with severe cerebral palsy, and to a daughter with learning difficulties. These challenges helped Nadella strengthen his empathy in the sense of the capacity of putting himself in his children's shoes and understand what their needs were; increase his openness to collaboration, as it happened with regard to how his family dealt with the situation, as well as with the supporting network of therapists and parents of disabled children around him; and develop his humility, by accompanying his children in their lifelong struggle with disability, made of achievements and failures (Nadella, Shaw, and Nichols 2017).

He believes human beings are wired to have empathy, and that's essential not only for creating harmony at work but also for making products that will resonate. "You have to be able to say, 'Where is this person coming from?'" he says. "What makes them tick? Why are they excited or frustrated by something that is happening, whether it's about computing or beyond computing?" (McCracken 2017).

### Conclusion

High-performing organizations (HPOs) exhibit a set of characteristics that are available to almost every company, regardless of the industry and scale of business.

HPOs operate as empowered networks, coordinated through culture, advanced digital technologies, and talent mobility (see Figure 8.5). Leaders need to continuously challenge their mental models in their efforts to build an HPO (Bawany 2018c).

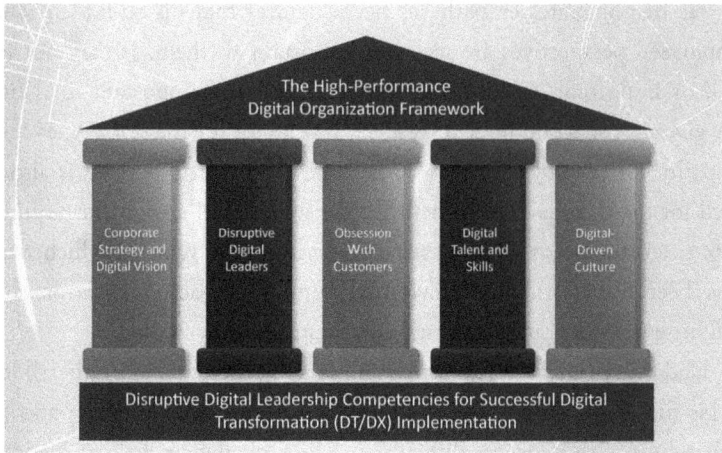

*Figure 8.5  The high-performance organization (HPO) framework*

HPOs are continuously focused on reinventing or redesigning the organization itself, studying and developing new models. They also invest considerable time, resources, and leadership commitment toward creating and executing a digital strategy that incorporates emerging digital ecosystems both inside and outside traditional industry boundaries to better guide and shape decision making (Bawany 2020).

For those companies embarking on digital transformation, it would be prudent for them to examine and benchmark every aspect of the business, including strategy, structure, people, climate, and processes, and take steps to bring their organizations in line with the digital-driven high-performance profile.

Leading an HPO in an increasingly VUCA-driven and disruptive business environment and workplace requires leaders to leverage their suite of disruptive leadership skills. This will enable the leader to connect emotionally with the team members to understand them better and ensure they always feel confident in what they are doing. The leader does not just feel for their people, they feel with them.

## Leveraging of Coaching for the Development of "Disruptive Leaders"

Today's dramatically changing work environment demands that organizations continuously ensure that there is a robust leadership pipeline ready to be deployed now and in the future. Identifying, assessing, selecting, and developing future leaders is, therefore, the critical strategic objective for ensuring a sustainable, competitive organization. The business case for doing so is clear as supported by extensive published research (Bawany 2019).

The high impact and cost of a new leader derailing within the first year are staggering. As Michael Watkins (2003) states in his book *The First 90 Days*, "studies have found that more than 40 to 50 percent of senior outside hires fail to achieve results" (p. 8). The reason for most of these failures is primarily not due to the lack of intelligence (IQ), ESI skills (EQ), or experience, but rather the inability of these executives to assimilate effectively into the new culture or new role and make the necessary "mindset shift" as they go through fundamental changes in roles.

Developing future leaders requires alignment between the achievement of business goals and leaders' skills to drive the achievement of those goals. To accomplish this, the organization needs to start with the creation of a business strategy, followed by a leadership strategy, followed by a leadership development strategy (Bawany 2019). It is important to know the distinctions:

> *Business strategy*: The roadmap for achieving the organization's business goals
>
> *Leadership strategy*: The organization's plan for assigning leaders to key job roles by defining the relevant competencies including skills, knowledge, and experiences required to achieve the organization's desired current and future business goals
>
> *Leadership development strategy*: The organization's plan for the development of current and future leaders at all levels to ensure that they, individually and collectively, have the crucial and relevant competencies and skills to lead and drive the organization's strategy successfully now and in the future.

## The Background of Coaching as a Leadership Developmental Tool

The history of coaching can be traced back as far as Socrates (427 BC to 347 BC). Socrates suggested that people learn best when they take personal responsibility and ownership of a given situation (Edwards 2003). The word "coach," however, originates from "Kocs," a village in Hungary, where high-quality carriages were produced. In the 19th century, English university students began to use this word as slang for tutors that helped them through their academic careers. They said they were in a carriage driven by their tutor (Wilson 2004).

Coaching first appeared in management literature in the 1950s. Managers began using coaching since it was understood that a manager was responsible for improving subordinates' performance through a sort of master–apprentice relationship. Coaching, at that time, often took the form of the manager supporting the development of their employees. In the mid-1970s, sports coaching was starting to make its way and being translated into the managerial situation. Since the 1980s, coaching has been presented as a training technique in the context of management development. Coaching literature nowadays makes a connection with mentoring, career development, management development over a long period, and generating team and individual performance (Evered and Selman 1989).

Athletes and actors have known the value of coaching for many years (King and Eaton 1999). As O'Shaughnessy (2001, 194) expressed, "as anyone who has watched a superbly-fought tennis match will testify, it is often down to how the contestants play a couple of crucial points." One might even say minimal differences in performance are of crucial importance in defining how someone's career will plan out.

In today's competitive world, no athlete should assume that it is possible to make it to the top without world-class coaching support (Burdett 1998). Mike Powell, an American long jump champion, gave credit for his achievements in the long jump event to a five-year scientific training plan, designed by his coach, Randy Huntington (Liu, Srivastava, and Woo 1998).

It is suggested that what is true in sports in general is also true in business (O'Shaughnessy 2001). In sports as well as in more conventional organizational models, individual excellence and teamwork are equally important. Teamwork is just as important as individual excellence since it is the ability to move beyond one's ego, showing a willingness to put the needs of the organization above personal gain, and a desire to win.

Today, business takes place in a highly competitive international arena, and the only way for companies to become successful is to push themselves to the very edge of their capability. There is only so much an organization can do productively, when downsizing or rightsizing, restructuring, focusing on the core business, and the like; ultimately the success of the organization depends on the people within it—building a winning team. As a result, coaching has become a secret weapon for many organizations (Burdett 1998).

According to Parsloe and Wray (2000, 41), coaching can be defined as follows:

> Coaching is a process that enables learning and development to occur and thus performance to improve. To be a successful coach requires knowledge and understanding of the process as the variety of styles, skills, and techniques that are appropriate to the context in which the coaching takes place.

## The Differences Between Managing, Coaching, Mentoring, Consulting, and Training

Managing, coaching, mentoring, consulting, and training are all related, and sometimes overlap. However, at their foundation, they are distinct in their focus.

A manager's primary attention is to achieve specific organizational results; this has been so for a long time (and will continue to be in this era of Industry 4.0). This would involve maximizing the output of the organization through administrative implementation through their direct reports by planning, organizing, staffing, directing (leading), and controlling. To that end, they may direct and/or develop those direct reports through developmental performance feedback and may use coaching skills (Bawany 2018b, 2019).

A professional coach's primary attention is to tap into the client's (also known as the "coachee") own vision, wisdom, and directed action in service of the client's self-identified agenda which often focuses on their professional endeavors. Today, coaching is rapidly being recognized as one of the best strategic weapons a company can have in its arsenal for improving business performance. It is therefore important to create a coaching environment that is founded on trust because on a normal working day, the executive works in a fast-paced, complex, and pressured environment and there is little time to sit back and reflect on the range of issues facing him or her (Bawany 2014b, 2018d).

A mentor's primary role is to help the mentee learn, much of which is enabled by the mentor guiding the mentee into learning situations and then helping them to reflect on and consolidate the learning (Bawany 2020). Mentoring is often thought of as a partnership largely because there are obligations, implicit or otherwise, that each party takes on and the key to a successful mentee–mentor relationship is to be aware of each other's obligations and take them seriously (Bawany 2014d).

A consultant's primary attention is to achieve organizational results (often large systems change) through the application of specific expertise. An external consultant is a professional contracted by the organization to conduct the evaluation or analyze specific organizational or business challenges and develop and implement the recommended plan of action as outlined in the agreed terms of reference (Bawany 2020). Consultants may or may not also be charged with transferring knowledge or skill sets to their clients through coaching or training. Consulting projects are often done in teams and can focus on a variety of areas, including strategy and technology implementations in digital transformation projects (Bawany 2019).

A training and development professional's primary attention is to ensure the successful transfer of specific information or skills to their clients. Training is an organizational development tool aimed at enhancing the performance of individuals and groups in an organizational setting (Bawany 2020). It is a combined role often called "human resources development" (HRD) meaning the development of "human" resources to remain competitive in the marketplace. Training focuses on upskilling (refers to retraining employees with new skills in their current roles) or reskilling (refers to training employees with new skills to upgrade their expertise and capabilities to prepare them for different roles and responsibilities). Both are crucial: As technology and digitalization impact the future of work, some jobs are going to become less relevant while others are going to suddenly become crucial. The trainer may well use a coactive approach, facilitation, and coaching skills (Bawany 2019).

# "Reverse Mentoring" in a Multigenerational Workplace

Changing demographics and diversity as one of the megatrends of disruption discussed earlier in the book would require adaptive methods of operation. Reverse mentoring is demonstrating itself as an efficient tool for navigating biases, sharing knowledge, creating engagement, and building intergenerational relations based on mutual acceptance and trust. This helps to promote a more team-oriented environment, where ideas and issues can be discussed openly. In this way, the adoption of reverse mentoring assists in meeting the demands of not only the new generation but everyone in this changing world of work.

Traditionally, many managers are in the position of providing leadership to employees who have more expertise in key business processes than they (the managers) do. As the future of work evolves in a multigenerational workplace, managers including those from the generation of baby boomers (born between 1946 and 1964) and Gen X (born between 1965 and 1980) are faced with increasing numbers of employees, in particular those from Gen Y or "millennials" (born between 1981 and 1994) and Gen Z or "digital natives" (born between 1995 and 2010), whom they must lead without an in-depth understanding of what these employees do. These younger generation employees are likely to be much more resilient and resourceful than their colleagues from the older generations (Bawany 2013a; Bawany and Bawany 2015).

Managers need to let go of the traditional and outdated practice of trying to be the expert—the person with the answers—and move to a position of enabling the learning of their employees and creating a knowledge-sharing culture both within their teams and across the larger organization.

Retaining the millennial talent and remaining to stay relevant to younger consumers continue to be key challenges for many organizations today. Leadership teams across various industries globally have found one solution to address these challenges by implementing "reverse mentoring," which is an organizational development practice where younger employees (millennials and digital natives) are matched to executive team members to mentor them on various topics of strategic and cultural relevance (Jordan and Sorell 2019).

While traditional mentoring has been around longer, reverse mentoring is a relatively new concept. It was notably popularized by the legendary late Jack Welch, former General Electric CEO and chairman back in the 1990s, when he realized that many of the newer and younger employees had much more expertise and knowledge about the newest technologies than their managers, including himself. As a result, he had all managers seek out mentors from the pool of younger employees (Allen 2019).

The primary objective of reverse mentoring is to enable these senior leaders to remain relevant with the emerging trends in the marketplace possibly those related to technology and the desired preferences and practices of the younger market segment in particular for those in the fast-moving consumer goods industry. Organizations that embarked on digital transformation are finding it of relevance as digital natives (as mentors) are helping their senior leaders (as mentees) to increase their technology skills (Bawany 2020).

The benefits for the younger mentor include exposing him or her to other areas and departments in the organization and providing an opportunity to expand his or her network, gaining access to the strategic thinking of more experienced leaders, which in turn results in developing greater insights into the organization's strategy. As for the mentee (senior leader) who is open and willing to shift his or her mental models, he or she will be able to learn new skills and insights from the millennials and/ or the digital natives in their workforce. Sometimes these skills are technical, of course, but there are other aspects of younger mentors' mindsets that can be leveraged too—new thinking, fresh perspective, and the sense of optimism and energy they often bring to working on something they are passionate about (Bawany 2020).

Mentoring can be an effective way to groom future leaders in companies. Pairing a more-senior employee with someone new can speed up the learning process and boost engagement. Research by the Centre for Executive Education (CEE) found that over 90 percent of mentors and mentees feel empowered by their mentoring relationships and have developed greater confidence (Centre for Executive Education 2020).

Reverse mentoring engages relatively junior employees in the mentoring process, equips them with leadership skills, and gives visibility and opportunities for further professional development. In reverse mentorship, a junior colleague mentors someone more senior or possibly a senior leader. The goal is to help the more senior colleague develop new skills and connect with the younger generation. This helps them gain new insights and perspectives on ways to improve their business. In addition, reverse mentoring also helps younger colleagues develop their skills and confidence. The additional perspective from seeing through the eyes of a different generation can be invaluable to their job and career.

The same research by the CEE (2020) unveiled that the younger generation may not be as experienced as their older counterparts, but they can bring fresh new insight to problems or concepts that more-senior leaders may not have thought of before.

This relationship aims to support the skill development of both colleagues. The junior team members also benefit from the knowledge and experience of their more-senior mentees. It also helps them develop their leadership skills.

In a traditional mentor–mentee relationship, the older and more experienced person acts as a mentor. But in reverse mentoring, the experienced person is the mentee and is paired up with a younger mentor. It's important to keep in mind that reverse mentoring doesn't always have to be based solely on age. Management level is also an important consideration.

Reverse mentoring helps companies address skills gaps. It also helps support efforts to upskill staff. This can help organizations stay competitive and relevant in an ever-changing global market.

Reverse mentoring could potentially be a solution to address the "Great Resignation" phenomenon. It refers to the higher-than-usual number of disgruntled employees voluntarily leaving their jobs since late 2020 and early 2021 during the COVID-19 pandemic largely due to unsatisfactory working conditions. Many of the younger employees feel that the relationship can give leaders a fresh perspective on rising trends in areas of technology or the future of work.

The other benefits that reverse mentoring offers include helping to reduce generational prejudice as the CEE research has shown that intergenerational prejudice can be a barrier to effective cooperation. Older colleagues might view millennials as spoiled and entitled. And younger team members may think baby boomers are resistant to change. With

Gen Z entering the workforce in large numbers, additional generational stereotypes are likely to form.

Reverse mentoring is not without challenges. First, the two parties must sort out expectations about how the relationship will work and if it will meet their respective needs. Importantly senior managers must be open to new ideas and suggestions from someone with significantly less experience.

The partnership must also reflect high levels of respect and low levels of conflict. Senior managers must be open to feedback about how they are seen at lower levels of the organization and the younger partner must have the confidence needed to relay such information. To be a successful mentor or mentee, both parties must be intentional in cultivating the professional relationship. It is encouraged that senior leaders participating in such reverse mentoring program be open-minded and allow their mentor—the up-and-coming leader—to drive the mentoring sessions.

The mentee (senior leader) needs to be vulnerable and authentic in sharing their own experiences. They need to recognize that often the unvarnished information that is necessary to move forward can be the most difficult to get. CEE research has shown that through mentoring relationships, senior leaders across various organizations are learning more about their businesses and how they operate by being exposed to different perspectives and experiences from the junior employees who are their mentors (Bawany 2020).

## Development of a Corporate-Wide Coaching Culture

Employees no longer expect company loyalty. Downsizing and layoffs have taught them otherwise. These events have also taught employees that they must be marketable at all times, and to be marketable they need to continually develop their skills and knowledge. Organizations that emphasize development are more likely to both attract and retain talented employees and at the same time build the critical capabilities the employees need to achieve business results. As those closest to employees, managers play a critical role in facilitating this development (Bawany 2019).

Today's workplace demands a change in the traditional manager's role. Thus, managerial coaching in organizations has been perceived as an important function of managers for the development and growth of employees leading to performance improvement. Managerial coaching has been given considerable attention in management and leadership and has consistently shown to have an impact on the development of high-performance organizations.

The current pace of change has resulted in the need for constant learning on the job. The shelf life of many skills and much knowledge is steadily decreasing. It used to be a common assumption that companies could hire MBAs and other professionals to bring the necessary knowledge into the organization. This is no longer true. Today, everyone needs to be learning constantly, and organizations and their managers need to be facilitating the learning process on the job.

According to the CEE,

> managerial coaching is about developing and maximizing an individual employee's potential which will consequently impact positively on the organization's performance. It is about more inquiry (ask) and less advocacy (tell) which means helping that individual to learn rather than teaching. Coaching sets out to embrace the employee as an individual and understands the organizational context in which the employee operates. It seeks to achieve alignment between the individual employee, team, and organizational goals. (Bawany 2015d)

According to a landmark research by the International Coaching Federation (ICF) in collaboration with Human Capital Institute (HCI) published in 2014, more and more organizations have recognized the value in building a culture of coaching that offers employees at all levels—not just executives and managers—the opportunity to grow their skills, enhance their value, and reach their professional goals. But not all coaching is equal. To ensure successful results that go beyond skills training and truly enable the company to increase employee engagement and retention, the organization must develop a comprehensive coaching plan that addresses both current and future needs. The challenge arises not only in determining the types of coaching that will be most impactful but also in attaining the internal buy-in and support for such a program.

Fundamentally, a coaching culture is an organizational development model that provides the structure that defines how the organization's members can best interact with their working environment and how the best results are obtained and measured. Organizational culture provides the stability and protocol for all interactions within the group. It serves as a mechanism that defines the acceptable parameters of behavior (what we do or say) and constraining activities to those that reinforce the espoused values of the organization (Bawany 2019).

Introducing coaching competencies into an organization is a very powerful strategy to create an adaptive workplace culture committed to the ongoing process of development and learning. Companies that have developed a coaching culture report significantly reduced staff turnover, increased productivity, and greater happiness and satisfaction at work.

There is a growing movement among organizations to develop a coaching culture as more companies realize the advantages of such a strategy. Once a luxury strictly for senior executives, coaching is now being extended to employees at all levels of the organization for developmental purposes through the managerial coaching approach, which will be elaborated on later.

Coaching continues to become an increasingly popular focus in business settings, underscoring the importance of exploring how organizations are cultivating a coaching culture.

A coaching culture needs the disciplines of building a shared vision, learning, and a desire for personal mastery to realize its potential. Building a shared vision fosters a commitment to the long term. Openness is required by all to unearth shortcomings in present ways. Team learning develops the skills of groups of people to look for the larger picture that lies beyond individual perspectives. And personal mastery fosters personal motivation to continually learn how our actions affect our world.

## Conducting Managerial Coaching Conversations: Leveraging on the "GROW" Model

The original GROW model was developed in the United Kingdom by three codevelopers: Alan Fine, Sir John Whitmore, and Graham Alexander. The original material primarily consisted of the basic GROW model, which is an acronym for the four stages of an effective coaching conversation. The model was the result of the collaborative efforts of all three individuals, each having joint ownership and intellectual property rights to the work.

For all the different versions of the *GROW* model, the first three letters are the same:

"*G*" is the *"Goal"* in which the managerial coach is helping the coachee (person or team member being coached) to articulate what he or she is seeking to achieve.

"*R*" is the *"Realities"* where the coachee describes his or her current situation in consideration of the context of the challenge to be resolved or decision to be made.

"*O*" is the *"Options"* open to the coachee through a brainstorming process with the managerial coach.

"*W*" is where the coachee identifies and selects one or more options explored in the preceding phase and develops an action plan. This phase has been interpreted differently by all three codevelopers of the model. Whitmore defined it as "Will" (Whitmore 2002), Alexander defined it as "Wrap-up" (Alexander and Renshaw 2005), although he also used "Wrap-up/Way forward"—and Fine defined it as "Way Forward" (Fine 2010).

## Sir John Whitmore's GROW Model

The GROW model is based on "The Inner Game" developed by Tim Gallwey. The Inner Game is a proven method to overcome the self-imposed obstacles that prevent an individual or team from accessing their full potential. The Inner Game takes place within the mind of the player and is played against such obstacles as fear, self-doubt, lapses in focus, and limiting concepts or assumptions (Gallwey 2001).

Whitmore and Alexander brought the Inner Game to Europe, with the blessing of Gallwey after they realized the value of the Inner Game for leaders and managers of organizations. As pioneers of coaching in the workplace, they spent much of the 1980s developing the methodology, concepts, and techniques for performance improvement in organizations. Wanting to make a real difference to people, they showed how it was possible to grow not just in performance but also in learning and enjoyment. Individuals become more aware and more responsible and gained a powerful sense of purpose in their work (Whitmore 2002).

In 1986, the management consulting firm McKinsey became their client. Many of the programs they ran for McKinsey included experiential coaching work on tennis courts. The coaching was so successful at improving performance and unlocking potential that McKinsey asked them to come up with an underpinning framework of coaching—a model on which to hang what was happening on the courts and elsewhere in the programs.

The GROW model is deservedly one of the most established and successful coaching models adopted globally by professional coaches and internal managerial coaches. It is popularized by the late Sir John Whitmore in his best-selling book, *Coaching for Performance* (Whitmore 2002).

Today, the GROW model is also "one of the tools Google uses to teach [its] managers about coaching conversations" (re: Work with Google 2018).

Utilizing a deceptively simple framework, the GROW model provides a powerful tool to highlight, elicit, and maximize inner potential through a series of sequential coaching conversations. The GROW model is renowned for its success in both problem solving and goal setting, helping to maximize and maintain personal achievement and productivity (Bawany 2015d).

Sir John Whitmore's GROW model, with the acronym standing for *(G)oals, (R)eality, (O)ptions, and (W)ill*, highlight the four key steps in the implementation of the GROW model. By working through these four stages, the GROW model raises an individual's awareness of their aspirations, a greater understanding of their current situation, the possibilities open to them, and the actions they could take to achieve their personal and professional goals. By setting specific, measurable, and achievable goals, and a realistic time frame for their achievement, the GROW model successfully promotes confidence and self-motivation, leading to increased productivity and personal satisfaction.

The implementation of the GROW model, by using carefully structured questions, promotes a deeper awareness and responsibility and encourages proactive behavior, as well as resulting in practical techniques to accomplish goals and overcome obstacles (Bawany 2015d).

The use of continuous and progressive coaching skills support provides the structure, which ultimately helps to unlock an individual's true potential by increasing confidence and motivation, leading to both short- and long-term benefits.

The GROW model (see Figure 8.6) has been seen to yield higher productivity, improved communication, better interpersonal relationships, and a better-quality working environment (Whitmore 2002).

Coaching is unlocking people's potential to maximize their performance. It is about raising awareness and responsibility—helping them to learn rather than teaching them. The GROW model is an elegantly simple way of structuring an effective coaching conversation and, as such, has become one of the best-loved models of coaching (Performance Consultants 2018).

For the managerial coach, the key to using GROW successfully is first to spend sufficient time exploring "G" until the coachee sets a goal that is both inspirational and stretching for them, then to move flexibly through the sequence, and revisit the goal if needed.

Performance Consultants International, a consulting firm cofounded by Sir John Whitmore, outlined the GROW model as follows (Performance Consultants 2018):

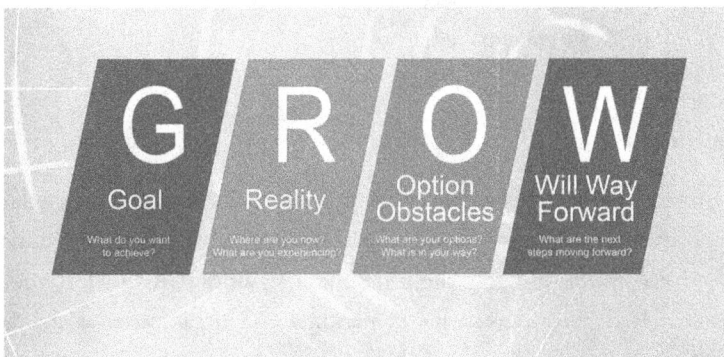

*Figure 8.6 The GROW coaching model*

**Step 1 of the GROW model: What are your Goals?**

- Identifies and clarifies the type of goal through an understanding of ultimate goals, performance goals, and progress goals along the way.
- It provides an understanding of principal aims and aspirations.
- Clarifies the desired result from the session.

**Step 2 of the GROW Model: What is the Reality?**

- Assesses the current situation in terms of the action taken so far.
- Clarifies the results and effects of previously taken actions.
- It provides an understanding of internal obstacles and blocks currently preventing or limiting progression.

**Step 3 of the GROW Model: What are your Options?**

- Identifies the possibilities and alternatives.
- Outlines and questions a variety of strategies for progression.

**Step 4 of the GROW Model: What Will you Do?**

- It provides an understanding of what has been learned and what can be changed to achieve the initial goals.
- Creates a summary and plan of action for the implementation of the identified steps.
- Outline possible future obstacles.
- Considers the continued achievement of the goals and the support and development that may be required.
- Estimates the certainty of commitment to the agreed actions.
- It highlights how accountability and achievement of the goals will be ensured.

## Conclusion

Managerial coaching is about creating the capacity for appreciative and supportive interaction that leads to the achievement of business results. Effective conversation sets the stage for a significant discussion about issues of leadership development, personal and organizational change, and creating capability through high-functioning people with enhanced emotional competence. For years, most organizational pundits have known that it is not how much you know but how well you relate to other people in the organization that matters (Bawany 2015d).

If organizations are going to be successful in improving employee performance over time, two-way conversations have to occur that allow employees to raise their level of self-awareness and identify problems and issues that prevent them from being as successful as possible through the process of performance coaching leveraging on the GROW model. If coaching is carried out effectively, individual employee performance is almost certain to increase, and as a result employee engagement, productivity, and sustainable organizational performance will be achieved in the longer term (Bawany 2016b).

In digitally driven organizations, coaching is highly effective when managers want to get buy-in from the stakeholders, particularly their direct reports when implementing change initiatives such as digital transformation at the workplace. It helps them identify when teamwork is important and to use their skills to foster it (Bawany 2020).

Coaching builds skills and capacities for effective working relationships. Coaching, through implementing and modeling coaching competencies, paves the way for leaders to create higher levels of organizational effectiveness through dialogue, inquiry, and positive interactions that create awareness, purpose, competence, and well-being among their team members. The value of coaching is a positive impact on the employee's engagement, productivity, organizational climate, and most importantly on the bottom line (Bawany 2019).

## Leveraging on Executive Coaching for the Development of Disruptive Leaders

Executive coaching is a concept that has moved from the world of sports to the executive suite and is designed as a means to help senior executives manage a constantly changing business environment and refine their leadership skills. But coaching is not limited to senior levels. Increasingly, people all over the world, at all levels, utilize executive coaches to help them achieve their full potential. The process focuses on the participant's goals, reinforces learning and change, and increases self-empowerment (Bawany 2019, 2020).

Executive coaching is one of the fastest-growing and most misunderstood professions of this decade. Coaching used to be an "executive perk" for senior executives in large companies to help them make better business decisions. Today, coaching is rapidly being recognized as one of the best strategic weapons a company can have in its arsenal.

Executive coaching focuses on developing a top executive's full potential by coaching them to think and act beyond existing limits and paradigms. Executive coaching is a highly individualized form of leadership development and support available. It is based on the understanding that to be maximally effective, executives must accurately identify their strengths and areas of development, examine the impact of their behavior on others, and regularly and intentionally reflect on their values, goals, and effectiveness (Bawany 2020).

The strength of executive coaching lies in the fact that it is almost exclusively an executive development strategy that builds leadership and management strength because it is ultimately concerned with understanding where the executive is, where it is that they want to go, and the things that they would have to do to get there. It is often lonely at the top for chief executives as they generally keep their own counsel, mainly because they find it difficult to discuss matters with colleagues and cannot or choose not to share their concerns with spouses and families. Executive coaching offers a way out of this by providing an opportunity for the executive to have an independent sounding board and strategic partner in a safe and confidential environment.

Executive coaching can be defined as a confidential, highly personal learning process, involving action learning and working in partnership, combining an executive coach's observations and capabilities with an executive's expertise. The result is that the executive achieves better and faster results-oriented outcomes. It is therefore important to create a coaching environment that is founded on trust because, in a normal working day, the executive works in a fast-paced, complex, and pressured environment and there is little time to sit back and reflect on the range of issues facing him or her (Bawany 2019).

Savvy organizations acknowledge that executive coaching is a proven effective leadership intervention tool of choice for future leaders, including high potentials, for the continuous development of their leadership skills, which is critical to organization-wide success.

A study by Manchester Inc. examined the impact of coaching in 56 companies with 100 executives (Manchester Inc. 2001). Their findings suggest that 74 percent of the sponsors and 86 percent of the participants were very satisfied with the process. From the survey of respondents who received coaching, it was estimated that coaching resulted in an average return of 5.7 times the initial investment. Furthermore, coaching contributed to a perception of increased productivity for 53 percent of respondents and improved quality of work for 48 percent of the respondents. When asked which workgroup relationships improved as a result of coaching, the results indicated that 77 percent reported improvement with direct reports, 71 percent reported improvement with immediate supervisors, and 63 percent reported improvement with peers. Of those receiving coaching, 61 percent reported a significant increase in their overall level of work and job satisfaction.

Executive coaching is typically seen as an ongoing relationship with no set time frame or definitive ending point. For example, the leader may have poor communication skills and is unintentionally undermining direct reports, which can lead to a loss of morale and retention issues. In corrective situations, the executive coach begins by completing a full diagnosis of the situation, through the identification of undesirable behaviors, such as berating or blaming others, and will then demonstrate the consequences these behaviors will have on the individual and the organization. The coach then helps the executive identify practical ways to strengthen his leadership impact, provides direct and objective feedback, and ensures the executive gets back on track and stays on track (Bawany 2019).

Whether the relationship starts with a derailment situation or as part of a corporate-wide initiative, executive coaching covers a wide range of situations with one common goal: the personal development of a leader through the support of a professional relationship. On the organizational level, executive coaches help companies avoid costly management turnover, develop their most talented people, and ensure that leaders perform at their maximum potential. In research published in Industrial and Commercial Training, it was reported that executives who received coaching are more likely to be promoted or received accelerated promotions than those who have not had one-on-one coaching (Parker-Wilkins 2006).

## Executive Coaching Versus Transition Coaching

Effective coaching is a major key to improving business performance. Executive coaching focuses on the qualities of effective leadership and improved business results. It is comprised of a series of structured, one-on-one interactions between a coach and an executive, aimed at enhancing the executive's performance in two areas (Bawany 2018e, 2019):

1. Individual personal performance
2. Individual organizational performance

When executives are first confronted by being coached, they are not always clear about how best to use their sessions and are quite unaware that it is they who set the agenda; in fact, some executives expect executive coaching to be like a one-on-one tailored training program where the executive coach initiates the agenda. Executive coaching teaches the beneficiary (coachee) to minimize, delegate, or outsource nonstrengths by changing ineffective behaviors or changing ineffective thinking (Bawany 2020).

The upfront purpose of executive coaching is to develop key leadership capabilities or focus required for their current role. But it can also be used as an instrument to prepare them for the challenges of the next level. The whole coaching experience is structured to bring about effective action, performance improvement, and personal growth for the individual executive, as well as better results for the institution's core business (Bawany 2019).

An executive coach only has one item on his agenda—the client's success. This means going where it might hurt and keeping a client accountable for achieving their goals. Coaching helps people grow personally and as professionals. This growth allows them to commit completely to the success of an organization. When professional coaches work with organizations, they can turn performance management into a collaborative process that benefits both the employee and the organization (Bawany 2020).

While many executives are familiar with executive coaching and may even have enlisted the help of external coaches at some point, few understand the right type of coaching approach required to address the challenges faced by leaders in transition situations. Many newly placed executives fail within their first two years in the position for reasons ranging from their inability to adjust to a new role and develop strong relationships, to a lack of understanding of the business imperatives. What new leaders do during their 90 days in a new role greatly determines the extent of their success for the next several years (Bawany 2010).

What if there was a proven process to support new leaders in their role while significantly increasing return on investment and ensuring a positive economic impact for the organization?

One such process is transition coaching, an integrated and systematic process that engages and assimilates the new leader into the organization's corporate strategy and culture to accelerate productivity (Bawany 2007, 2010).

Transition coaching encompasses the goals of executive coaching but focuses on a specific niche, the newly appointed leader (either being promoted from within or being hired externally). Leadership transitions are among the most challenging situations executives face. Take the case of a leader who might enter a new position thinking he or she already has all the answers; or just the opposite, the leader might lack a clear understanding of what to expect from the role. The goal of transition coaching is to reduce the time it takes for new leaders to make a net contribution to the organization and establish a framework for ongoing success.

Those promoted from within will have to be mindful that a smooth and effective role-to-role transition is critical to the organization's business performance. The organization depends on leaders to execute and meet objectives and has placed its bet that internal candidates are better valued and have less risk. Organizations understand that successful transitions ensure future capability (Bawany 2018e).

An unsuccessful transition can negatively impact an organization through poor financial results, decreased employee morale, and costly turnovers. So rather than risk this sink-or-swim gamble, organizations can improve the assimilation process through transition coaching (Bawany 2019).

Transition coaching is also recommended when organizations assign managers to the role, for the first time, of leading digital transformation projects. If organizations use the right transition strategies, the leader will not only help prevent failure but also create additional value by accelerating the new leader's effectiveness. Transition coaching engages the new disruptive leader in the organization's corporate strategy and culture to accelerate performance.

## The Potential Pitfalls of Leadership Transitions

The biggest trap that new leaders fall into is believing that they will continue to be successful by doing what has made them successful in the past. There is an old saying, "To a person who has a hammer, everything looks like a nail" (Bawany 2019). So too it is for leaders who have become successful by relying on certain skills and abilities. Too often they fail to see that their new leadership role demands different skills and abilities. And so they fail to meet the adaptive challenge. This does not, of course, mean that new leaders should ignore their strengths. It means that they should focus first on what it will take to be successful in the new role, then discipline themselves to do things that don't come naturally if the situation demands it (Bawany 2020).

Another common trap is falling prey to the understandable anxiety the transition process evokes. Some new leaders try to take on too much, hoping that if they do enough things, something will work. Others feel they have to be seen as "taking charge," and so make changes to put their stamp on things. Still others experience the "action imperative"—they feel they need to be in motion, and so don't spend enough time upfront engaged in diagnosis. The result is that new leaders end up enmeshed in vicious cycles in which they make bad judgments that undermine their credibility (Bawany 2018e, 2019).

New leaders are expected to "hit the ground running." They must produce results quickly while simultaneously assimilating into the organization. The result is that many newly recruited or promoted managers fail within the first year of starting new jobs.

From the extensive executive and transition coaching engagements over the past 20 years by the CEE's panel of executive and transition coaches, it has been discovered that many newly promoted leaders in transition fail due to one or more of the following factors (Bawany 2019):

1. They do not fit into the organizational culture.
2. They don't build a team or become part of one.
3. They are unclear about their stakeholder's and their bosses' expectations.
4. They fail to execute the organization's strategic or business plan.
5. They lack savvy in maneuvering and managing internal politics.
6. There is no formal process to assimilate them into the organization.

A proven assimilation process is critical as it provides support to the newly hired executive and helps the organization protect its investment.

## Success Strategies for the Assimilation of New Disruptive Leaders

Successful new leaders redefine their need for power and control. Team members normally value a certain amount of freedom and autonomy. People want to influence the events around them and not be controlled by an overbearing leader. When the manager is an individual contributor, he or she is close to the work itself and is the master in control of his or her circumstances; the manager's performance has a big effect on his or her satisfaction and motivation.

The situation is different when the managers are promoted and become a leader. Their contribution is less direct as they often operate behind the scenes. Leaders create frustration for everyone when they try to be involved in every project and expect team members to check in before beginning every task. World-class leaders delegate. They learn to trust. This means giving up some control. Leaders learn to live with the risks and know that someone else may do things a little differently. Every person is unique, and they will individualize certain aspects of their work. When leaders don't empower and delegate, they can become ineffective and overwhelmed. In turn, team members feel underutilized and therefore less motivated (Bawany 2019).

Finally, leaders learn to transition in other critical ways. They learn how to live with occasional feelings of separation and that people don't always accept their decisions when faced with gut-wrenching situations. Leaders have a view of the big picture in mind. But the challenge for leaders lies in balancing the needs of many stakeholders: owners, employees, customers, and community. Because of this challenge, team members can feel alienated when unpopular decisions must be made. Leadership can be hard. It is impossible to please everyone all the time. While the need for belonging and connecting with the group is important, leaders know the mission and vision take precedence. Sometimes a leader should make waves, champion change, and challenge people's comfort zone. Leaders may not always relish conflict, but they are not afraid of it either. Leaders are guided by standards, principles, and core values. Leaders focus on what is right, not who is right.

Leaders know they cannot make people happy. People have to take ownership and control of their happiness. Leaders do not focus on personality factors. At times, the individual self-interests of a team member may be in opposition to the interests of the group. Leaders concentrate on shared interests and team goals. Consequently, the driving force behind a team is a leader who treats team members with respect, while keeping the vision in mind. People are different and you have to treat people differently yet fairly (Bawany 2019).

## What Are the Skills Required for Disruptive Leaders in Transition?

In the literature and research on leadership transitions and helping leaders to accelerate themselves into new roles, early findings indicate that new leaders gain leverage by putting in place the right strategies, structures, and systems. Transitions could be viewed as an engineer would approach a challenging design problem: advising leaders to identify the right goals, developing a supporting strategy, aligning the architecture of the organization, and figuring out what projects to pursue to secure early wins (Bawany 2010, 2018e).

The current research and perspectives of the competencies and skills expected to be demonstrated by disruptive leaders (e.g., Bawany 2019, 2020; Freakley 2019; Gibson, West, and Pastrovich 2020; Harvard Business Review 2015; Korn Ferry 2019; Mortlock et al. 2019; Wade, Tarling, and Neubauer 2017) include a combination of attributes and skills such as the ability to envision the future, agility, ESI skills such as empathy and relationship management (social skills), results driven, engagement, agility and adaptability, innovativeness and courage to experiment, and resilience.

ESI competencies such as empathy and social skills are essential building blocks in a disruptive leader's ability to establish the right organizational climate when leading a digital transformation project and collaborating with various stakeholders. Leaders at all levels of the organization must constantly demonstrate a high degree of EI in their leadership roles. Emotionally intelligent leaders create a climate or a workplace environment of positive morale and higher productivity (Goleman 1998).

The reality confronting leaders in transition is that the relationships with their bosses, peers, direct reports, and external constituencies must be seen as good, to be a good source of leverage. These elevated relationships and the energy they can mobilize (or drain the leader) to the forefront can help leaders enter and gain momentum to meet the challenges of the new roles.

This is not to say, of course, that strategies, structures, and systems are unimportant; usually, they are critical. But if the new leader hopes to put in place the right strategies, structures, and systems, he or she must first secure victory on the relationship front. This means building credibility with influential players, gaining agreement on goals, and securing their commitment to devote their energies to helping the new leader achieve those goals.

In the leader's new situation, relationship management or social skills are critical as they aren't the only ones going through a transition. To varying degrees, many different stakeholders, both inside and outside the leader's direct line of command, are affected by the way he or she handles his or her new role. Inside the new leader's direct line of command are people who report directly to the leader, as well as employees from other groups. While some may feel apprehensive about the new leader's arrival, all must adjust to the leader's communication and managerial style and expectations (Bawany 2018e, 2019).

Outside the new leader's direct line of command are senior executives, peers, and key external constituencies such as customers, suppliers, and distributors. The new leader will likely have no "relationship capital" with these individuals, that is, there are no existing support or obligations upon which the leader could draw. The leader will need to invest extra thought and energy in gaining their support. Leverage through relationships is an essential foundation for effectiveness in a new leadership role.

## Transition Coaching Approach for the Development of Disruptive Leaders

Transition coaching has three overall goals: to accelerate the transition process by providing just-in-time advice and counsel, to prevent mistakes that may harm the business and the leader's career, and to assist the leader in developing and implementing a targeted, actionable transition plan that delivers business results (Bawany 2010, 2020).

While many of the issues covered by transition coaching are similar to those included in executive coaching, such as sorting through short- and long-term goals and managing relationships upwards as well as with team members, transition coaching is focused specifically on the transition and designed to educate and challenge new leaders. The new leader and coach will have to work together to develop a transition plan and a roadmap that will define critical actions that must take place during the first 90 days to establish credibility, secure early wins, and position the leader and team for long-term success (Bawany 2018e).

The transition coaching relationship also includes regular meetings with the new leader as well as ongoing feedback. Frequently, the coach conducts a "pulse check" of the key players, including the boss, direct reports, peers, and other stakeholders, after four to six weeks to gather early impressions so that the new leader can make a course correction if needed.

The transition coaching framework (refer to Figure 8.7) developed by the CEE with the complete transition coaching process provides new leaders with the guidance to take charge of their new situation, achieve alignment with the team, and ultimately move the business forward (Bawany 2020).

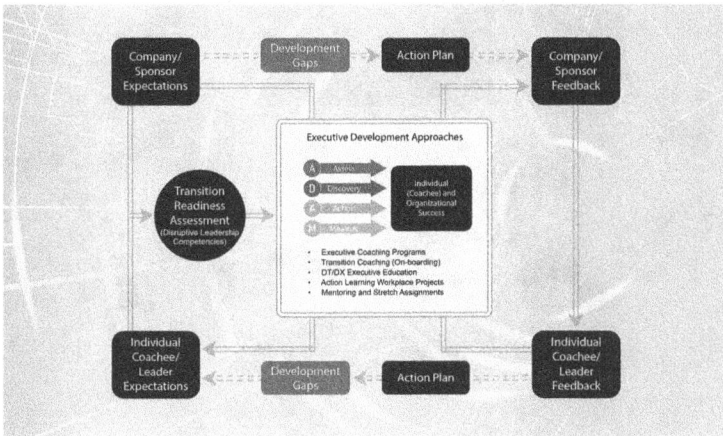

*Figure 8.7  The transition coaching framework*

The "transition readiness assessment" is designed for the evaluation of the desired disruptive leaders' competencies as stated earlier, which includes the ability to envision the future, agility, ESI skills such as empathy and relationship management (social skills), cognitive readiness, critical thinking, engagement, agility and adaptability, innovativeness and courage to experiment, and resilience, among others.

## The ADAM Coaching Methodology

The ADAM coaching methodology (see Figure 8.8) also developed by the CEE is a structured approach to executive coaching. This consists of a four-step process that is firmly grounded in leadership development best practices.

### "A"ssess

- A series of psychometric assessments and information gathering from a series of stakeholders' interviews, including the immediate manager of the disruptive leader being coached (known as the coachee), will be conducted.
- The primary objective is to determine how the coachee's performance links to current business goals.

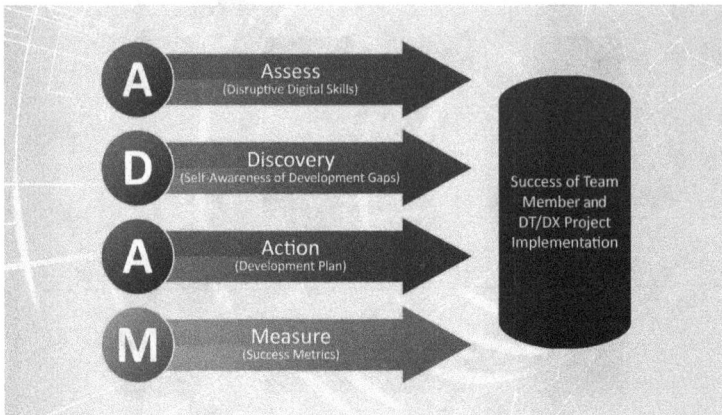

*Figure 8.8  The "ADAM" coaching methodology*

- An assessment of the coachee's competencies, skills, styles, values, and leadership effectiveness forms the basis of the action plan.
- Gather background on the situation, identify the purpose of the coaching engagement, and discuss expected outcomes.
- Conduct an in-depth coachee interview, including life and career history, self-perceived behavioral and leadership strengths and shortcomings, and desire to close the gap on weaknesses and further develop the strengths.
- Hold a tripartite session with coachee and sponsor (the coachee's immediate manager), to obtain the senior management's commitment, and define the degree of confidentiality.
- Provide an overview of the coaching process, timetable, and parameters of the engagement.

### "D"iscovery

- Meetings are scheduled to review the assessment data.
- The coachee will be provided with feedback based on the results of the assessments that have been undertaken.
- Development objectives are discussed between the coachee and the coach to link the feedback received, with the agreed business goals and professional objectives.

- Based on the key objectives identified, coaching activities and timelines are developed jointly between the coachee and the coach.
- The coachee, with the support of the coach, will develop an action plan that will enable coachees to determine what to do to close the gaps in their leadership capability.
- The coach and the coachee form a working alliance where the coach provides the stimulus and environment for the coachee who will write the action plan.
- The plan is formalized and shared by the coachee with the sponsor for agreement and support of the action plan and expected development outcomes.
- The sponsor will sign off on the development plan to ensure that there is alignment with the business objectives.

### "A"ction Plan

- The coachee will implement the development plan by taking well-defined action steps and regular feedback during scheduled monthly coaching sessions with the coach, which enables the coachee to move toward measurable goals.
- "Shadowing" or observation of the coachee at work (as needed and if appropriate).
- Specific actions are taken to develop the key skills and knowledge agreed to in the development plan. These actions may include:
- Behavior modification and efforts to use new behaviors.
  - Building new skills and competencies while refining others.
  - Developing key relationships within the sponsoring organization.
  - Communication strategies for successful networking and being an ambassador for the sponsoring organization.
- The sponsor and coach communicate, in person, by phone, or through e-mail, to discuss specific situations and maintain focus on the objectives of the development plan.

- There is also an opportunity for contact with the sponsor to monitor progress, as defined within the parameters of the sponsoring organization's/coach confidentiality agreement.

### "M"easure

- A full evaluation of the coaching process and engagement based on the agreed success metrics at the beginning of the assignment yields objective measures of business results and professional outcomes for both the organization and the coachee.
- Periodically, and after the coaching program, the coachee and the coach will discuss progress against the plan and determine action plans as appropriate.
- A final tripartite coaching meeting will be held, where the results of the coaching engagement will be presented to the sponsor.
- The recommended next step for the continuous professional development of the coachee will be discussed and agreed upon with the sponsor.
- The consistent ADAM coaching delivery methodology ensures that every coachee receives the same degree of insightful business analysis, personalized consideration, and performance-driven priority.

## Case Study on Transition Coaching of a Newly Appointed Disruptive leader

The following case study illustrates how the ADAM coaching methodology has been successfully applied in the development of a newly appointed disruptive leader that has been identified through the Assessment & Development Centre (ADC) to be the project leader for an organization-wide digital transformation project (see Figure 8.8).

### The Situation: Leading an Innovation and Digital Transformation Project at Workplace

The said manager, belonging to Generation X (born between 1964 and 1979), has been with the organization for over 15 years. He was promoted to the role of vice president of operations and technology at a global bank. The manager has a solid record of success in his previous roles where a hands-on, controlling style with staff direct reports was an effective managerial tool. However, in his new position, he faced broad operational responsibilities and managed multiple stakeholders both internally and externally. The manager needed to lead cross-functionally by bringing together departments throughout the organization including strategy, finance, marketing, distribution, IT, and technical operations. The make-up of the majority of the employees from these various functions is those of Generation Y (born between 1981 and 1994).

With significantly more Gen Yers under his leadership, the manager's communication style was soon found to be confrontational and abrasive and often prevented him from building trusting relationships with his newly formed project management team to drive the digital transformation project, which the CEO had deemed to be critical to the success of the organization. His style also jeopardized negotiations with existing and potential key business alliances, channels of distribution, and vendors.

Several of the senior leadership team members including the chief information officer (CIO), chief data officer (CDO), and chief technology officer (CTO) perceived that the manager was unwilling or unable to adapt to his new role. It was soon apparent that if left unchecked, the situation could impact not only the manager's career but most importantly the corporation's strategic objectives. Not counting the loss of productivity, the loss of crucial digital talent and their replacement costs alone are expected to be substantial.

The chief human resources officer (CHRO) recommended to the CEO that an external professional executive coach will be a useful resource for addressing the managerial challenges faced by this newly promoted manager. The CEO, who is a strong advocate for the development of future leaders, believed that the manager, whom he has known over the years, can be developed. Hence, upon reviewing the business case put up by the CHRO and the human resource business partner (HRBP), the CEO agreed to the engagement of an executive coach.

## Coaching Strategy: Assessment, Feedback, and Development of New Behavioral Skills

During the first stage of the coaching process, the manager completed a group of assessments including a 360-degree feedback leadership effectiveness profile to provide objective information about his communication and leadership style. Feedback from project team members, peers, and direct reports, combined with constructive 1:1 conversation with the CIO, CDO, CTO, and CEO, provided a clear insight into the style, competencies, and behaviors that are expected from the role of a project leader in driving digital transformation initiatives. These data enabled the manager to see the impact his behavior had on others and how it could impact his success in building relationships and reaching business outcomes of the specific digital transformation project that he was leading.

A developmental plan was written by the manager and reviewed with his executive coach to address gaps in areas of communication, collaboration, developing others (coaching), relationship management (social skills), empathy, conflict management, and strategic leadership. More effective techniques and approaches were role-played with the coach, and the manager was encouraged to use these new behaviors by leveraging the GROW model during the managerial coaching conversations that he had planned weekly, individually with each team member as well as in project team meetings. He also began to use them with business associates outside the organization. The coaching goal was to increase the manager's effectiveness in all his business endeavors and to increase his ability to improve the organization's success through managing the stakeholders as well as leading and engaging his project team in a much more effective manner than before.

## Results: Tremendous Improvement in the Leader's Communication Style Observed

Feedback received by the CHRO and the other senior leadership team members was that there is much more open and trust-based communication between the manager and his team members as well as with the other stakeholders; key sensitive strategic alliances were successfully negotiated, resulting in the implementation of the digital transformation project in a much more effective manner and ahead of the timeline for several of the tasks.

The manager was better able to communicate with and facilitate information transfer among his project team of primarily Gen Yers. Over six months, he was able to transform them into a high-performance team by adopting the SCORE™ framework for high-performing teams, which is found in Chapter 9. A follow-up 360-degree leadership assessment was conducted where a positive change in the manager's leadership and communication style was perceived by the various stakeholders.

Due to the success of this coaching intervention, both executive and transition coaching are being used more broadly as a tool to enhance leadership development among future digital disruptive leaders as well as high-potential talent for other functional roles throughout the organization, resulting in the achievements of both tactical and strategic objectives of the organization (Bawany 2020).

## Conclusion

The development of future disruptive leaders includes the process of transitioning them effectively into a leadership position. This could be smoother if new leaders develop a sense of optimism and monitor and manage their outlook and perspective. Executive or transition coaching, mentoring, action learning workplace projects, leadership masterclass training, stretch assignments, and executive education along with the relevant tools and systems are very important for the effective development of these future leaders. However, without the right outlook and unwavering support from the senior leadership team, new and even seasoned leaders will experience serious difficulties and unrest (Bawany 2010).

New leaders need to reflect on and examine their leadership attitude and perspective and develop a plan to work on areas that need improvement. Whether a manager is moving into a new position or looking to get back on the road to success, executive or transition coaching can work to bring out the best in the new leaders through the support of a professional relationship. The relationship has to be built on a foundation of trust and confidentiality. The ability of coaches to provide leaders as an outside resource that can also act as a sounding board can help them become the successful leaders they were meant to be (Bawany 2018d).

Organizations must clearly define the purpose of coaching, gauge the process, and evaluate the results. Coaching is not just about providing support. Ultimately, coaching should deliver what any business needs— real results (Bawany 2019).

# CHAPTER 9

# Leading High-Performance Teams

## Introduction

Digital transformation is being increasingly implemented by organizations in their quest to achieve sustainable competitive advantage in the fast-changing marketplace as it can help organizations cut costs and boost productivity, often with remarkable results. Those who failed to achieve similar results realized that simply implementing innovative technology is not enough to increase value.

Digital transformation initiatives require *people, process, and technology* (PPT), which refers to the methodology in which the disruptive leader's role as the project leader is to achieve the balance of people, process, and technology, to drive action:

1. *People* perform a specific type of work for an organization using processes (and often, technology) to streamline and improve these processes. The people are the project leader and his team who do the work. Without people, nothing can happen.
2. *Processes* could be viewed as a series of actions or steps that need to happen to achieve a particular goal. People are ineffective without processes in place to support their decisions.
3. *Technology* will not make existing problems go away without the people and processes around to support it. Too often, companies invest in technology and try to retrofit the people and processes, but that is backward logic.

Many digital transformation efforts do not achieve their desired results because they concentrate on the process improvement strategies with the technology as an enabler but they ignore the people aspect of the change initiative.

## Teams Versus Working Groups

To understand how digital transformation project teams deliver extra performance, it is important to distinguish between teams and other forms of working groups. That distinction turns on performance results. A working group's performance is a function of what its members do as individuals. A team's performance includes both individual results and what is called "collective work products." A collective work product is what two or more members must work on together, such as interviews, surveys, or experiments. Whatever it is, a collective work product reflects the joint, real contribution of team members (Bawany 2019).

Working groups are both prevalent and effective in large organizations where an individual's accountability is most important. The best working groups come together to share information, perspectives, and insights, to make decisions that help each person do his or her job better, and to reinforce individual performance standards. But the focus is always on individual goals and accountabilities. Working-group members don't take responsibility for results other than their own. Nor do they try to develop incremental performance contributions requiring the combined work of two or more members (Katzenbach and Smith 1993).

Teams differ fundamentally from working groups because they require both individual and mutual accountability. Teams rely on group discussion, debate, and decision making, but more on sharing information and best-practice performance standards. Teams produce discrete work products through the joint contributions of their members. This is what makes possible performance levels greater than the sum of all the individual team members. Simply stated, a team is more than the sum of its parts.

Katzenbach and Smith (1993) stated that ". . . a team is a small number of people with complementary skills who are committed to a common purpose, performance goals, and approach for which they hold themselves mutually accountable" (p. 45). Let's examine this definition further.

*A small number of people*: The optimal number of people in a team is generally between five and nine. While more team members bring a greater diversity of perspectives and ideas, the difficulty of consensus decision making increases dramatically. Subgroups can be created, but then the entire team is at risk of losing sight of the big picture.

*Complementary skills*: In establishing a team, it is critical to ensure that there is a mix of diverse, yet complementary, skills such as technical, functional, and interpersonal abilities.

*Committed to a common purpose*: Without a unified purpose, the team has no yardstick against which to measure performance.

*Common performance goals*: Teams share performance goals or objectives; if a goal or objective is not achieved, the entire team is accountable. Commitment to these common performance objectives results in higher productivity and raises motivation levels.

*Common approach*: Objectives represent the "task" element of performing successfully; a common approach represents the "group process" element of working together. Neither is more important than the other, but without agreeing on how the team will interact, the chances of completing the task are pretty low!

*Mutually accountable*: This refers to the shared ownership and responsibility that is fundamental to real teamwork. If something goes wrong, there should not be any finger-pointing but rather a group effort to fix the current situation and prevent future problems. Everyone should feel free to ask for help, just as they should feel free to offer assistance. In a team, individual and team success are the same.

## Importance of Teams in a Disruptive and Digital-Driven Workplace

Like any good team, each individual's role in achieving digital transformation must complement one another and benefit the greater good. As Jim Collins says in his book *Good to Great*: Leaders of companies that go from good to great start not with "where" but with "who." First the people, then the direction (Collins 2001).

High-performing teams have become a principal building block of the successful digital transformation strategy. While teams are at the core of any change initiatives, success will often depend on how well each team member operates and collaborates with others.

Today's highly disruptive as well as VUCA-driven networked business environment not only provides a challenging environment for leaders to operate but would need to depend on their teams, which are critically important to getting work done (Bawany 2016a). Yet, not all teams are created equal. Some fail to perform or they perform below expectations. Some start well but later lose their focus and energy. Teams are extremely valuable if they are working well. They are very costly if they are not. Disruptive digital leaders must find ways to ensure their teams are working effectively and are achieving their results (Bawany 2020).

In most teams, the energies of individual members work at cross-purposes. Individuals may work extraordinarily hard, but if their efforts do not translate into a team effort, this would result in wasted energy. By contrast, when a team becomes more aligned, a commonality of direction emerges, and individual energies harmonize. You have a shared vision and an understanding of how to complement each other's efforts. As jazz musicians say, "You are in the groove."

A team can have everything going for it—the brightest and most qualified people, access to resources, a clear mission—but still fail because it lacks group emotional intelligence.

Moreover, managers need to develop the self-awareness and interpersonal skills associated with a high level of emotional intelligence, as do teams. One way for leaders to help their teams build this capability is to understand and ensure that their teams move successfully through the stages of small-group development: membership, control, and cohesion. These stages are experienced by all teams. If teams are not well led and facilitated through them, their chances of achieving their results are substantially reduced (Bawany 2014a).

## Characteristics of Effective Teams

An organization and its leaders put a great deal of effort into assembling high-performing teams. This means that the power of a team must lie in its capacity to perform at levels and deliver results, greater than the sum of its parts. Considerable resources are often expended to ensure those teams reach their potential. For team members, as well as other people in an organization, recognizing when a team is doing well is important. When improvement is needed, it is important to make positive changes. However, sometimes it is helpful to take a step back to recognize when a team is working effectively. The workings of a highly effective team are not always obvious or intuitive to everyone. Highly effective teams are likely to have the five characteristics described below.

1. **Well-Defined Team Charter and Operating Philosophy**
   The single most important ingredient in team success is a clear, common, compelling task. The power of a team flows out of a purpose with which every team member is aligned. The task of any team is to accomplish an objective and to do it at exceptional levels of performance. Teams are not ending in themselves, but rather a means to an end. Therefore, high-performance teams should be mission-directed and ultimately judged by their results. This would include the team's mission, shared purpose and values, and goals. Effective teamwork includes having a synergistic social entity that works toward a common goal or goal. Often, high-performance teams exemplify a total commitment to the work as well as a total commitment to each other.

   Katzenbach and Smith (1993) stated, "Common sense suggests that teams cannot succeed without a shared purpose" (p. 2). While this may be an obvious statement, teams often form (or are developed) without a clear direction or meaning even though many researchers have explained that employees are inclined to do better when they know how to do their jobs and why they are doing them. Teams that seek higher levels of performance should ensure that each member understands and supports the true meaning and value of the team's mission and vision. Clarifying the purpose in this manner, and linking each individual's role and responsibilities, is a major contributor to tapping into team potential (Bawany 2020).

2. **Clarity of Roles and Performance Standards of Team Members**
   High-performance teams are also characterized by crystal clear roles. Every team member is clear about his or her particular role, as well

as those of the other team members. Roles are all about how we design, divide, and deploy the work of the team. While the concept is compellingly logical, many teams find it very challenging to implement in practice. There is often a tendency to take role definition to extremes or not take it far enough. But when they get it right, team members discover that making their combination more effective and leveraging their collective efforts are key to synergistic results.

Clear performance standards are essential to high-performing teams. Such standards provide a system of accountability, which also feeds into the performance ethic (Katzenbach and Smith 1993). This is an ethic that supports results for customers, employees, and shareholders, recognizing that each is of critical importance and must be balanced with great care and consideration.

Driving standards are certain pressures. These pressures include the individual's performance expectations, team pressure to perform, team leader pressure, the consequences of success or failure, and other external pressures (e.g., the larger organization, the crowd) that compel one to excel. According to Larson and LaFasto (1989), "people with high standards are those people who extraordinarily do ordinary things" (p. 100). When helping people reach the extraordinary, it is important to remember that setting standards must be a flexible process. Larson and LaFasto also provided three common features of developing standards of excellence: setting standards that include a variety of variables; variables that include individual commitment, motivation, self-esteem, and performance mutual accountability and dedication to reviewing and reworking standards to keep them fresh and valuable for the team.

3. **Shared Norms and Culture**

Like rules that govern group behavior, norms can help assist team development and performance. For example, Jehn and Mannix (2001) proposed that high-performance teams build "open discussion" norms to promote task conflict—a type of conflict associated with high-performance teams. Other norms of high-performance teams include high levels of respect among members and a cohesive and supportive team environment. Any number of norms may exist for a given team, but high-performing teams use norms, in general, to help govern behavior. In addition to having team norms, teams also benefit from organizing their team standards. As asserted by Larson and LaFasto (1989), "openly articulated or haphazardly applied, standards define those relevant and very intricate expectations that eventually determine the level of performance a team deems acceptable" (p. 95). Standards change the nature of performance by setting the bar at a new level—a level that is clearly defined.

Teams should be recognized and integrated within their organizations (Pearce and Ravlin 1987). Organizations need to clearly define their expectations and mechanisms of accountability for all teams (Sundstrom, De Meuse, and Futrell 1990). Organizational culture needs to transform shared values into behavioral norms (Blechert, Christiansen, and Kari 1987). For example, team success is fostered by a culture that incorporates shared experiences of success. In times of economic rationalism, there may be cultural conflict and inconsistency between norms of maintaining the standards and adhering to the organization's mission. Team members with higher status also have less regard for team norms and may exacerbate internal conflict.

4. **Excellent Communication and Collaboration**

Communication is the very means of cooperation or collaboration between team members. One of the primary motives for companies to implement teams is that team-based organizations are more responsive and move faster. A team, or the organization in which it resides, cannot move faster than it communicates. Fast, clear, and accurate communication is a hallmark of high levels of team performance. Such teams have mastered the art of straight talk; there is a little wasted motion from misunderstanding and confusion. Ideas move like quicksilver. The team understands that effective communication is key to thinking collectively and finding synergy in team solutions. As a result, team members approach communication with determined intentionality. They talk about it a lot and put a lot of effort into keeping it good and getting better (Bawany 2020).

While high-performing teams experience certain types of healthy conflict, and while they are said to be good communicators, research studies indicate that different types of communication, even different levels of perceptions of the amount of conflict, can have different types of effects. Different communication strategies appear to yield different results (including satisfaction) among those who participated, suggesting that the best forms of communication are dependent upon the workgroup and its goals and objectives. Open communication in high-performing teams means a focus on coaching instead of directing (Regan 1999). The value of coaching has emerged over the past several years as a process for helping individuals think for themselves. Coaching is seen as a facilitative process where team leaders or members help facilitate the process of self and group discovery. By utilizing coaching more frequently, individuals become less dependent and more able to take greater levels of responsibility.

5. **Effective Leadership**

The more complex and dynamic the team's task, the more a leader is needed. Leadership should reflect the team's stage of development. Leaders need to maintain a strategic focus to support the organization's vision, facilitate goal-setting, educate, and evaluate achievements (Proctor-Childs, Freeman, and Miller 1998). When leaders delegate responsibility appropriately, team members become more confident and autonomous in their work.

One of the leader's roles is to ensure that the team has the right number of members with the appropriate mix and diversity of tasks and interpersonal and complementary skills. A balance between homogeneity and heterogeneity of members' skills, interests, and backgrounds is preferred (Hackman 1990). Homogenous teams are composed of similar individuals who complete tasks efficiently with minimal conflict. In contrast, heterogeneous teams incorporate membership diversity and therefore facilitate innovation and problem solving (Pearce and Ravlin 1987).

High-performing leaders usually accompany high-performance teams. High-performing teams have leaders who, when times are certain and peaceful, can take a proactive stance and help the team stay ahead. Regan (1999) encouraged team leaders to create a sense of distress and urgency so as not to be surprised when confronted by external crises.

Regan purported those essential leadership qualities include the following:

i. Having a vision—meaning one should see the crisis before it happens and act upon it
ii. Convincing the opinion leaders of the importance of the goals at hand
iii. Organizing quantitative goals
iv. Being persistent in asking for the goals to be met
v. Endurance testing—whereby leaders must remain steadfast among team members trying to test the leader's commitment
vi. The ability to induce creativity once goals are set
vii. Staying out of the team's way

Katzenbach and Smith (1993) cited six elements necessary for good team leadership:

i. Team leaders must keep the purpose, goals, and approach relevant and meaningful.
ii. Team leaders should continue to build commitment and confidence.
iii. Team leaders must ensure that their members are always enhancing their skills—skills that include technical, problem solving, decision making, interpersonal, and teamwork skills.
iv. Effective team leaders are skillful at managing relationships from the outside, with a focus on removing obstacles that get in the way of team performance.
v. Team leaders provide opportunities for others and are the last to seek credit.
vi. Team leaders don't shy away from getting in the trenches and doing the real work.

While the authors contend that most individuals can develop effective skills to be a team leader, they suggest these components as a guideline for success.

In the earlier chapters, we have discussed the crucial competencies of disruptive digital leaders, which include but are not limited to agility, adaptability, emotional resilience and social skills, empathy, cognitive readiness, critical thinking, driving for results, innovativeness, and resilience. He or she also needs to lead and engage the team by having regular managerial coaching sessions both individually and as a team by leveraging tools such as the GROW model.

## Why Do Teams Fail?

In *The Five Dysfunctions of a Team: A Leadership Fable*, Patrick Lencioni tells the story of Kathryn Petersen, DecisionTech's CEO, who faces the ultimate leadership crisis: how to unite a team that is in such disarray that it threatens to bring down the entire company. Will she succeed? Will she be fired? Lencioni's tale serves as a timeless reminder that leadership requires courage and insight (Lencioni 2002).

As difficult as it is to build a cohesive team, it is not complicated. Keeping it simple is critical, whether you run the executive staff of a multinational company or a small department within a larger organization or even if you are merely a member of a team that needs improvement. Lencioni reveals the five dysfunctions that are at the very heart of why teams—even the best ones—often struggle. He outlines a powerful model (see Figure 9.1) and actionable steps that can be used to overcome these common hurdles and build a cohesive, effective team (Lencioni 2002).

According to Lencioni, most teams unknowingly fall victim to five interrelated dysfunctions. Teams that suffer from even one of the five are susceptible to the other four. Solving all five is required to create a high-functioning team. The five dysfunctions are displayed in a pyramid.

> *Dysfunction One: Absence of Trust.* When team members do not trust one another, they are unwilling to be vulnerable within the team. A team can't build a foundation for trust when team members are not genuinely open about their mistakes and weaknesses.
> *Dysfunction Two: Fear of Conflict.* Failure to build trust sets the stage for the second dysfunction. Teams without trust are unable to engage in passionate debate about ideas. Instead, they are guarded in their comments and resort to discussions that mask their true feelings.
> *Dysfunction Three: Lack of Commitment.* Teams that do not engage in healthy conflict will suffer from the third dysfunction. Because they

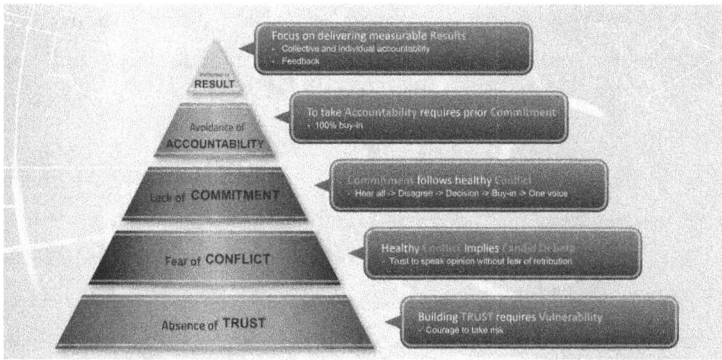

*Figure 9.1 Lencioni's framework of five dysfunctions of teams*

do not openly express their true opinions or engage in open debate, team members will rarely commit to team decisions, though they may feign agreement to avoid controversy or conflict.

*Dysfunction Four: Avoidance of Accountability.* A lack of commitment creates an atmosphere where team members do not hold one another accountable. Because there is no commitment to a clear action plan, team members hesitate to hold one another accountable for actions and behaviors that are contrary to the good of the team.

*Dysfunction Five: Inattention to Results.* The lack of accountability makes it possible for people to put their own needs above the team's goals. Team members will focus on their own career goals or recognition for their departments to the detriment of the team.

A weakness in any one area can cause teamwork to deteriorate. The model is easy to understand, and yet can be difficult to practice because it requires high levels of discipline and persistence.

## Resolving the Challenges in Leading High-Performing Teams

### 1. Building Trust

Lencioni states that trust lies at the heart of a functioning, cohesive team and that, without trust, teamwork is all but impossible. As a leader, you must encourage members of the teams to admit their weaknesses, take risks by offering one another feedback and assistance, focus their energy on important issues, and be willing to ask for help.

Teamwork begins by building trust. And the only way to do that is to overcome our need for invulnerability (putting up a front). Trust is the confidence among team members that their peers' intentions are good and that there is no reason to be protective or careful around the group. In essence, teammates must get comfortable being vulnerable to each other.

2. **Removing the Fear of Conflict**

Teams that avoid conflict often do so to avoid hurting team members' feelings and then end up encouraging dangerous tension as a result. When team members do not openly debate and disagree with important ideas, they often turn to back-channel personal attacks, which are far nastier and more harmful than any heated argument over issues. The leader must call out sensitive issues and force the team members to work through them.

When the leader sees that people engaged in healthy conflict are uncomfortable, he should remind them that what they are doing is necessary—this can keep them encouraged. At the end of the discussion, remind the participants that the healthy conflict they just engaged in is good for the team. The leader should restate the agreements and goals arrived at and restate everyone's commitments and actions expected.

3. **Achieving Commitment**

According to Lencioni, commitment is a function of clarity and buy-in. Leaders need to ensure that their teams make timely and clear decisions with buy-in from all team members, even those who do not agree with the decision. Teams with commitment have common objectives, move forward without hesitation, change direction when necessary, and learn from their mistakes.

To reach commitment, the five dysfunctions model recommends techniques such as establishing clear deadlines and communicating the team's goals throughout the organization. This happens through effective discussion, which is a reflection of feedback. Feedback involves active listening and understanding other team members' concerns and viewpoints. It also includes adapting communication to match the styles of other team members.

4. **Ensuring Accountability**

Accountability requires team members to call their peers on performance or behaviors that might hurt the team. Teams that hold one another accountable identify problems quickly by questioning one another's actions, hold one another to the same standards, and avoid needless bureaucracy around managing performance. Members of great teams improve their relationships by holding one another accountable, thus demonstrating they respect each other and have high expectations for one another's performance.

One of the best and healthiest motivators for a team is peer pressure. Clarify publicly exactly what the team needs to achieve. The enemy of accountability is ambiguity. Perform simple and regular progress reviews. Shift rewards away from individual performance to team achievement. That will create a culture of accountability because a team is unlikely to stand by quietly and fail when a peer is not pulling his or her weight. Once a leader has crafted a culture of accountability on a team, he or she must then be willing to become the ultimate arbiter of discipline when the team itself fails. An optimistic outlook is critical since it communicates confidence to other team members and the rest of the organization that the team is on the right track. An optimistic team is more likely to hold one another accountable for achieving its goals.

5. **Driving Results**

The ultimate dysfunction is when members put their status or personal goals above the best interests of the team. Teams that focus on results minimize this type of self-centered behavior. The key is to make the collective ego greater than the individual one. When everyone is focused on results and using those to define success, it is difficult for the ego to get out of hand. If the team loses, everyone loses. Eliminate ambiguity by having agreed-on and set goals. (A sports team knows at the end of the game how well it did based on the results.)

Adopt a set of common goals and measurements, then use them to make collective decisions daily. Publicly declaring the team's results and offering results-based rewards are techniques for managing this dysfunction. Without personal conscientiousness, perseverance, flexibility, and optimism, it would be difficult if not impossible for teams to achieve results. Innovation is another competence that is particularly important for achieving results. Teams that are creative and generate innovative products and solutions will inevitably achieve results that are superior to those of their competitors.

## The SCORE™ Framework for Developing High-Performance Teams

Despite society's emphasis on individuality, the critical work of business today is undertaken by teams, whether real or virtual. The success of organizations can be closely linked to how well these teams of diverse individuals perform, and it is clear that some teams truly do excel. Based on studies from extensive consulting engagements by the Centre for Executive Education (CEE) over a decade, several key elements have been identified as critical in high-performance organizations. These elements constitute the SCORE™ framework for high-performing teams (see Figure 9.2).

A high-performing team demonstrates a high level of synergism—the simultaneous actions of separate entities that together have a greater effect than the sum of their individual efforts. It is possible, for example, for a team's efforts to exemplify an equation such as $2 + 2 = 5$! High-performing teams require a complementary set of characteristics known collectively as "SCORE™"—cohesive strategy, clear roles and responsibilities, open communication, rapid response, and effective leadership—as outlined in Table 9.1.

In high-performing teams, leadership shifts during the stages of team development based on team needs. Unlike organizational leadership, which remains somewhat constant, team leadership can shift from very directing, when the team is being formed, to more delegating, when the team is functioning effectively. When you have assessed your team's current performance level and needs, you will be ready to move on to building your dream team in whatever SCORE™ category you choose to begin (Bawany 2020).

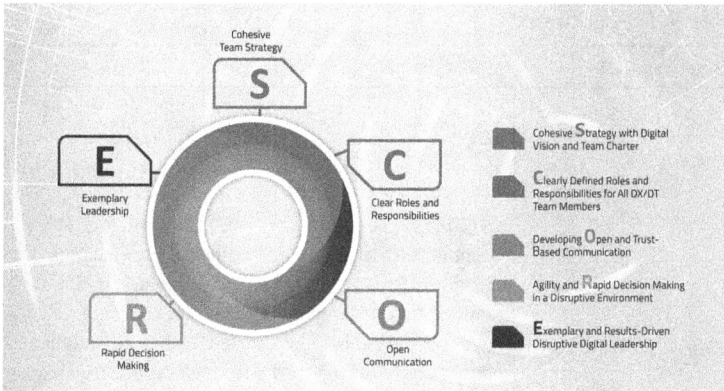

*Figure 9.2 The SCORE™ framework for developing high-performing teams*

*Table 9.1 "SCORE™" characteristics of high-performing teams*

| Characteristics | Descriptions |
|---|---|
| S: Cohesive Strategy | High-performing teams with a cohesive strategy will demonstrate why they are in existence by articulating a strong, uniting purpose that is common to all team members. They will describe how they work together by *defining team values and ground rules also known as team charter, which will guide the team's actions.* Finally, they will be clear about what they do by defining key result areas (KRAs) and performance standards |
| | Digital transformation is the integration of digital technology into all areas of a business, fundamentally changing how an organization operates and delivers value to customers. The role of the disruptive digital leader as a project leader is to define the project objectives or terms of reference in collaboration with the sponsors (CEO or other designated C-level executive). He or she would also need to relate to the team members how the project is being undertaken to the organization's broader digital transformation agenda and also how it is aligned to the overall organization's corporate strategy |
| C: Establishing Clear Roles and Responsibilities | Successful teams determine overall team competencies and then *clearly define individual member roles and responsibilities.* High-performing teams examine each individual's responsibilities in terms of the key competencies of the role, resulting in an accurate understanding of each member's accountability and contribution to the team |

(Continued)

*Table 9.1 (Continued)*

| Characteristics | Descriptions |
|---|---|
| | Digital transformation projects would typically involve various C-suite executives such as the chief digital transformation officer (CDTO), chief digital officer (CDO), chief technology officer (CTO), chief information officer (CIO), and chief marketing officer (CMO). While the CDTO as the project leader is accountable for the implementation of the project and operational activities, business transformation is a strategic initiative requiring the complete collaboration of the entire C-suite including the chief executive officer (CEO) and the chief finance officer (CFO). Hence, there is a need to clearly define the role and contribution of each of these C-suite executives to the project to avoid potential conflict, which will impact the morale of the project team members |
| O: Developing Open Communication and Trust | Communication is the key component in facilitating successful team performance; its lack limits team success. Effective communication includes *flexing and adapting one's style of communication* to suit the other team members. Also, a cohesive culture is attained when interpersonal interactions flow smoothly and individual differences are also respected and leveraged to enhance overall team functioning <br><br> Delivering any digital transformation project depends on effective collaboration and communication. Collaboration acts as a catalyst to move digital transformation efforts forward, while new digital processes bring about new ways of working together. Greater collaboration is needed to access the information required in digital transformation projects. For many organizations, data still exist in silos and proprietary technologies can still limit how it's shared within an organization <br><br> As businesses move to a more customer-centric culture, breaking down silos becomes crucial. This is where collaborative tools play their part. The information created and unleashed by digital transformation will require unified communications tools that access the data, whether it's a document, e-mail, or multimedia recording, and distribute it to another project team member or company-wide. Team members won't be able to collaborate effectively using legacy tools, and digital transformation goes a long way in enabling successful collaboration |

| Characteristics | Descriptions |
|---|---|
| **R**: Rapid Response to Problem Solving and Decision Making | A high-performing team responds quickly, as necessary, to changes in the environment, by shifting their mental models with creativity and "outside-the-box" thinking. When faced with a problem, these teams brainstorm possible solutions and create innovative resolutions leveraging disruptive leadership competencies including *agility, adaptability, cognitive readiness, and critical thinking skills* |
| | Organizations faced with digital transformation often neglect how it will impact their way of making decisions. There is a growing need to gain a competitive advantage by making decisions faster. Digital transformation requires operational agility from organizations that reach into decisions and decision making. In general, decision making has already moved to more agile environments such as WhatsApp and other instant messaging applications, which have made overall communication more informal and unstructured. However, there hasn't been a tool to specifically support complex problem solving and decision making, particularly for large, complex organizations |
| | The frequency and pace of change from digital disruption necessitate that companies can no longer rely on traditional planning and decision-making models. A rapid decision must be made in a timely and confident manner that will not only meet customer expectations but also exceed them, resulting in a competitive advantage for the organization. Any delay, interruption, or downtime, inside and outside the network, can accumulate a cost that is detrimental to the organization |
| | Adopting a rapid response approach in decision making will allow the project team to adapt, adjust, and, when necessary, pivot in real time on how to approach the implementation of the digital transformation project. This will result in delivering the project key performance indicators (KPIs) or desired outcomes, which will ultimately drive growth for the organization |

*(Continued)*

*Table 9.1  (Continued)*

| Characteristics | Descriptions |
|---|---|
| E: Exemplary and Effective Leadership | An effective team leader can adjust his or her leadership style *leveraging on the results-based leadership (RBL) framework* as necessary depending on the task at hand and the skill level of each team member performing that task. The team leader also demonstrates effective emotional and social intelligence competencies including *empathy and relationship management/social skills* as well as plays a critical role in raising morale by *having coaching conversations with team members* (leveraging on GROW model) and *providing developmental feedback* to improve individual and team performance. Finally, the team leader takes an active role in guiding the team through each stage of team development by using team-building activities and celebrating the success of early wins |
| | The key to success for any digital transformation is team leadership commitment. The leader needs to demonstrate an innovative mindset to test and apply new technologies and techniques that can be used to streamline existing business processes and lead the business forward |
| | They would need to create a culture where their team members exhibit behaviors such as a sense of urgency, calculated risk taking, increased collaboration, customer centricity, continuous learning, and an open and trust-based work environment where their team members have a say on where digitization could and should be adopted or which business processes to be redesigned |
| | The disruptive digital team leader needs to communicate the project vision with the "storytelling" approach to assist team members, and the other employees organization-wide, to better understand the business case for implementing the digital transformation initiatives, where it is heading, and why the changes are important. Leaders that follow this practice are likely to achieve higher success in their digital transformation projects |
| | Finally, the disruptive digital team leader has the greatest influence on the success of the digital transformation projects by ensuring that there are clear targets for KPIs and clear communication of the transformation's timeline |

# Best-Practice Toolkit: The Five-Step "AGREE" Framework to Achieve Collaboration

The CEE has developed the five-step "AGREE" process (see Figure 9.3) for achieving commitment to team collaboration at the workplace as well as resolving conflict and negotiation situations as driven by the use of communication skills.

## A: Acknowledge

The critical first step in achieving team collaboration or resolving conflict is for all parties to acknowledge that a conflict exists. This is particularly important when any of the involved parties or team members prefer an avoiding conflict management style. Acknowledging that a difference in the way of working or conflict exists and inviting parties to collaborate help set the tone for productive interaction.

**Example:** "I sense that we see this issue very differently, and I believe it is an important matter. Would it be helpful, from your perspective, to spend some time focusing on this? Who else should we involve to help us find a workable solution or work toward resolving this?"

## G: Ground Rules

Ground rules help establish the tone, climate, and time frame for a discussion toward a collaboration process. By establishing rules up-front, the

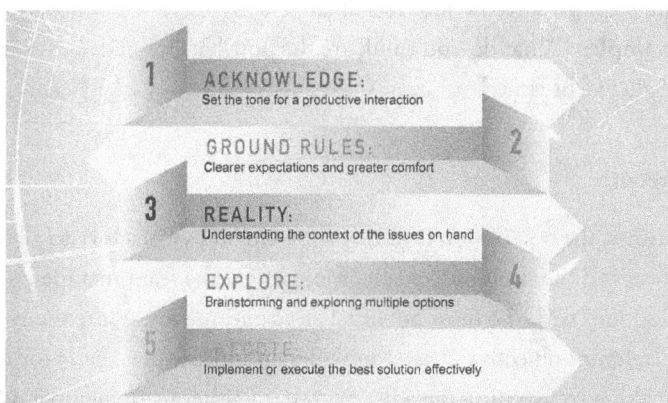

*Figure 9.3  The "AGREE" framework to achieve team collaboration*

parties begin the discussion with clearer expectations and a greater degree of comfort. Teams may also leverage their "team charter" if this has been established.

**Examples:** Listen to understand; question to clarify; maximize participation; silence means assent; speak for yourself; be respectful.

### R: Reality

Establishing the context and understanding the current reality related to the issues or conflict in question is the most critical step in achieving team collaboration. It is used to move from the destructive side of collaboration (blame or winning at the other person's expense) to the constructive side (resolving problems). In this phase, each team member demonstrates empathy and article listening by clearly articulating their understanding of the other person's position and must consciously put any emotion aside and reconsider the situation from all perspectives.

**Example:** "If I am understanding you correctly, you are saying . . ."

### E: Explore

Team member rarely sees a need for numerous options when they see that other members already know the right option, which is his or her position. Brainstorming and exploring multiple options gives parties room to explore alternatives from the other member's perspectives and support a problem-solving focus. The goal is to create as many options as possible that are responsive to the interests of all parties.

**Example:** "What do you think are the possible alternatives to resolve this challenge or issue?"

### E: Execute

Sometimes, the best option is readily apparent and satisfactory to all team members and the decision is made. More often, the team members select those options with the most potential and continue to explore them. The use of relevant objective criteria provides an independent basis for decision making by avoiding the will or power of either team member. Once the best solution has been identified and agreed upon, the final step will be to implement or execute it effectively. Have a follow-up discussion regularly to enhance collaboration.

**Example:** Possible objective criteria include cost, timeline, and customer demand.

## Case Study: Turnaround of a Highly Dysfunctional Project Team

### Background

An established and reputable institution of higher learning in Asia realized that rapid digital innovation has significantly disrupted all aspects of higher education, fundamentally changing how universities operate.

The rise of online and blended learning and the development of free online courses have transformed the higher education sector. Online learning emerged over two decades ago as a technology category that enables a range of potentially disruptive business models. No longer do students need to convene at a central location to enjoy a real-time, interactive experience with a teacher and peers. They can instead participate from anywhere in the world, more affordably and conveniently.

Digital technology is already providing solutions that have the potential to revolutionize tertiary education—at least if adopted widely enough. Distance learning platforms, virtual learning environments (VLE), learning management systems, and massive online open courses (MOOCs) are all ways of allowing that scarce resource—the domain expert (lecturers) with good teaching skills—to deliver teaching to a class over the Internet in an engaging, multimedia fashion. No longer do students necessarily have to be in the classroom; instead, they can watch video streams of lectures whenever and wherever they happen to be. The platforms enable them to interact with other students and instructors, download extra materials, upload completed assignments, and more.

The president of the university understood the impact of this disruption and therefore decided to appoint a project team headed by one of the senior faculty from the computer science department with the mandate to design and implement a digital transformation project to build digital capability throughout the institution, with the primary objective to develop a distinctive competitive advantage, by enhancing the student learning experience and positioning the university as the university of choice among the Gen Z (digital natives).

Following the announcement of the digital transformation project, students and staff including the faculty members expected personalized digital experiences, whether in their learning, teaching, research, or administrative services.

### Project Implementation and Challenges

The project leader, who is the head of the Computer Science Department, is a brilliant and academically qualified engineer who recruited the members of his team from other departments and also hired external talent with the relevant digital skills sets to drive specific initiatives.

He developed the digital strategy with the support of the chief information officer (CIO) and the head of the Information Technology (IT) Department. The project involves the deployment of advanced digital technologies such as cognitive computing, machine learning, virtual reality, and augmented reality, to transform the university into a digital environment.

The project leader was frequently directive and micro-managing his team with requests for frequent updates at times on an hourly basis for critical initiatives that he has assigned to his team members. He used to shout across the office to call his team members.

Within six months into the project, several of the project team had frequent misunderstandings between themselves and also with the stakeholders, including the other department, particularly the teaching staff who were apprehensive as to how their role will be impacted and possibly made redundant; hence there was no support or buy-in for the said digital transformation project. Several of the valued team members who were hired externally with the much-desired digital skills decided to leave the institution.

The project was subsequently delayed and the president being the sponsor was unhappy with the state of affairs and decided to engage an organizational development and digital transformation consultant from the CEE to investigate and made the relevant recommendation to address the problems.

## The Key Issues

The consultant conducted a series of individual and focus group interviews with the project leader and the team members as well as the other stakeholders, including the heads of department (HODs) and faculty members.

It was discovered that although the specific digital strategies were developed with the massive investment and shift toward using new technologies, there was resistance by the stakeholders due to the lack of buy-in to the vision of the project. This was a result of poor communication by the project leader in articulating the business case for digital transformation, and his reliance on the heavy investment in the IT systems regrettably does not deliver the expected outcomes.

He failed to realize that he needs support from many departments, not just the president, the CIO, and the head of the IT Department. There was also a lack of digital literacy among academics, students, and staff, meaning that early engagement and interaction to build the right support networks is essential to achieving sustainable change across the entire institution.

The high employee turnover, especially among the mission-critical talent, had created misalignment in what was once initially a strong performing team. There was a lack of direction and clarity on the respective project team members' roles and responsibilities compounded by the relatively ineffective team communication, which resulted in frequent conflict leading to poor performance and results.

## Recommended Actions

The project leader was provided with individualized executive coaching to raise his level of self-awareness of his leadership and communication style and how it has impacted the team members' morale and level of engagement.

The SCORE™ framework was introduced through the facilitation of a series of team effectiveness meetings and workshops; the project team achieved breakthrough results in employee satisfaction and interteam collaboration.

The project leader made efforts to engage directly with the HODs and other stakeholders. The team's KPIs were achieved with shortened response times and improved communication project delivery within the allocated budget.

Regular coaching conversations were conducted between the project leader and his team at an individual level as well as with the whole team. He adopted a much more consultative leadership style and empowered his team members who are knowledge workers with both the digital skills and know-how to carry out the assigned tasks.

The team's emotional intelligence was enhanced and relationship management became second nature as team members became more cohesive and leading to the projects being back on track. The team leveraged the "AGREE" framework whenever there was disagreement or potentially contentious issues to be resolved among themselves.

A survey with the stakeholders confirmed acknowledgment of the value that digital transformation will bring to the institution and how it would support the university's mission of enhancing the student's learning experience and making the institution a choice among the Gen Z or digital natives.

The project team's ultimate proof of transformation was its unanimous decision to distribute among all team members annual performance bonuses previously assigned to a select few. This presents some evidence that high-performance teams impact not only the organization and stakeholders but above all the gratified individuals that constitute them.

## Conclusion

The success of a team should be measured at regular intervals so that team spirit can be encouraged, either through celebrating achievements or by sharing problems. In terms of measuring success, it is perhaps easier to gauge the progress of a sports team than it is to rate the performance of work-based teams; for example, the performance of a sports team can usually be tracked by league tables.

Working as part of a successful team makes work enjoyable. It provides employees with a supportive work environment and enables them to address constructively any conflict that might arise. In high-performing teams, leadership shifts during the stages of team development based on team needs.

Unlike organizational leadership, which remains somewhat constant, team leadership can shift from very directing, when the team is being formed, to more delegating, when the team is functioning effectively. To transform into high-performance teams, easily implementable frameworks such as SCORE™ and AGREE would assist in achieving that end goal.

# CHAPTER 10

# Are You Ready for the Next Crisis?

## Introduction

We are living in an era of constant disruptions and crises!

First, the COVID-19 pandemic: It upended lives and livelihoods as it turned our lives and economies upside down—and it is not over. The continued spread of the virus could give rise to even more contagious or worse, more lethal variants, prompting further disruptions—and further divergence between rich and poor countries.

Second, the war: Russia's invasion of Ukraine, devastating for the Ukrainian economy, is sending shockwaves throughout the globe. Above all is the human tragedy—the suffering of ordinary men, women, and children in Ukraine, among them millions of displaced people. The economic consequences from the war spread fast and far, to neighbors and beyond, hitting hardest the world's most vulnerable people. According to the managing director of the International Monetary Fund (IMF), hundreds of millions of families were already struggling with lower incomes and higher energy and food prices. The war has made this much worse and threatens to further increase inequality (International Monetary Fund 2022b).

She further adds that:

for the first time in many years, inflation has become a clear and present danger for many countries around the world. This is a massive setback for global recovery. In economic terms, growth is down and inflation is up. In human terms, people's incomes are down and hardship is up.

These double crises—pandemic and war—and our ability to deal with them are further complicated by another growing risk: fragmentation of the world economy into geopolitical blocs—with different trade and technology standards, payment systems, and reserve currencies.

Such a tectonic shift would incur painful adjustment costs. Supply chains, R&D, and production networks would be broken and need to be rebuilt. Poor countries and poor people will bear the brunt of these dislocations. This fragmentation of global governance is perhaps the most serious challenge to the rules-based framework that has governed international and economic relations for more than 75 years and helped deliver significant improvements in living standards across the globe (International Monetary Fund 2022b). It is already impairing our capacity to work together on the two crises we face. And it could leave us wholly unable to meet other global challenges—such as the existential threat of climate change.

As the most recent UN climate report highlights, the threat to our planet is not going away (UN Climate Change 2022a). On the contrary, it is getting worse. We must mitigate it everywhere, adapt where necessary, and build resilience against the shocks to come.

We know what needs to be done: a comprehensive approach including carbon pricing and investment in renewables, with compensation and new opportunities for those adversely affected by the green transition. These measures can also bolster energy security (UN Climate Change 2022b).

The IMF Executive Board approved the creation of a new Resilience and Sustainability Trust. By providing affordable longer-term funding and catalyzing private investment, it will help address macro-critical challenges such as climate change—and future pandemics (International Monetary Fund 2022b).

The news of the grounding of a large container ship in the Suez Canal in March reminds us how fragile supply chain operations can be. The cost of the disruption to international trade is yet to be finalized but estimated losses due to the blockage could cost global trade between $6 billion and $10 billion a week and reduce annual trade growth by 0.2 to 0.4 percentage points (BBC 2021).

There are other disruptions including the COVID-19 pandemic; rising tensions in the Middle East and Europe including the Russian–Ukrainian war; humanitarian crises notably in Yemen, Venezuela, and elsewhere; and a growing list of climate events such as hurricanes, wildfires, and earthquakes across the globe.

Sadly, many of these events are not new. The World Economic Forum (WEF) studies global, emerging, and geopolitical issues and produces a Global Risks Report every year (World Economic Forum 2022). Interestingly, they predicted the risk of a pandemic and other health-related risks back in 2006 and since then we have lived through Swine Flu, Ebola, SARS, MERs, and now COVID-19. These risks are derived from the expertise of the forum's extensive network of business, government, civil society, and thought leaders. Their Global Risks Perception Survey (GRPS) extends to multi-stakeholder communities (including the Global Shapers Community), the professional networks of its advisory board, and members of the Institute of Risk Management. As a point of reference for global risk, the WEF makes for a credible starting point when talking about future risk.

As 2023 begins, COVID-19 and its economic and societal consequences continue to pose a critical threat to the world: vaccine inequality and a resultant uneven economic recovery risk compounding social fractures and geopolitical tensions. In the poorest 52 countries—home to 20 percent of the world's people—only 6 percent of the population had been vaccinated as of January 2022 when the GRPS results were published. By 2024, developing economies (excluding China) would have fallen 5.5 percent below their prepandemic expected GDP growth, while advanced economies would have surpassed it by 0.9 percent—widening the global income gap (World Economic Forum 2022).

The COVID-19 crisis has also had extensive collateral health impacts, partly because other diseases were deprioritized. The pandemic led to an additional 53 million cases of major depression globally (Lancet 2021).

According to the same GPRS report, the resulting global divergence will create tensions—within and across borders—that risk worsening the pandemic's cascading impacts and complicating the coordination needed to tackle common challenges including strengthening climate action, enhancing digital safety, restoring livelihoods and societal cohesion, and managing competition in space.

McKinsey's Global Institute published a report on supply chain (McKinsey 2020b), which argues that as climate change makes extreme weather more frequent and/or severe, it also increases the annual probability of events that are more intense than manufacturing assets are constructed to withstand, therefore increasing the likelihood of supply chain disruptions.

The report features a case study of an automotive original engineering manufacturer (OEM) that uses leading-edge semiconductor chips sourced from countries in the western Pacific like Korea and Taiwan. McKinsey's modeling suggests that by 2040, the company can expect that hurricanes sufficient to disrupt its suppliers will become two to four times more likely. Some of these disruptions may last for several months.

At the other end of the scale is the example in the McKinsey report of a commodity supplier of heavy rare earth elements, for example, chromium or nickel. This supplier faces the prospect that the probability of severely disrupted production from extreme rainfall may increase two- or even threefold by 2030.

Typically, the more specialized the supply chain, the more severe the impact could be for a downstream player; especially if the supply of a critical material may only be available from the source that has been disrupted. However, the more commoditized the supply chain is, the larger the number of downstream players that may be affected by spiking prices from a sudden reduction in supply.

Interestingly, the report also models how a well-prepared company fares against a poorly or nonprepared competitor. In a scenario of a 1 in 100 hurricane year, the poorly prepared company can suffer a 35 percent reduction in revenue while the well-prepared company is modeled to lose only 5 percent of revenue (McKinsey 2020b).

It is worth noting that while we focus on the risk, there is the other side of the coin, that is, the opportunity. Climate change can also create opportunities such as the opening of northern polar shipping routes cutting transit times (albeit with new geopolitical tensions) or deployment of "greener" modes of transport increasing company credentials and appeal.

# Negotiating the Rebalancing of Risk and Resilience in Global Value Chains

In recent decades, value chains have grown in length and complexity as companies expanded around the world in pursuit of margin improvements. Since 2000, the value of intermediate goods traded globally has tripled to more than $10 trillion annually. Businesses that successfully implemented a lean, global model of manufacturing achieved improvements in indicators such as inventory levels, on-time-in-full deliveries, and shorter lead times (McKinsey 2020b).

However, these operating model choices sometimes led to unintended consequences if they were not calibrated to risk exposure. Intricate production networks were designed for efficiency, cost, and proximity to markets but not necessarily for transparency or resilience. Now they are operating in a world where disruptions are regular occurrences. Averaging across industries, companies can now expect supply chain disruptions to last a month or longer to occur every 3.7 years, and the most severe events take a major financial toll.

The said McKinsey report explores the rebalancing act facing many companies in goods-producing value chains as they seek to get a handle on risk. Instead of focusing on ongoing business challenges such as shifting customer demand and suppliers failing to deliver or on ongoing trends such as digitization and automation, companies should consider risks that manifest from exposure to the most profound shocks, such as financial crises, terrorism, extreme weather, and, yes, pandemics.

The risk facing any particular industry value chain reflects its level of exposure to different types of shocks, plus the underlying vulnerabilities of a particular company or in the value chain as a whole. We, therefore, examine the growing frequency and severity of a range of shocks, assess how different value chains are exposed, and examine the factors in operations and supply chains that can magnify disruption and losses. Adjusted for the probability and frequency of disruptions, companies can expect to lose more than 40 percent of a year's profits every decade, based on a model informed by the financials of 325 companies across 13 industries (McKinsey 2020b). However, a single severe shock causing a 100-day disruption could wipe out an entire year's earnings or more in some industries—and events of this magnitude can and do occur.

Trade tensions between the United States and China as well as between Russia and European companies (as a fall-out of the Russian invasion of Ukraine in February 2022) and now the COVID-19 pandemic have led to speculation that companies could shift to more domestic production and sourcing. We examined the feasibility of movement based on industry economics as well as the possibility that governments might act to bolster domestic production of some goods they deem essential or strategic from a national security or competitiveness perspective. Moving the physical footprint of production is only one of many options for building resilience, which we broadly define as the ability to resist, withstand, and recover from shocks. Technology is challenging old assumptions that resilience can be purchased only at the cost of efficiency. The latest advances offer new solutions for running scenarios, monitoring many layers of supplier networks, accelerating response times, and even changing the economics of production. Some manufacturing companies will no doubt use these tools and devise other strategies to come out on the other side of the pandemic as more agile and innovative organizations.

To understand the full range of potential disruptions and avoid the trap of "fighting the last war," companies must look beyond the latest disaster. Not all shocks are created equal. Some pass quickly, while others can sideline multiple industry players for weeks or even months. Business leaders often characterize shocks in terms of their source. These may include force majeure events, such as natural disasters; macropolitical shocks, such as financial crises; the work of malicious actors, such as theft; and idiosyncratic shocks, such as unplanned outages. But characteristics beyond the source of a shock determine its scope and the severity of its impact on production and global value chains.

Today, much of the discussion about resilience in advanced economies revolve around the idea of increasing domestic production. But the interconnected nature of value chains limits the economic case for making large-scale changes in their physical location. Value chains often span thousands of interconnected companies, and their configurations reflect specialization, access to consumer markets around the world, long-standing relationships, and economies of scale.

# Reshaping Your Organization in an Era of Constant Crisis and Disruption

As it turned out, COVID-19 was less a "black swan" (catastrophic but highly improbable) than a "gray rhino"—a big grey beast lumbering along the horizon and then suddenly charging ahead as a high-likelihood, high-impact event. The COVID-19 crisis proved to us all that resilience alone was not enough to survive disruption. Firms also needed to be able to adapt to the uncertainty of the "new normal": They needed to be agile.

Building organizational agility into "business-as-usual" has been a challenge for decades, and organizations are often impeded by the leaders' and managers' lack of disruptive mental agility and suite of disruptive leadership competencies. Many of them have a misguided belief that agility and resilience cannot work together. On the contrary, our research has shown that the two can be complementary.

Today's business environment demands organizations to adopt organizational learning as a source of sustainable competitive advantage. This means they need to learn to scale and deliver growth at clock speed while enabling agility and sustainability.

Enabling growth today in an era of constant disruptions and crises would require a deliberate focus on elasticity: building agility and sustainability into the design of the organization while ensuring that the business can meet strategic business objectives and goals. Companies need to adhere to evolving societal standards and operate using sustainable business practices to scale and drive growth. Opting in or opting out of sustainability is no longer an option. Sustainable organizations expand the term "performance" to optimize environmental, social, and governance (ESG) outcomes as well as financial results. Since the relative emphasis on these outcomes changes over time along with the methods for achieving them, there is no sustainability without agility. Indeed, the digital era has revealed the implications for the effective design and implementation of agile and sustainable organizations.

Organizations must be prepared for future disruptions which would evolve into crises if they are not prepared and those. that place importance on resilience now, only to let become an afterthought later, will do so at their peril. COVID-19, with all its indirect impacts, is the most immediate critical event organizations face so far in this decade, but it is hardly the only one. There will be other potential forces that are creating new and constant waves of disruption—creating both opportunities and risks as outlined earlier in Chapter 2.

Companies experiencing fast growth must build an agile and sustained organization designed to rapidly deploy and redeploy talent and resources without denigrating operational capability in other areas. Capability building includes everything from training on how to run virtual meetings and executive coaching to workshops focused on teaching fundamentals around how to lead change. While companies face a significant opportunity to expand and realize revenue and profit growth, they may not always readily have the organizational capabilities to do so effectively. Why? For one, external disruptions to a given market (e.g., new regulations, innovations, and customer performance requirements) can quickly make current business and/or operating models less viable. Organizational designs must be able to outpace disruptive changes of environmental jolts, economic shocks, and more classical reorganizations.

To evolve, organizations need to develop continuous change capabilities. For organizations seeking to scale and grow, not only should their leaders inspire change and be effective "change agents," but they also need to adopt an integrative and future-focused approach to their strategic redesign, allowing them to integrate structure, people, process, and technology (PPT) as leverage points to drive growth. Engaging leaders at all levels and aligning their growth and disruptive mindsets and providing the relevant incentives to reinforce new behaviors go a long way toward executing large-scale organizational design efforts and growing the company.

Research by the Centre for Executive Education (CEE) and the Disruptive Leadership Institute (DLI) on best-in-class organizations that have successfully navigated the disruptive challenges showed that they took concrete steps to dramatically improve their capacity to anticipate, respond to, and capitalize on the disruptive forces heading their way. As a result, both CEE and DLI have developed the *"L.E.A.DE.R." framework* (see Figure 10.1) for organizations to prepare for the era of constant disruption and crises ahead that could threaten the organization's sustainability.

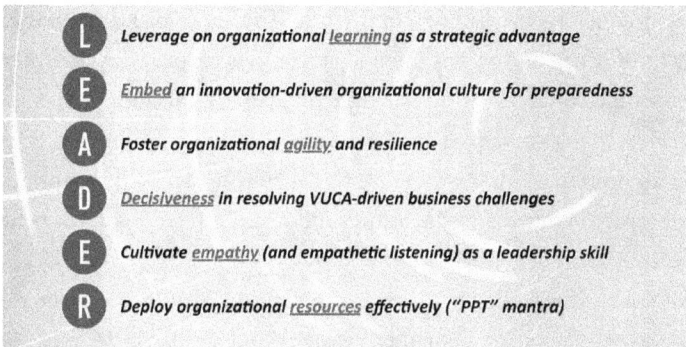

**L** Leverage on organizational *learning* as a strategic advantage

**E** *Embed* an innovation-driven organizational culture for preparedness

**A** Foster organizational *agility* and resilience

**D** *Decisiveness* in resolving VUCA-driven business challenges

**E** Cultivate *empathy* (and empathetic listening) as a leadership skill

**R** Deploy organizational *resources* effectively ("PPT" mantra)

*Figure 10.1 Navigating disruptive challenges with the "L.E.A.D.E.R." framework*

### L: Leverage Organizational "Learning" as a Strategic Advantage

Organizational learning and management are at a transition point because of the shift in disruptive digital innovations. There is widespread recognition that investing in organizational learning drives change and innovation. Today's organizations are operating in an environment characterized by high uncertainty, risk, and turbulence, for example, natural disasters, terrorist attacks, corporate scandals, and major product defects, to name a few.

These unanticipated crisis events, small or large scale, naturally occurring or human induced, have a far-reaching and significant impact on organizations and individuals within.

Avoiding or reducing such impact requires not only effective crisis management practice but also significant learning effort from everyone in the organization. Meanwhile, as the environment grows in complexity, it is more apparent that the rate at which organizations learn may become the determining factor in their ability to survive or adapt. Within such a context, constant and continuous learning has become a necessity rather than an option for organizational survival, adaptability, competitiveness, and long-term viability.

### E: Embrace "Experimentation" and an Innovation-Driven Organizational Culture for Preparedness

Change is imperative. Yet many organizations' large-scale transformation initiatives meet with setbacks, delays, and even failure. Those that succeed are soon confronted with a painful truth: They are not leapfrogging. At best, transformation can put these organizations on par with their newer, more nimble competitors. As the pace of change continues to accelerate, organizations across various industries are seeking a way forward. Developing an innovative-driven organizational culture can help organizations to withstand disruption in the future, and it also offers important benefits today.

While all innovation requires creativity and action to deliver value, crisis-driven innovation demands creativity and action under pressure—and oftentimes constraint—in response to a disruptive event or trend. Understanding the psychology of crisis-driven innovation is an essential component of building a more resilient future and creating crisis-driven innovation principles. Successful organizations run through the crisis-driven innovation principles by applying the "think, do, apply" model, cycle testing different scenarios and ways of working as you explore new ideas and potential solutions. They keep learning and experimenting.

### A: *Foster Organizational "Agility" and Speed*

Organizational agility requires a cadre of *disruptive leaders* that can anticipate business changes, stay flexible to adapt to shifts in the market, and initiate change in their organizations. It's the dynamic organizations that have a much better chance of surviving—and even thriving—in the shifting business environment. Embracing new ways of working and making decisions can help firms avoid becoming mired in the bureaucracy, which can bring change to a screeching halt.

It seems obvious that when faced with a crisis, organizations should simply ramp up more speed and agility to seize an opportunity. But not all organizations do. Speed is not simply an attribute of an organizational activity tied to clock time. Rather, speed is a complex, performance-enhancing organizational capability that requires a holistic approach to its development and execution. Speed alone enables companies to operate quickly only in already established product domains. During a crisis, companies must also demonstrate agility, a capability that allows the organization to pivot to adjacent or entirely new product domains.

## D: "Decisiveness" and Rapid Decision Making

Agile organizations navigated the initial impact of a disruptive event and crisis better than most. One reason is that they delegate decision making to frontline employees and to other critical roles where value and risk are concentrated. Yet, delegating does not mean leaving people on their own; rather, it is about coaching (not micromanaging) decision makers to make successful decisions, providing guardrails, and empowering them to make final decisions.

Making decisions faster inevitably means mistakes will happen. However, organizations should adopt experimentation and give employees room to make those mistakes—as long as they don't threaten the business. Our research unveiled that best-in-class organizations take steps to build risk mitigation into their decision processes. This lets them continue to move with speed: moving forward with implementation and quick test-and-learn cycles that allow for nimble adjustments and open doors to opportunities.

## E: "Empathy" and Empathetic Listening

Empathy affects our ability to adapt and achieve results. It is the capacity to understand what someone else is experiencing. Leaders who practice empathy consider what people in the organization are experiencing through their frame of reference. When leaders are being profoundly impacted personally and professionally, it's important to check in with people regularly. Asking someone how they're doing takes on a whole new meaning and dimension during a time of massive disruption.

When you take a moment to connect with someone, you create the right experience for employees. During times of crisis, empathy is of great importance as our research has shown that leading companies that pivot from marketing to helping and from fulfilling customer desires to meeting customer needs have achieved great results. These socially conscious organizations across sectors and geographies are finding ways to get involved and support their customers and communities. By consciously providing empathy and care during this crisis, companies can build a foundation of goodwill and long-lasting emotional connections with the communities they serve.

### R: "Resilience" in Navigating Disruptive Change

During times of disruption, embedding resilience at the heart of the organization is crucial for building a foundation for growth and innovation and pursuing new opportunities. Both leaders and employees at large need to be empowered to take positive action during a crisis, and organizations can achieve this by equipping them with the right skills and competencies. By rehearsing different risk-type scenarios, crisis management or response teams can develop the ability to operate effectively, even under the most challenging disruptive conditions.

At the same time to successfully navigate extreme uncertainty, effective crisis structures, plans, and processes must be developed to help absorb and recover from the impact of unprecedented or extraordinary events. By managing the response, owning the data, and making better decisions, the organization can move through a crisis and emerge stronger. As a result, even in a worst-case scenario, you can navigate extreme disruption; protect your people, customers, and business; and build trust with your stakeholders, regulators, and wider society.

## Best Practices for Building Organizational Resilience

There are several actions that leaders could consider how to steer their organization toward resilience in an era of constant disruption and crises:

1. **Demonstrate Strategic Foresight**
   Leveraging cognitive readiness skills and disruptive mental agility where the leader could anticipate, predict, and prepare for their organizational future. This could involve activities such as learning to scan the external business environment, listen, monitor, notice, and learn from events, or things that can affect the organization. Strategic foresight seeks to help leaders think through uncertainty. It employs scenarios to consider how trends and developments in several areas may come together in different ways ("connecting the dots" to affect the operating environment of an organization both positively and negatively).

2. **Demonstrate Cognitive Readiness and Critical Thinking**
   Next, the leader must be able to critically evaluate and analyze the data collected to develop insights, in other words, be able to interpret

and respond to the present conditions. Building situational awareness and searching for latent problems and errors are two key skills in this space. Adopt the inspirational leadership style by encouraging experimentation and people to report anomalies, mistakes, and concerns, and providing confidence that these will be addressed is a fundamental part of this stage and may require a step change in the organization's culture. This will enable people to explore the problem and encourage novel solutions, which might shift people's mental models and adopt growth mindsets. (*Someone with a growth mindset views intelligence, abilities, and talents as learnable and capable of improvement through effort whereas, on the other hand, someone with a fixed mindset views those same traits as inherently stable and unchangeable over time.*)

3. **Adopt System Thinking and Connect the Dots**

   Here, the organization must learn to monitor and review what has happened and assess the changes and implications from both risk and sustainability perspectives. This can be achieved by putting in place a robust process for identifying, prioritizing, sourcing, managing, and monitoring the organization's critical risks and ensuring that the process is continually improved as the external or macro-business environment changes. Systems thinking offers a way to better predict future outcomes—based not on past events, but on a more intimate understanding of the surrounding structure and its elements. Structure, to a large extent, determines the behavior and actions of the leader.

4. **Adopt Organizational Learning and Knowledge Management**

   This is about being able to correct organizational practices by learning from experience and past mistakes which is part of the organization's knowledge management (KM) system. Future performance can only be enhanced if your organization is willing and able to change behavior as a result of experience. In simple terms, reflecting on an event is not about where the fault lies but what could have been done differently. Through KM, organizations seek to acquire or create potentially useful knowledge and to make it available to those who can use it at a time and place that is appropriate for them to achieve maximum effective usage to positively influence organizational performance. It is generally believed that if an organization can increase its effective knowledge utilization by only a small percentage, great benefits will result.

# Conclusion

The recent COVID-19 pandemic with its devastating consequences has tested political and business leaders globally and has exposed deficits in crisis communication, leadership, preparedness, and flexibility. Extraordinary situations abound, with global supply chains suddenly failing, media communicating contradictory information, and politics playing an increasingly bigger role in shaping each country's response to the crisis. The pandemic threatens not just our lives and livelihoods but also our economy and liberty as we have experienced during the lockdowns or travel restrictions.

It has also imposed at times ethical dilemmas and emotional stress on both the business leaders and the employees at large. Nevertheless, the pandemic and other past crises including the Asian Financial Crisis in 1997, the 9/11 Terrorist Attacks in 2001, and Global Financial Crisis in 2008–2009 also provide an opportunity for organizations, leaders, and governments to learn from their mistakes and to place their businesses, countries, and institutions in a better position to face future challenges.

Organizations should have a sense of optimism (but grounded in reality) and should not have a bleak view of the business landscape characterized by the threat of new start-ups at every turn and the potential disruptive impact these start-ups would potentially have on their business. Digitalization is shaping the way organization operates today and, to serve customers better, businesses must understand how to leverage digital technologies to innovate and better serve them.

New start-ups and budding entrepreneurs are leveraging digital technologies to disrupt the marketplace by developing creative and innovative solutions that are delivering on and exceeding customer expectations. However, these digital technologies also present golden opportunities for established organizations to transform their businesses and become disruptors themselves as we have seen how DBS Bank (in Chapter 7) achieved this when faced with the emergence of "fintech" and platform-based competitors.

Every business today needs to embark on digital transformation if they have not done so already. Digitalization is not just about how technology is being incorporated into the organization; it's about how technology can be leveraged to create new opportunities for the business and also ensure the organization serves the customer of today and tomorrow. Digital transformation is for all sizes and types of organizations as it provides opportunities to innovate, retain, and capture more market share in the segments that they are currently serving or in the new ones that they are entering. Digitalization would also be able to streamline the way the organization currently works by developing and implementing effective and efficient systems and processes that would result in increased productivity, profitability, and sustainable growth for the business.

# References

Alexander, G. and B. Renshaw. 2005. *SuperCoaching: The Missing Ingredient for High Performance*. London, UK: Random House.

Allen, R.B. November 21, 2019. "Get on Board With Reverse Mentoring." *Chief Learning Officer*. www.chieflearningofficer.com/2019/11/21/get-on-board-with-reverse-mentoring/ (accessed on December 2, 2022).

Almond, G.A., S. Flanagan, and R. Mundt, eds. 1973. *Crisis, Choice, and Change: Historical Studies of Political Development*. Boston: Little Brown.

Amadeo, K. April 21, 2020. "Oil Price Forecast 2020-2050." *The Balance*. https://www.thebalance.com/oil-price-forecast-3306219 (accessed on November 13, 2022).

Anaya, P., N. Blyth, R. Hanspal, M. McAdoo, S. Ramachandran, K. Ramadurai, and S. Schram. September 17, 2020. *The $10 Trillion Case for Open Trade*. Boston Consulting Group.

Anthony, S.D., A. Trotter, and E.I. Schwartz. September 24, 2019. "The Top 20 Business Transformations of the Last Decade." *Harvard Business Review*.

Ardern, J. 2020. "Major Steps Taken to Protect New Zealanders From COVID-19 [Press Release]." www.beehive.govt.nz/release/major-steps-taken-protect-new-zealanders-covid-19 (accessed on December 2, 2022).

Aten, J. March 20, 2020. "Marriott's CEO Shared a Video With His Team and It's a Powerful Lesson in Leading During a Crisis." *Inc.* www.inc.com/jason-aten/marriotts-ceo-shared-a-video-with-his-team-its-a-powerful-lesson-in-leading-during-a-crisis.html (accessed on December 12, 2022).

Baculard, L.P. January 2, 2017. "To Lead a Digital Transformation, CEOs Must Prioritize." *Harvard Business Review*. Harvard Business School Publishing.

Bass, B.M. and R.M. Stogdill. 1990. *Bass & Stogdill's Handbook of Leadership: Theory, Research, and Managerial Applications*. New York, NY: Free Press, Collier Macmillan.

Bawany, S. September–October 2007. "Winning the War for Talent." *Human Capital*, pp. 54–57. Singapore Human Resources Institute.

Bawany, S. September 2010. "Maximizing the Potential of Future Leaders: Resolving Leadership Succession Crisis With Transition Coaching." In *Coaching in Asia—The First Decade*. Candid Creation Publishing LLP.

Bawany, S. January 24, 2013a. "Unlocking the Benefits of a Multi-Generational Workforce in Singapore." *Singapore Business Review*. https://sbr.com.sg/hr-education/commentary/unlocking-benefits-multi-generational-workforce-in-singapore (accessed on November 22, 2022).

Bawany, S. 2013b. "Harnessing the Potential of Multigenerational Workforce in Singapore." *Today's Manager*, no. 2. Singapore Management Institute.

Bawany, A. August 2014. "Generation Y and Practical Guidelines to Deal With Their Expectations." *Leadership Excellence Essentials*, no. 8.

Bawany, S. 2014a. "Building High Performance Organizations With Results-Based Leadership (RBL) Framework." *Leadership Excellence Essentials* 31, no. 11, pp. 46–47.

Bawany, S. 2014b. "Transforming the NextGen Leaders: Leadership Pipeline for Succession Planning." *Leadership Excellence Essentials* 31, no. 7, pp. 30–31.

Bawany, S. 2014c. "Building High Performance Teams Using SCORE Framework." *Talent Management Excellence* 2, no. 4, pp. 23–24.

Bawany, S. 2014d. "Mentoring & Leadership Development: Benefits of Having a Mentor." *Leadership Excellence Essentials* 31, no. 8, p. 52.

Bawany, S. 2014e. "Leadership Communication: Great leaders are good communicators". *Leadership Excellence Essentials* 31, no. 9, p.31.

Bawany, S. and A. Bawany. 2015. "Inspiring Your Future Workforce: How to Lead and Engage Gen Y and Z Effectively." *Talent Management Excellence Essentials* 32, no. 2, pp. 14–16.

Bawany, S. 2015a. "Results-Based Leadership: Putting Your Employees First Before Customer & Profits." *Leadership Excellence Essentials* 32, no. 5, pp. 22–23.

Bawany, S. 2015b. "What Makes a Great Leader? The Emotional & Social Intelligence Competencies of Highly Effective Leaders." *Leadership Excellence Essentials* 32, no. 12, pp. 5–6.

Bawany, S. 2015c. "Inspiring Your Future Workforce: How to Lead and Engage Gen Y and Z Effectively." *Talent Management Excellence Essentials* 32, no. 2, pp. 14–16.

Bawany, S. 2015d. "Creating a Coaching Culture: Leveraging on Corporate Coaching Skills." *Leadership Excellence Essentials* 32, no. 1, pp. 43–44.

Bawany, S. 2016a. "NextGen Leaders for a VUCA World." *Leadership Excellence Essentials* 33, no. 7, pp. 39–40.

Bawany, S. 2016b. "Time to Stop Performance Appraisals? Reinventing Performance Management With a Performance Coaching Culture." *Leadership Excellence Essentials* 33, no. 1, pp. 23–24.

Bawany, S. 2017. "The Art and Practice of Servant Leadership: Importance of Empathy as an Emotional & Social Intelligence Competency for Servant Leaders." *Leadership Excellence Essentials* 34, no. 11, pp. 34–35.

Bawany, S. 2018a. "Leading in a Disruptive VUCA World." *Expert Insights Series*. New York, NY: Business Express Press (BEP) Inc. LLC, United States of America.

Bawany, S. 2018b. "What Makes a Great Nextgen Leader?" *Expert Insights Series*. New York, NY: Business Express Press (BEP) Inc. LLC, United States of America.

Bawany, S. 2018c. "Developing a High-Performance Organization in a VUCA World." *Expert Insights Series*. New York, NY: Business Express Press (BEP) Inc. LLC, United States of America.

Bawany, S. 2018d. "Coaching of NextGen Leaders: The 'ADAM' Coaching Methodology." *Leadership Excellence Essentials* 35, no. 4, pp. 54–57.

Bawany, S. 2018e. "Transition Coaching of Leaders for First 90 Days." *Leadership Excellence Essentials* 35, no. 5, pp. 52–56.

Bawany, S. 2019. *Transforming the Next Generation of Leaders: Developing Future Leaders for a Disruptive, Digital-Driven Era of the Fourth Industrial Revolution (Industry 4.0)*. New York, NY: Business Express Press (BEP) Inc. LLC, United States of America.

Bawany, S. 2020. *Leadership in Disruptive Times*. New York, NY: Business Express Press (BEP) Inc. LLC.

BBC. March 29, 2021. *The Cost of the Suez Canal Blockage*. www.bbc.com/news/business-56559073 (accessed on November 27, 2022).

BBC. February 24, 2022. "Ukraine Conflict: Russian Forces Attack From Three Sides." www.bbc.com/news/world-europe-60503037 (accessed on October 14, 2022).

Bennett, N. and J. Lemoine. 2014. "What VUCA Really Means for You?" *Harvard Business Review* 92, no. 1/2.

Bernstein, P. February 4, 2014. "Did Netflix Really Put Blockbuster Out of Business? This Infographic Tells the Story." *Indiewire*. www.indiewire.com/article/did-netflix-put-blockbuster-out-of-business-this-infographic-tells-the-real-story (accessed on April 17, 2020).

Blain, J. and Speculand, R. 2019. "Transforming Your Company into a Digital-Driven Business." Performance Works International & Bridges Business Consultancy Int.

Blechert, T.F., M.F. Christiansen, and N. Kari. 1987. "Intraprofessional Team Building." *American Journal of Occupational Therapy* 41, no. 9, pp. 576–582.

Bolt, J.F. and B. Hagemann. 2009. "Lessons From the Front Line—Harvesting Tomorrow's Leaders." *Training & Development*, pp. 53–57.

Božič, K. and V. Dimovski. 2019. "Business Intelligence and Analytics for Value Creation: The Role of Absorptive Capacity." *International Journal of Information Management* 46, pp. 93–103. https://doi.org/10.1016/j.ijinfomgt.2018.11.020.

Bradley, C., J. Seong, S. Smit, and J. Woetzel. 2022. *On the Cusp of a New Era?* New York City, NY: McKinsey Global Institute, McKinsey & Company.

Brohi, N. 2022. "One Nation Under Water." *The Atlantic*. www.theatlantic.com/international/archive/2022/10/pakistan-flood-cop27-climate-change/671664/ (accessed on December 2, 2022).

Burdett, J.O. 1998. "Forty Things Every Manager Should Know About Coaching." *Journal of Management and Development* 17, no. 2, pp. 142–152.

Campbell, M. and R. Smith. 2010. *High Potential Talent: A View From Inside the Leadership Pipeline.* Colorado Springs, CO: Center for Creative Leadership.

Centers for Disease Control and Prevention. February 14, 2022a. Recent Bird Flu Infections in U.S. Wild Birds and Poultry Pose a Low Risk to the Public. Centers for Disease Control and Prevention, National Center for Immunization and Respiratory Diseases (NCIRD). Atlanta, GA: U.S. Department of Health & Human Services.

Centers for Disease Control and Prevention. November 3, 2022b. "U.S. Approaches Record Number of Avian Influenza Outbreaks in Wild Birds and Poultry: Some People Should Take Preventive Measures to Protect Against Bird Flu Viruses." Centers for Disease Control and Prevention, National Center for Immunization and Respiratory Diseases (NCIRD). Atlanta, GA: U.S. Department of Health & Human Services.

Centre for Executive Education. 2015. "Inspiring Your Future Workforce: How to Lead and Engage Gen Y and Z Effectively." Research Report. Singapore: Centre for Executive Education Pte Ltd.

Centre for Executive Education. December 22, 2020. "Best Practices in Implementing a Successful Digital Transformation at the Workplace During the Pandemic." CEE Quarterly Research Briefings. Singapore: Centre for Executive Education Pte Ltd.

Centre for Executive Education. December 29, 2021. "Leading and Engaging Your Multigenerational Talent in the Post-Pandemic 'New Normal' Workplace." CEE Quarterly Research Briefings. Singapore: Centre for Executive Education Pte Ltd.

Centre for Executive Education. October 11, 2022. "Research on Negotiating the New Balance—Corporate Sustainability & Enterprise Risk Management (ERM) in an Era of Constant Disruption and Crisis." CEE Quarterly Research Briefings. Singapore: Centre for Executive Education Pte Ltd.

Chamorro-Premuzic, T., S. Adler, and R.B. Kaiser. October 3, 2017. "What Science Says About Identifying High-Potential Employees?" *Harvard Business Review.* Harvard Business School Publishing.

Charan, R., S. Drotter, and J.L. Noel. 2000. *The Leadership Pipeline: How to Build the Leadership Powered Company.* Indianapolis, IN: Jossey-Bass.

Chartrand, J., H. Ishikawa, and S. Flander. 2018. "Critical Thinking Means Business: Learn to Apply and Develop the #1 Workplace Skill of the 21st century!" White Paper, Pearson TalentLens.

China Power. August 2, 2017. "How Much Trade Transits the South China Sea?" Washington, DC: Center for Strategic and International Studies, China Power. https://chinapower.csis.org/much-trade-transits-south-china-sea/ (accessed January on 15, 2023).

Christensen, C.M. 1997. *The Innovator's Dilemma: When New Technologies Cause Great Firms to Fail.* Boston, MA: Harvard Business School Press.

Christensen, C.M., M. Raynor, and R. McDonald. 2015. "What Is Disruptive Innovation?" *Harvard Business Review* 93, no. 12, pp. 44–53. Harvard Business School Publishing.

Chui, M., J. Manyika, and M. Miremadi. April 12, 2017. "The Countries Most (and Least) Likely to Be Affected by Automation." *Harvard Business Review.* Harvard Business School Publishing.

Chui M., R. Roberts, and L. Yee. 2023. "Generative AI Is Here: How Tools Like ChatGPT Could Change Your Business." *Quantum Black, AI by McKinsey.* December 2022. New York City, NY: McKinsey & Company.

Clark, A. July 28, 2006. "Wal-Mart Pulls Out of Germany." *The Guardian.* www.theguardian.com/business/2006/jul/28/retail.money (accessed on January 12, 2023).

Clark, D. August 13, 2013. "The New Freelance Economy: How Entrepreneurship Is Disrupting Unemployment." *Forbes.* www.forbes.com/sites/dorieclark/2013/08/13/the-new-freelance-economy-how-entrepreneurship-is-disrupting-unemployment/ (accessed on January 12, 2023).

Clarkson, K. September 1, 2017. "Four Lessons in Leadership from the World's Favorite Entrepreneur." *Virgin Group Leadership Blog.* www.virgin.com/entrepreneur/four-lessons-leadership-worlds-favourite-entrepreneurs (accessed on May 28, 2020).

Collins, J.C. 2001. *Good to Great: Why Some Companies Make the Leap and Others Don't.* New York, NY: Harper Business.

Corporate Leadership Council. 2005. *Realizing the Full Potential of Rising Talent (Volume 1): A Quantitative Analysis of the Identification and Development of High Potential Employees.* Washington, DC: Corporate Executive Board.

Coyle, D. Feburary 2, 2023. "Preempting a Generative AI Monopoly." *Project Syndicate.* www.project-syndicate.org/commentary/preventing-tech-giants-from-monopolizing-artificial-intelligence-chatbots-by-diane-coyle-2023-02 (accessed on February 13, 2023).

Davenport, T.H. and J.G. Harris. 2007. *Competing on Analytics: The New Science of Winning.* Harvard Business Press.

DBS. September 27, 2019. "DBS Among Top 10 Business Transformations of the Decade: Harvard Business Review." Press Release. www.dbs.com/newsroom/DBS_among_top_10_business_transformations_of_the_decade__Harvard_Business_Review_19 (accessed on December 10, 2022).

DBS. 2022. "Corporate Profile." *About Us.* DBS Bank Ltd. www.dbs.com/default.page (accessed on November 10, 2022).

Deloitte. 2020a. *COVID-19: Managing Supply Chain Risk and Disruption.* Deloitte Development LLC. www2.deloitte.com/ca/en/pages/finance/articles/covid-19-managing-supply-chain-risk-and-disruption.html (accessed on December 21, 2022).

Deloitte. 2020b. *Perspectives: 2020 Engineering and Construction Industry Outlook.* Deloitte Development LLC.

Deloitte Insights. 2020. *The Journey of Resilient Leadership.* Deloitte Development LLC.

DeSimone, P. March 31, 2014. "Board Oversight of Sustainability Issues: Study of S&P 500." Sustainable Investments Institute (Si2), Investor Responsibility Research Center Institute (IRRCI).

Desjardins, J. July 2014. "How Bitcoin Can and Will Disrupt the Financial System." *Visual Capitalist.* www.visualcapitalist.com/how-bitcoin-can-and-will-disrupt-financial-system (accessed on January 12, 2023).

Disruptive Leadership Institute. 2022. *Crisis Leadership Lessons Learned From the Front Lines: Navigating the Disruptive Leadership Challenges of the COVID-19 Pandemic & the Fourth Industrial Revolution (Industry 4.0) at the Workplace.* Singapore: Disruptive Leadership Institute. www.disruptiveleadership.institute/research-reports/ (accessed on January 3, 2023).

Doheny, M., V. Nagali, and F. Weig. May 2012. "Agile Operations for Volatile Times." *McKinsey Quarterly.*

Drennan, L. and A. McConnell. 2007. *Risk and Crisis Management in the Public Sector.* London: Routledge.

Dweck, C.S. 2006. *Mindset: The New Psychology of Success.* Random House.

Economist. 2018. *How Digitization Is Paying for DBS.* March 8, 2018 edition. London, UK: The Economist Newspaper Limited.

Economist. 2019a. *A Wary Respect: A Special Report on China and America.* October 24, 2009 edition. London, UK: The Economist Newspaper Limited.

Economist. 2019b. *Xi Jinping Wants China's Armed Forces to Be "World-Class" by 2050.* June 27, 2009 edition. London, UK: The Economist Newspaper Limited.

Edmondson, C.A. March 6, 2020. "Don't Hide Bad News in Times of Crisis." *Harvard Business Review.*

Edwards, L. 2003. "Coaching the Latest Buzzword or a Truly Effective Management Tool?" *Industrial and Commercial Training* 35, no. 7, pp. 298–300.

Evered, R.D. and J.C. Selman. 1989. "Coaching and the Art of Management." *Organizational Dynamics* 18, no. 2, pp. 16–33.

Faus, J. March 17, 2020. "This Is How Coronavirus Could Affect the Travel and Tourism Industry." *The World Economic Forum.*

Feldscher, K. August 12, 2021. "COVID's Future: From Pandemic to Endemic?" Harvard Gazette, Harvard University. https://news.harvard.edu/gazette/story/2021/08/what-will-it-be-like-when-covid-19-becomes-endemic/ (accessed on January 10, 2022).

Feyrer, J. October 2019. "Trade and Income—Exploiting Time Series in Geography." *American Economic Journal: Applied Economics* 11, no. 4, pp. 1–35. American Economic Association.

Fine, A. 2010. *You Already Know How to Be Great: A Simple Way to Remove Interference and Unlock Your Greatest Potential.* New York, NY: Penguin Group.

Firestein, D. August 9, 2016. "The U.S.–China Perception Gap in the South China Sea." *The Diplomat.* Arlington, VA: Diplomat Media Inc.

Fisher, M. April 8, 2020. "Why Coronavirus Conspiracy Theories Flourish. And Why It Matters." *The New York Times.* www.nytimes.com/2020/04/08/world/europe/coronavirus-conspiracy-theories.html (accessed on January 12, 2022).

Freakley, S. April 4, 2019. "7 Skills Every Leader Need in Times of Disruption." *The World Economic Forum.*

Friedman, U. April 19, 2020. *New Zealand's Prime Minister May Be the Most Effective Leader on the Planet: Jacinda Ardern's Leadership Style, Focused on Empathy, Isn't Just Resonating With Her People; It's Putting the Country on Track for Success Against the Coronavirus.* Washington, DC: The Atlantic. www.theatlantic.com/politics/archive/2020/04/jacinda-ardern-new-zealand-leadership-coronavirus/610237/ (accessed on January 10, 2022).

Gallup. 2018. "The Engaged Workplace: A Highly Engaged Workforce Means the Difference Between a Company That Outperforms Its Competitors and One That Fails to Grow." *Gallup.* www.gallup.com/services/190118/engaged-workplace.aspx (accessed on January 12, 2023).

Gallwey, W.T. 2001. *The Inner Game of Work: Focus, Learning, Pleasure, and Mobility in the Workplace.* New York, NY: Random House.

Gangadhar, S. April 12, 2017. "Coca-Cola Nears Biggest Showdown With India Activists." *Nikkei Asia.* https://asia.nikkei.com/Politics/Coca-Cola-nears-biggest-showdown-with-India-activists (accessed on November 25, 2022).

Gartner. February 7, 2022. *Gartner Predicts 25% of People Will Spend At Least One Hour Per Day in the Metaverse by 2026: Metaverse Hype to Transition into New Business Models that Extend Digital Business.* Press Release. www.gartner.com/en/newsroom/press-releases/2022-02-07-gartner-predicts-25-percent-of-people-will-spend-at-least-one-hour-per-day-in-the-metaverse-by-2026 (accessed on January 12, 2023).

General Electric. 2021. *2021 Sustainability Report: Sustainability at Core.* Boston, MA: General Electric Company.

Gibson, P., K.W. West, and R. Pastrovich. April 1, 2020. *Disruptive Leaders: An Overlooked Source of Organizational Resilience.* Chicago, IL: Heidrick & Struggles Knowledge Center, Heidrick & Struggles International, Inc.

Goleman, D. 1995. *Emotional Intelligence.* New York, NY: Bantam Books.

Goleman, D. November–December 1988. "What Makes a Leader?" *Harvard Business Review*, pp. 93–102. Harvard Business School Publishing.

Goleman, D. 1998. *Working With Emotional Intelligence.* New York, NY: Bantam Books.

Goleman, D. March–April 2000. "Leadership That Gets Results." *Harvard Business Review*, pp. 15–29. Harvard Business School Publishing.

Goleman, D. 2002. *Primal Leadership: Realizing the Power of Emotional Intelligence*. Boston, MA: Harvard Business School Press.

Google. 2019. "66% of People Say They Are Interested in Using AR for Help When Shopping." *Google Consumer AR Survey, Global*. www.thinkwithgoogle. com/consumer-insights/consumer-trends/ar-shopping-interest-statistics/ (accessed on January 12, 2023).

Graham-Harrison, E. February 6, 2020. "The Whistleblower Doctor Who Fell Victim to China's Coronavirus." *The Guardian*. www.theguardian.com/ world/2020/feb/06/li-wenliang-coronavirus-whistleblower-doctor-profile (accessed on January 2, 2023).

Gulati, R., N. Nohria, and F. Wohlgezogen. 2010. "Roaring Out of Recession." *Harvard Business Review*, March 2010 Issue.

Hackman, J.R., ed. 1990. *Groups That Work (and Those That Don't)*. San Francisco, CA: Jossey-Bass.

Hagemann, B. and S. Bawany. 2016b. "Enhancing Leadership and Executive Development—Latest Trends & Best Practices." *Leadership Excellence Essentials* 33, no. 3, pp. 9–11.

Hamilton, E. J., and B. C. Rathbun. 2013. "Scarce Differences: Toward a Material and Systemic Foundation for Offensive and Defensive Realism." *Security Studies* 22, no. 3, pp. 436–465.

Harris, K. 2018. "Labor 2030: The Collision of Demographics, Automation and Inequality: The Business Environment of the 2020s Will Be More Volatile and Economic Swings More Extreme." Boston, MA: Bain & Company, Inc.

Harvard Business Review. 2015. "Driving Digital Transformation: New Skills for Leaders, New Role for the CIO." *Harvard Business Review*. Analytic Services Report. Harvard Business School Publishing.

Hitachi. 2021. *Hitachi Sustainability Report 2021*. Tokyo, Japan: Hitachi Limited.

Hoyt, R.E. and A.P. Liebenberg. 2011. "The Value of Enterprise Risk Management." *Journal of Risk and Insurance* 78, no. 4.

Hsiung, J.C. July 2018. "The South China Sea Disputes and the US–China Contest." *Series on Contemporary China: Volume 43*. Singapore: World Scientific Publishing Co Pte Ltd.

Huang, N. September 26, 2022. "A Taiwan Perspective on What Is at Stake After Nancy Pelosi's Visit to Taiwan." *Taiwan-U.S. Quarterly Analysis series*. Washington, DC: The Brookings Institution.

International Monetary Fund. October 11, 2022a. *World Economic Outlook Report October 2022*. International Monetary Fund (IMF). www.imf.org/ en/Publications/WEO/Issues/2022/10/11/world-economic-outlook-october-2022 (accessed on January 4, 2023).

International Monetary Fund. April 14, 2022b. *Facing Crisis Upon Crisis: How the World Can Respond*. April 14, 2022 by Kristalina Georgieva, IMF Managing Director. International Monetary Fund (IMF).

Isaacson, W. June 25, 2012. "The Leadership Lessons of Steve Jobs." *Harvard Business Review*. https://hbr.org/2012/06/the-leadership-lessons-of-stev.html (accessed May 30, 2020).

Janda, K.F. 1960. "Towards the Explication of the Concept of Leadership in Terms of the Concept of Power." *Human Relations* 13, pp. 345–363.

Jehn, K.A. and E.A. Mannix. 2001. "The Dynamic Nature of Conflict: A Longitudinal Study of Intragroup Conflict and Group Performance." *Academy of Management Journal* 44, no. 2, pp. 238–251.

Johansen, R. 2012. *Leaders Make the Future: Ten New Leadership Skills for an Uncertain World*, 2nd ed. San Francisco, CA: Berrett-Koehler Publishers.

Jordan, J. and M. Sorell. October 3, 2019. "Why Reverse Mentoring Works and How to Do It Right." *Harvard Business Review*. Harvard Business School Publishing.

Kaganer, E., R.W. Gregory, and C. Codrean. 2015. *Driving Digital Transformation at the DBS Bank*, IESE, SI-195-E, 10/2016.

Kane, G.C., D. Palmer, A. N. Phillips, D. Kiron, and N. Buckley. July 2016. "Aligning the Organization for Its Digital Future." *2016 Digital Business Report, MIT Sloan Management Review*. Massachusetts Institute of Technology.

Kane, G.C., D. Palmer, A.N. Phillips, D. Kiron, and N. Buckley. July 13, 2017. "Achieving Digital Maturity: Adapting Your Company to a Changing World." *2017 Digital Business Report, MIT Sloan Management Review*. Massachusetts Institute of Technology.

Katzenbach, J.R. and D.K. Smith. 1993. *The Wisdom of Teams: Creating the High-Performance Organization*. New York, NY: Harper Business.

Kets de Vries, M.F. 2004. "Putting Leaders on the Couch." A conversation with M.F.R. Kets de Vries. Interview by Diane L. Coutu. *Harvard Business Review* 82, pp. 64–71, 113.

Khoury, E. 2017. "*Recent Trends in the South China Sea Disputes*." Asia Focus#16—Asia Programme, Insititut de relations internationales et stratégiques.

King, P. and J. Eaton. 1999. "Coaching for Results." *Industrial and Commercial Training* 31, no. 4, pp. 145–148.

Klann, G. 2003. *Crisis Leadership: Using Military Lessons, Organizational Experiences, and the Power of Influence to Lessen the Impact of Chaos on the People You Lead, Center for Creative Leadership*. NC: Greensboro.

Klemash, S., J. Smith, and J. Lee. October 7, 2018. *The Board's Role in Confronting Crisis, Harvard Law School Forum on Corporate Governance*.

Korn Ferry. 2019. *The Self-Disruptive Leader*. Korn Ferry Institute.

Lancet. October 8, 2021. *Global Prevalence and Burden of Depressive and Anxiety Disorders in 204 Countries and Territories in 2020 Due to the COVID-19 Pandemic* 398, pp. 1700–1712. https://doi.org/10.1016/.

Larson, C.E. and F.M.J. LaFasto. 1989. *Teamwork: What Must Go Right, What Can Go Wrong?* Newbury Park, CA: Sage Publications.

Lau, J. July 28, 2022. *Preparing for the Next Pandemic.* Boston, MA: Harvard T.H. Chan School of Public Health, Harvard University. www.hsph.harvard.edu/news/features/preparing-for-next-pandemic-g7-pact/ (accessed on January 12, 2023).

Lencioni, P.M. 2002. *The Five Dysfunctions of a Team, A Leadership Fable.* San Francisco, CA: Jossey-Bass.

Letzing, J. July 26, 2021. *How Long Will People Live in the Future?* World Economic Forum (WEF).

Lichtheim, M. 1973. *Ancient Egyptian Literature: A Book of Readings* 1. London: Berkeley, The Old and Middle Kingdoms.

Lioudis, N. April 21, 2020. "What Causes Oil Prices to Fluctuate?" *Investopedia.* www.investopedia.com/ask/answers/012715/what-causes-oil-prices-fluctuate.asp (accessed on January 13, 2023).

Liu, J., A. Srivastava, and H.S. Woo. 1998. "Transference of Skills Between Sports and Business." *Journal of European Industrial Training* 22, no. 3, pp. 93–112.

Lu, D. April 1, 2020. *The Hunt for Patient Zero: Where Did the Coronavirus Outbreak Start?* The New Scientist.

Luecke, R. and L. Barton. 2004. *Crisis Management: Master the Skills to Prevent Disasters.* Boston, MA: Harvard Business School Press.

Mair, V.H. 2007. *Danger + Opportunity ≠ Crisis: How a Misunderstanding About Chinese Characters Has Led Many Astray.* Pinyin.info.

Manchester Inc. 2001. *Executive Coaching Yields Return on Investment of Almost Six Times Its Costs,* pp. 2–3.

Marvin, R. April 1, 2019. "The New Entertainment Giants: Welcome to the Streaming-Industrial Complex." *P.C. Magazine.* www.pcmag.com/news/the-new-entertainment-giants-welcome-to-the-streaming-industrial-complex (accessed April 15, 2020).

McCracken, H. September 18, 2017. "Satya Nadella Rewrites Microsoft's Code." *Fast Company.* Long Read. www.fastcompany.com/40457458/satya-nadella-rewrites-microsofts-code (accessed January 12, 2023).

McKinsey. October 1, 2011. *The Business of Sustainability.* McKinsey Global Institute. New York City, NY: McKinsey & Company.

McKinsey. March 2017. "The Digital Reinvention of an Asian Bank: The CEO of DBS Says It's Not Enough to Apply Digital 'Lipstick'." *McKinsey Quarterly,* March 2017 Issue. New York City, NY: McKinsey & Company.

McKinsey. July 2020. *Prioritizing Health: A Prescription for Prosperity.* McKinsey Global Institute. New York City, NY: McKinsey & Company.

McKinsey. August 6, 2020b. *Could Climate Become the Weak Link in Your Supply Chain?* McKinsey Global Institute. New York City, NY: McKinsey & Company.

McKinsey. 2022a. "Value Creation in the Metaverse: The Real Business of the Virtual World." *McKinsey Report June 2022*. New York City, NY: McKinsey & Company.

McKinsey. 2022b. "The Board Perspective: A collection of McKinsey Insights Focusing on Boards of Directors." *McKinsey Report Spring 2022*, no. 3. New York City, NY: McKinsey & Company.

McKinsey. January 19, 2023. "What Is Generative AI?" *McKinsey Report January 2023*. New York City, NY: McKinsey & Company.

McNulty, E.J. and L. Marcus. June 20, 2019. "What Boards Can Do to Prepare for Crises." *Harvard Business Review*.

Mendiluce, M. November 10, 2022. "A Guide to Achieving Net Zero Emissions." *Harvard Business Review*. Harvard Business School Publishing.

Mercer, D. April 22, 2020. "Coronavirus: Scientists in China Find 33 Mutations of Virus in Warning to Vaccine Developers." *Sky News*. https://news.sky.com/story/coronavirus-has-mutated-into-more-than-30-strains-say-scientists-in-china-11976380 (accessed on January 2, 2023).

Mistry, P. October 8, 2017. "Richard Branson: Clients Do Not Come First. Employees Come First." *The HR Digest*. www.thehrdigest.com/richard-branson-clients-do-not-come-first-employees-come-first/ (accessed on January 10, 2023).

Mortlock, L., A. Murphy, K.A. Razak, K. Ermelbauer, and I. Anderson. 2019. *Transformation Leadership in a Digital Era*. Ernst & Young LLP.

Mottl, J. May 19, 2020. *Why Retailers Should Embrace Augmented Reality in the Wake of COVID-19*. Retail Customer Experience.com. www.retailcustomerexperience.com/articles/why-retailers-should-embrace-augmented-reality-in-the-wake-of-covid-19/ (accessed on January 12, 2023).

Mudhar, R. February 10, 2015. "Canadian Business to Benefit from Robots: Report." *The Star*. www.thestar.com/business/2015/02/10/canadian-business-to-benefit-from-robots-report.html (accessed May 30, 2020).

Nadella, S., G. Shaw, and J.T. Nichols. 2017. *Hit Refresh: The Quest to Rediscover Microsoft's Soul and Imagine a Better Future for Everyone*. New York, NY: Harper Collins Publishers.

Needham, E.G. July 28, 2022. *US Economy Enters Technical Recession: GDP Drop of 0.9% in Q2, Investment Week, July 28, 2022*. www.investmentweek.co.uk/author/7bf4cdf2-550e-4d6c-9def-f918496ca01e/elliot-gulliver-needham (accessed on December 2, 2022).

Ngai, E.W.T., L. Xiu, and D.C.K. Chau. 2009. "Application of Data Mining Techniques in Customer Relationship Management: A Literature Review and Classification." *Expert Systems With Applications* 36, no. 2, pp. 2592–2602. https://doi.org/10.1016/j.eswa.2008.02.021.

O'Shaughnessy, S. 2001. "Executive Coaching the Route to Business Stardom." *Industrial and Commercial Training* 33, no. 6, pp. 194-197.

Parker-Wilkins, V. 2006. "Business Impact of Executive Coaching: Demonstrating Monetary Value." *Industrial and Commercial Training* 38, no. 3, pp. 122–127.

Parsloe, E. and M. Wray. 2000. *Coaching & Mentorship: Practical Methods to Improve Learning.* London, UK: Kogan.

Pearce, J.A. and E.C. Ravlin. 1987. "The Design and Activation of Self-Regulating Work Groups." *Human Relations* 40, no. 11, pp. 751–782.

Performance Consultants. 2018. "GROW Model: GROWing People, Performance and Purpose." *Performance Consultants International.* www.performanceconsultants.com/wp-content/uploads/GROW-Model-Guide.pdf (accessed on January 12, 2022).

Platt, G. October 1, 2018. "World's Best Banks 2018: DBS Named Best Bank in the World." *Global Finance Magazine.* www.gfmag.com/magazine/october-2018/worlds-best-banks-2018 (accessed on December 10, 2022).

Procter & Gamble. December 2021. *P&G Ambition 2030 Report.* Cincinnati, OH: The Procter & Gamble Company.

Proctor-Childs, T., M. Freeman, and C. Miller. 1998. "Visions of Teamwork: The Realities of an Interdisciplinary Approach." *British Journal of Therapy and Rehabilitation* 5, no. 12, pp. 616–635.

Pulley, M.L. and M. Wakefield. 2001. *Building Resiliency: How to Thrive in Times of Change.* Greensboro, NC: Center for Creative Leadership.

PwC. 2020. *2020 Global Digital I.Q Report.* PwC Research and Insights.

Raditio, K.H. 2019. *Understanding China's Behaviour in the South China Sea: A Defensive Realist Perspective.* Singapore: Palgrave Macmillan, Springer Nature Singapore Pte Ltd.

re:Work with Google. 2018. *Coach With the GROW Model.* https://rework.withgoogle.com/guides/managers-coach-managers-to-coach/steps/coach-with-the-grow-model (accessed on December 2, 2022).

Ready, D.A., J.A. Conger, and L.A. Hill. June, 2010. "Are You a High Potential?" *Harvard Business Review* 88, pp. 78–84.

Ready, D.A., C. Cohen, D. Kiron, and B. Pring. January 21, 2020. "The New Leadership Playbook for the Digital Age. Findings From the 2020 Future of Leadership Global Executive Study and Research Project." *MIT Sloan Management Review.*

Regan, M.D. 1999. *The Journey to Teams: A Practical Step-by-Step Implementation Plan.* New York, NY: Holden Press.

Research and Markets. May 16, 2022. *Global Metaverse Technology Use Cases by Industry 2022: Revenue Opportunities Across Multiple Verticals.* Press Release. www.globenewswire.com/en/news-release/2022/05/16/2443639/28124/en/Global-Metaverse-Technology-Use-Cases-by-Industry-2022-Revenue-Opportunities-Across-Multiple-Verticals.html (accessed on January 9, 2023).

Saitto, S. December 5, 2014. "Uber Valued at $40 Billion in $1.2 Billion Equity Funding." *Bloomberg*. www.bloomberg.com/news/articles/2014-12-04/uber-valued-at-40-billion-with-1-2-billion-equity-fundraising (accessed on October 17, 2022).

Salovey, P. and J.D. Mayer. 1990. "Emotional Intelligence." *Imagination, Cognition, and Personality* 9, pp. 185–211.

SAP Center for Business Insight and Oxford Economics. July 11, 2017. "SAP Digital Transformation Executive Study: 4 Ways Leaders Set Themselves Apart. Four Traits Set Digital Leaders Apart From 97% of the Competition." Insights. SAP News Center, SAP Insights, SAP.

Sattarkhanova, A. 2021. "The Four Case Studies on the Effects of Corporate Social Responsibility on Water Pollution: Do Conflicts Affect a Company's CSR Policy?" *International Journal of Engineering Applied Sciences and Technology* 5, no. 9, pp. 30–43.

Schumpeter, J. 1942. *Capitalism, Socialism, and Democracy*. New York, NY: Harper & Bros.

Schwab, K. 2017. *The Fourth Industrial Revolution*. New York, NY: Crown Publishing Group.

Scott, A. and P. Cobban. November 25, 2021. "3 Tactics to Accelerate a Digital Transformation." *Harvard Business Review*. Harvard Business School Publishing.

Shear, M.D. and M. Haberman. February 27, 2020. "Pence Will Control All Coronavirus Messaging From Health Officials." *The New York Times*. www.nytimes.com/2020/02/27/us/politics/us-coronavirus-pence.html (accessed on January 14, 2023).

Shen, M. January 31, 2022. "Sexual Harassment in the Metaverse? Woman Alleges Rape in Virtual World." *USA Today*.

Shih, G. April 7, 2022. "How War in Ukraine Turned Sri Lanka's Economic Crisis Into a Calamity." *Washington Post*. www.washingtonpost.com/world/2022/04/17/sri-lanka-crisis-default-ukraine (accessed on November 17, 2022).

Sia, S.K., C. Soh, P. Weill, and Y. Chong. 2015. "Rewiring the Enterprise for Digital Innovation: The Case of DBS Bank." *Asian Business Case Centre*. Ref. ABCC-2005-004.

Silzer, R. and A. H. Church. 2009. "The Pearls and Perils of Identifying Potential." *Industrial and Organisational Psychology* 2, pp. 377–412.

Sridhar, D. October 26, 2022. "Five Ways to Prepare for the Next Pandemic: COVID-19 and Other Infectious-Disease Outbreaks Can Teach Us How to Respond to Future Threats." *Nature*. Spinger Nature Ltd.

Standard Chartered. 2022. "Just in Time: Financing a Just Transition to Net Zero." *Standard Chartered Report*. www.sc.com/en/insights/just-in-time/ (accessed on November 24, 2022).

Stephenson, N. 1992. *Snow Crash*, First ed. New York, NY: Bantam Books.

Stiehm, J.H. and N.W. Townsend. 2002. *The U.S. Army War College: Military Education in a Democracy*, p. 6. Temple University Press.

Sun, L. September 1, 2018. "Alibaba Is Expanding Its E-Commerce Platform into These 4 Markets." *The Motley Fool*. www.fool.com/investing/2018/09/01/alibaba-is-expanding-its-e-commerce-platform-into.aspx (accessed on January 12, 2023).

Sundheim, D. April 23, 2020. "When Crisis Strikes, Lead With Humanity." *Harvard Business Review*.

Sundstrom, E., K.P. De Meuse, and D. Futrell. 1990. "Work Teams: Applications and Effectiveness." *American Psychologist* 45, no. 2, pp. 120–133.

Taleb, N.N. 2007. *The Black Swan: the Impact of the Highly Improbable*. New York, NY: Random House.

Tan, J. June 4, 2014. "Piyush Gupta Demands a Shift to Digital Banking in Singapore." *Forbes Asia*. www.forbes.com/sites/forbesasia/2014/06/04/piyush-gupta-wants-a-shift-todigital-banking-in-singapore/ (accessed on January 10, 2023).

Tan, S.K. December 1, 2020. "China's Export Control Law to Become 'Key Dynamic' in US Relations." *Nikkei Inc.* https://asia.nikkei.com/Economy/China-s-export-control-law-to-become-key-dynamic-in-US-relations (accessed on November 16, 2022).

Thomas, Z. February 13, 2020. "WHO Says Fake Coronavirus Claims Causing 'Infodemic'." *BBC News*. www.bbc.com/news/technology-51497800 (accessed January 3, 2023).

Tzu, S. 2005. *The Art of War by Sun Tzu—Special Edition*. El Paso Norte Press.

UN Climate Change. November 6, 2022a. "COP27 in Sharm el-Sheikh to Focus on Delivering on the Promises of Paris." *UN Climate Press Release*. https://unfccc.int/news/cop27-in-sharm-el-sheikh-to-focus-on-delivering-on-the-promises-of-paris (accessed on December 3, 2022).

UN Climate Change. October 26, 2022b. "Climate Plans Remain Insufficient: More Ambitious Action Needed Now." *UN Climate Press Release*. https://unfccc.int/news/climate-plans-remain-insufficient-more-ambitious-action-needed-now (accessed on December 3, 2022).

UNICEF. November 3, 2022. "Schools for More Than 2 Million Children in Pakistan Remain Inaccessible Due to Devastating Floods." *UNICEF Press Release*. www.unicef.org/press-releases/schools-more-2-million-children-pakistan-remain-inaccessible-due-devastating-floods (accessed on December 17, 2023).

United Nations. 2018. "Defining a 'Large City' as Having More Than One Million Inhabitants. Projections From World urbanization Prospects: The 2018 Revision." *UN Population Division*.

United Nations. April 1, 2020a. "COVID-19: Disrupting Lives, Economies and Societies." *World Economic Situation and Prospects: April 2020 Briefing*, no. 136.

United Nations. July 7, 2022. *The Sustainable Development Goals Report 2022*. New York, NY: United Nations Department of Economic and Social Affairs, United Nations.

United Nations. September 13, 2022b. "The End of the COVID-19 Pandemic Is in Sight: WHO." *UN News*. United Nations. https://news.un.org/en/story/2022/09/1126621 (accessed on January 12, 2023).

Volini, E., J. Schwartz, I. Roy, M. Hauptmann, Y. Van Durme, B. Denny, and J. Bersin. April 11, 2019. "Leadership for the 21st Century: The Intersection of the Traditional and the New–2019 Global Human Capital Trends." *Deloitte Insights*.

Wade, M.R., A. Tarling, and R. Neubauer. March, 2017. *Redefining Leadership for a Digital Age*. IMD.

Walch, K. December 15, 2019. "You've Heard of Robots; What Are Cobots." *Forbes*. www.forbes.com/sites/cognitiveworld/2019/12/15/youve-heard-of-robots-what-are-cobots/ (accessed on January 5, 2022).

Watkins, M. 2003. *The First 90 Days*. Boston, MA: Harvard Business School Press.

Whiteman, W.E. 1998. *Training and Educating Army Officers for the 21st Century: Implications for the United States Military Academy*. Fort Belvoir, VA: Defense Technical Information Center.

Whitmore, J. 2002. *Coaching for Performance: GROWing People, Performance and Purpose*, 3rd Ed. London; Naperville, USA: Nicholas Brealey.

Wiles, J. October 21, 2022. *What Is a Metaverse? And Should You Be Buying In?* Gartner Inc. Stamford, CT. www.gartner.com/en/articles/what-is-a-metaverse (accessed on November 2, 2022).

Willingham, E. May 25, 2021. "Humans Could Live up to 150 Years, New Research Suggests." *Scientific American*.

Wilson, C. 2004. "Coaching and Coach Training in the Workplace." *Industrial and Commercial Training* 36, no. 3, pp. 96–98.

Wipro Digital. 2019. *Wipro 2019 Digital Transformation Survey: Barriers to Success*. Wipro. https://transformationsurvey.wiprodigital.com/ (accessed on December 11, 2022).

World Economic Forum. January 11, 2022. *The Global Risks Report 2022*, 17th Edition. World Economic Forum (WEF).

World Health Organization March 11, 2019. "8 Things to Know About Pandemic Influenza." World Health Organization (WHO). www.who.int/news-room/feature-stories/detail/8-things-to-know-about-pandemic-influenza (accessed on January 12, 2022).

World Health Organization. 2020a. "Coronavirus Disease (COVID-19) Pandemic." World Health Organization (WHO). www.who.int/emergencies/diseases/novel-coronavirus-2019 (accessed on January 12, 2022).

World Health Organization. 2020b, "Coronavirus Disease (COVID-19) Outbreak Situation." World Health Organization (WHO).

World Health Organization. 2022. "Coronavirus Disease (COVID-19) Pandemic." https://www.who.int/emergencies/diseases/novel-coronavirus-2019 (accessed January 12, 2022)

World Health Organization. October 17, 2022a. *WHO Coronavirus (COVID-19) Dashboard.* World Health Organization (WHO). https://covid19.who.int/ (accessed on December 12, 2022).

World Health Organization. September 9, 2022b. "New Fund for Pandemic Prevention, Preparedness and Response Formally Established." World Health Organization (WHO).

World Health Organization. 2022c. "Strategic Preparedness, Readiness and Response Plan to End the Global COVID-19 Emergency in 2022." World Health Organization (WHO).

Yukl, G.A. 1989. "Managerial Leadership: A Review of Theory and Research." *Journal of Management* 15, pp. 251–289.

# About the Author

**Professor Sattar Bawany** is the chief executive officer of the Disruptive Leadership Institute and the Centre for Executive Education (CEE).

He is also concurrently the managing director as well as certified C-suite master executive coach (CMEC) with Executive Development Associates (EDA Inc.).

Professor Bawany was awarded the "2019 Executive of the Year for Human Resources Consulting" at the Singapore Business Review (SBR) Management Excellence Awards 2019.

He is currently the professor of practice and adjunct professor with various universities globally.

Over the past 35 years, working with global clients across various industries, professor Bawany has delivered coaching engagement as well as developed a series of professional development and initiatives designed to enhance leaders' capabilities leading and engaging the workforce in the highly disruptive and digital-driven World-of-Work (WOW).

He has assumed various senior management roles with leading global consulting firms such as Hay Group (now part of Korn Ferry), Mercer, Forum, and DBM (now part of Adecco).

Professor Bawany is an astute advisor to executives who need to know how they are perceived and want to focus on what is most important in their professional and personal lives. He has coached a range of leaders, from CEOs to senior vice presidents, and high-potential managers. His current work in organizations focuses on encouraging individual initiative and leadership from a systemic perspective to achieve clearly defined business results. His specialty is effectively linking people processes to business outcomes.

He holds an executive MBA from Golden Gate University, San Francisco, CA, and a bachelor in business administration (marketing) from Curtin University, Perth, Western Australia.

He is a Fellow of the International Professional Managers Association (IPMA) and the Chartered Institute of Marketing (CIM). He is a professional member of the Society for Human Resource Management (SHRM) and the Chartered Institute of Personnel and Development (CIPD). He is also a practicing member of the International Coaching Federation (ICF) and the International Association of Coaching (IAC).

# Index

www.ingramcontent.com/pod-product-compliance
Lightning Source LLC
Chambersburg PA
CBHW061128220326
41599CB00024B/4202